Full Employment and Public Policy: The United States and Sweden

Full Employment and Public Policy: The United States and Sweden

Helen Ginsburg
Brooklyn College—City
University of New York

LexingtonBooks
D.C. Heath and Company
Lexington, Massachusetts
Toronto

Library of Congress Cataloging in Publication Data

Ginsburg, Helen.
 Full employment and public policy.

 1. United States—Full employment policies. 2. Sweden—Full employment
policies. 3. Unemployment—United States. 4. Unemployment—Sweden.
5. United States—Economic policy—1981-   . 6. Sweden—Economic policy.
7. United States—Social policy—1980-   . 8. Sweden—Social policy.
I. Title.
HD5724.G51696   1983   339.5'0973   76-55536
ISBN 0-669-01318-8

Second printing, April 1985

Published simultaneously in Canada

Printed in the United States of America

International Standard Book Number: 0-669-01318-8

Library of Congress Catalog Card Number: 76-55536

To my husband, Nathan,
and my mother, Anna Lachs

Contents

Contents

Tables

Preface

Can there be jobs for all? At a time when unemployment is higher than it has been since the Great Depression, that may appear to be a frivolous question. Yet if one looks closely at the U.S. scene, the need for full employment becomes more evident than ever. Sections of the country, like the industrial midwest, are dying a slow death because so many of their residents are out of work. In ghettos and *barrios* throughout the land, unemployment has led to hopelessness, despair, crime, and the need for welfare; young people in those areas hold no hope for the future. Middle-aged and older workers, victims of plant closings, wonder what they will do when their meager unemployment benefits run out. Disabled workers who hope to join the labor force scarcely stand a chance when the able-bodied are being rejected. Native Americans are suffering from endemic and massive unemployment. Mothers who want to work can find no affordable place to leave their children. Young college teachers are being terminated because of declining enrollment. Civil servants are the victims of budget cuts. These are just a few examples of the impact of unemployment.

The other side of the picture is a United States that has work to be done. There is a need to build and repair bridges, roads, water mains, sewers, and subways; there is a need to provide rural and urban public transportation and to expand and rebuild the country's deteriorating physical infrastructure. Housing for low- and middle-income persons is in short supply. There is also a need for services for the disabled, for the aged, for children and their parents; for an expansion of health and education in certain fields and locations; and so on. Meanwhile, much of our existing productive capacity remains idle.

Are there alternatives? Can a full-employment policy work? Can we use our idle labor and idle resources to improve the quality of life in the United States? Do the adverse international economic trends preclude consideration of full employment?

Sweden, faced with adverse trends in the international economy, has nevertheless maintained a full-employment policy. Its unemployment rate rarely rises much above 2 percent—with 3 percent considered catastrophic. Yet the United States has tolerated higher levels of unemployment for decades; the current near-depression is actually an acute crisis superimposed on a quiet crisis of unemployment that has persisted for many years.

Why the difference between the two countries? What is full employment? What is the history of full employment and unemployment in the United States? How does the Swedish situation contrast with the American? Why has government policy in the United States often been used to create unemployment rather than to create jobs for all who want to work? These are some of the questions this book asks.

Part I deals with the U.S. experience, and part II deals with Sweden. Throughout the book, the emphasis is on the underlying philosophical, economic, political, and social issues surrounding full employment and unemployment, which contrast sharply in the two countries. This book provides a full analysis of the unsuccessful struggle for full employment in the United States in the 1940s, a consequence of the Great Depression of the 1930s, and the reemergence of the struggle in the 1970s. The politics and economics that led to the passage of a vitiated version of the Humphrey-Hawkins Full Employment and Balanced Growth Act of 1978—and to its subsequent neglect—are also explored in depth. The contours and dimensions of unemployment since World War II are fully documented, as are the staggering human and social costs that stem from this unemployment. Then the scene shifts, and the historical, social, political, and economic roots of Swedish full-employment policy are traced. There is also detailed information on the techniques Sweden uses to attain full employment. There is a dearth of such material in English and much we can learn from the Swedish methods. This is not a symmetrical book. I have given relatively little detailed information on U.S. programs such as the Comprehensive Employment and Training Act (CETA) compared to Swedish programs because an extensive literature in English already exists. More important, none of the U.S. programs to date has had full employment as its aim, nor has any been part of an overall strategy to attain full employment. Indeed, they have often worked at cross-purposes with other policies that create unemployment. By contrast, in Sweden these programs flow from a commitment to provide jobs for all.

Sweden's effort to achieve full employment is not solely a matter of economics. It is rooted in political power and in a deep-seated commitment to the dignity of every individual, as well as in a desire to use the labor of the jobless to improve the quality of life in the country.

Realistically, however, what happens to those Swedes who live in regions where unemployment is high—by Swedish standards? What happens to disadvantaged groups? to women? to immigrants? to the disabled? to youth? to older workers? to families and children in a full-employment society? What is done for them? These chapters present problems as well as successes. There are hurdles to overcome. Achieving full employment is not a simple task, even in a country committed to that goal. An important point about the Swedish story, however, is that even in a world beset by unemployment, policy can make a difference. It may not be able to solve all the problems, but it can overcome many of them.

The final section of this book considers the future of full employment in Sweden and the United States. It offers a bold political and economic strategy in the case of the United States.

My initial interest in full employment came from my research and writing on poverty. An earlier book, *Poverty and Society* (Little, Brown, 1972; University Press of America, 1981) examined different perspectives on poverty and the condition of the poor. I later did research on unemployment, subemployment, and income-maintenance policies. From both these research efforts, the need for jobs at decent wages for all who want to work became more and more apparent. In the 1970s I was engaged in an effort to secure full-employment legislation in the United States. That effort piqued my interest in the Swedish full-employment system.

It took the efforts of many to realize passage of the Full Employment and Balanced Growth Act of 1978. Now, however, although the act is nominally law, its spirit appears to be dead. I hope that this book will revive interest in the 1980s in the idea of full employment as a feasible alternative to the present policy of unemployment. The United States does not have to tolerate a situation in which nearly 11 million people are officially out of work and millions more unofficially jobless. Full employment would help this country solve many of its overriding problems, such as poverty, urban decay, crime, racism, sexism, and ageism. It cannot do the whole job; it is not a panacea for all the ills of the economy and society. It would, however, be a long step toward alleviating some of them.

Acknowledgments

This book could not have been written without the help of many people. I was a founding member of the National Committee for Full Employment and participated during the 1970s in the movement for full employment. So many of the people I met through that experience, especially Representatives Augustus Hawkins of California and John Conyers of Michigan, provided me with information, knowledge, and perspectives that were instrumental in shaping my ideas about full employment that it would take another book to list them all. Therefore, I shall simply thank all the other economists; members of Congress and their staffs; public officials; members of religious, civil-rights, environmental, labor, social-welfare, women's, senior citizens', civic, academic, and other organizations who helped in one way or another—and all others concerned about unemployment, especially the unemployed themselves.

I am grateful to the Swedish Bicentennial Fund for a grant that enabled me to visit Sweden. Marna Feldt of the Swedish Information Service in New York has been especially helpful to me for many years, and Charlotte Ganslandt of the Swedish Institute in Stockholm provided invaluable assistance. In Sweden, many people gave generously of their time and willingly shared their expertise and ideas. I shall list these in the order in which I saw them.

In Östersund: Gert Korths-Aspergren (director) and Kjell Risberg of the Jämtland County Employment Board; Kerstin Johansson and Christer Ägren, JAVI, the Rehabilitation Center in Jämtland; the director and staff of the Labor Market Training Center; Judith Jädeberg; Jan Bjorkland, Jämtland County Administration; and the management and workers at the Vinetta plant.

In Sundsvall: Erling Jacobsson, director, Västernorrland County Labor Market Board; Curt Landén, manager of the Public Employment Service; Åke Dahlberg of the Social Democratic party and head of the Sundsvall Employment Committee; Birgitta Hendriksson, Sundsvall Equality Committee; Mona Wohlin, director of the Institute for Back Pain; and the management and workers at the Sunds plant, especially Lennart Edström, Moje Westberg, and all the members of the Sunds adjustment group.

In Stockholm: Agnetta Dreber of the National Committee on Equality; Sven Ove Hansson of the Social Democratic party; Lars Ettarp and Anders Reuterswärd, Ministry of Labor; Åke Norlander, member, National Labor Market Board (AMS), and general director, Swedish Engineering Employers' Association; Kjell Treslow, Swedish Engineering Employers' Association; Bertil Rehnberg, general director of AMS; Ingrid Jonshagen, Åke Dahlberg, Torbjörn Sundquist, Ingeborg Jöhnsson, Leif Tallskog,

Alan Read, and Britta Koch Ericson of AMS; Gunnar Lindström of the Swedish Employers' Confederation (SAF); Alva Myrdal; Gunnar Myrdal; Göran Borg, then of the Swedish Confederation of Trade Unions (LO); Per Granstedt, Center party member of Parliament and its Labor Market Committee; Marianne Pettersson of the Center for Working Life; Sten Markusson of the Swedish Confederation of Professional Associations (SACO/SR); and the late Margareta Carlestam of the Central Organizations of Salaried Employees (TCO).

In Malmö: Björn Pettersson, director, and Ronny Nilsson of the County Labor Market Board; Ulf Farnok and Mats Ohrström, county administration; Sylvia Hyrenium, Malmö immigration officer; Gilbert Andersson, director, and faculty and staff of the Furulund Labor Market Training Center; Carl-Axel Johansson of the Employment Service; all the members of the Youth Guarantee program; Jan-Olaf Henriksson, head of the Consultant Group on Youth Unemployment and member of the Board of Education.

In Lund: Eskil Wadensjö, then at Lund University (now at the Swedish Institute for Social Research).

Finally, thanks go to all the unemployed and trainees whom I met at Labor Market Training Centers, employment offices, and rehabilitation centers.

In the United States I thank the following people: in the U.S. Department of Labor, Bureau of Labor Statistics: Joyanna Moy, Division of Foreign Labor Statistics; Lillian Kohlrieser, Solidelle Wasser, and Patricia Bommicino of the Middle Atlantic Regional Office; Florence Kramer, office of Congressman Benjamin Rosenthal; and the staffs of the Brooklyn College Library and the Brooklyn Public Library. My special thanks go to Bertram Gross, distinguished professor emeritus at Hunter College and visiting professor at St. Mary's College of California. He encouraged me to continue this project and willingly shared with me his expertise on the subject of full employment. He also kindly provided me with preliminary drafts of a full-employment bill (discussed in chapter 9) that he and Professor Stanley Moses of Hunter College are helping Representative John Conyers to prepare.

It is with deep appreciation that I thank those who read and commented on parts of an earlier draft of this manuscript. Their suggestions and critical comments have made this a better book. I take full responsibility, however, for its contents, interpretations, and any remaining errors. In the United States: Paul Bullock, University of California, Los Angeles, Bertram Gross and Sumner Rosen, Columbia University. In Sweden: Marianne Pettersson, Center for Working Life; Anne-Marie Qvarfort, Ministry of Labor; Bertil Rollén, AMS; Eskil Wadensjö, Swedish Institute for Social Research; and Fredrik Winter, AMS. Thanks also to Sune Åhlen of the Swedish Embassy and Anne-Marie Ringertz of AMS.

Some of the ideas in this book were first developed in articles and an earlier monograph. I wish to thank *Current History* for permission to reprint excerpts from "Needed: A National Commitment to Full Employment"; *The Nation* for permission to reprint excerpts from "Deliberate Unemployment: The Strategy of Misery," copyright 1975; "Jobs for All: Congressional Will o' the Wisp," copyright 1977; and "Full Employment: Swedish Style," copyright 1980; New York University for permission to reprint excerpts from *Unemployment, Subemployment and Public Policy*, which I wrote while I was at its Center for Studies of Income Maintenance Policy; and the Rockefeller Foundation and the Rockefeller Brothers Fund for their support of my research on unemployment while at the center. Finally, I thank Samuel M. Ehrenhalt, U.S. Department of Labor, Bureau of Labor Statistics, for permission to reprint part of his speech on "The Outlook for the New York City Labor Market."

Another debt of gratitude is owed to Margaret Zusky, my editor at Lexington Books, who encouraged me and showed great patience, and to Susan Lasser, editorial assistant.

The final and deepest thanks are due to my husband, Nathan Ginsburg. His suggestions and penetrating criticisms at every stage have improved this book. It could not have been written without his continuous cooperation and encouragement—and endurance.

Part I
The United States

1

Full Employment: The Origin of an Issue

On October 27, 1978, in an impressive ceremony in the White House, President Jimmy Carter signed the Humphrey-Hawkins Full Employment and Balanced Growth Act into law.[1] Passage of the act was the culmination of the second attempt in three decades to commit the U.S. government to the goal of full employment.

Crowded into the East Room of the White House to witness the historic event were the bill's sponsors, Senator Muriel Humphrey of Minnesota, widow of Hubert Humphrey, and Representative Augustus Hawkins of California. Also in the East Room were Secretary of Labor Ray Marshall; Leon Keyserling, the bill's drafter and chairman of the Council of Economic Advisers under President Harry Truman; Coretta Scott King, widow of the slain civil-rights leader; Representative John Conyers of Michican; and other congressional supporters, as well as leaders of civil-rights, labor, religious, women's, and other groups that had been active in the campaign for passage of the bill.

Coretta King—present in her capacity as cochairperson of the Full Employment Action Council, a group organized in the mid-1970s to work for full-employment legislation—noted that the event not only marked a milestone on the road to full employment but also represented a fulfillment of the dream of her late husband, Dr. Martin Luther King, Jr. The event, King observed, was at least as significant as the signing into law of the Civil Rights and Voting Rights acts of 1964 and 1965, because the Humphrey-Hawkins Act deals with the most basic of all human rights—the right to a job.[2] Calling the bill's enactment a victory for the American people, Labor Secretary Marshall added that he could think of no societal problem that would not be immeasurably relieved by achieving its full-employment goals.[3]

Despite these impressive comments, the bill had generated intense controversy in Congress, as had an earlier attempt to enact full-employment legislation in the mid-1940s. Even the Democratic president was, at best, an unenthusiastic supporter. The goal of full employment had far from universal support. To complicate matters, the term *full employment* had come to have a variety of meanings, often light years apart, so that even persons claiming to support full employment did not have the same perception of the target.

3

Concepts of Full Employment

What is full employment? The answer to that question is not readily apparent. Full employment can mean different things to different people.

In an influential report written during World War II, *Full Employment in a Free Society*, the British economist Sir William Beveridge defined full employment as "having always more vacant jobs than unemployed men [sic], not slightly fewer jobs."[4] These jobs, Beveridge stressed, should pay fair wages and be located where the unemployed could be expected to take them. Beveridge allowed for the existence of some unemployment, but only of a very temporary nature, since those who lose jobs must be able to find "new jobs within their capacity, without delay."[5]

Beveridge clearly defined full employment in terms of the human beings who are out of work. An employer who has difficulty buying labor suffers at worst from an inconvenience or reduction of profit, whereas a worker unable to find a job is being told "he [sic] is of no use"; it is a "personal catastrophe" even if an adequate income is provided by unemployment insurance.[6] Even short-term unemployment is not to be lightly regarded, according to Beveridge, because no one can know that he or she is one of the short-term unemployed until he or she has found work again. In Beveridge's view, the government should guarantee full employment through its economic policies. Full employment thus becomes the foundation of the welfare state, in which jobs are to be made available for those who can work. And social-welfare programs ensure an adequate income for those who cannot work because of old age or illness, or for other reasons. They provide health care, social services, and children's allowances regardless of employment status. The Beveridge plan guided the British Labor party government after World War II. Although in later decades it sometimes just limped along, the most concerted attempt to destroy this model came under Prime Minister Margaret Thatcher's Conservative government.

The late Russell Nixon, a Columbia University economist and social-welfare expert, who worked with Representative Hawkins on the earliest version of the Full Employment Bill, viewed full employment as an expanding concept, one with progressively higher standards reflecting advances in social and economic perceptions. He identified four phases.[7]

At the simplest level, full employment means jobs for all, with the emphasis on giving everybody the opportunity to work so that no one who is able and willing to work lacks employment. It is a purely quantitative goal, in which wages, working conditions, and duration of employment are not considerations. Even someone forced to work less than a normal work week because of an inability to find full-time work would be considered employed.

A slightly higher concept is the idea of a good job at a living wage for all. Such a goal implies that jobs with substandard wages and working conditions or involuntary part-time work would not be considered adequate to meet the full-employment goal.

A still higher standard is "jobs for all with decent pay and conditions and realistic opportunities for upward mobility and work at full capacity."[8] The additional emphasis here is on utilization of the abilities and skills of workers. This would mean, for example, that female (or male) college graduates would not end up as clerical workers; and that job ladders, as another example, would enable unskilled hospital workers to receive training and the opportunity to advance to more skilled jobs.

In Nixon's view, the ultimate concept of full employment is not achieved until there is also "full development and full utilization of the total voluntary potential of human resources over time."[9] This concept focuses on time as an important dimension, which can be used to overcome handicaps of all sorts—physical, mental, and social. Adjustments can be made to overcome barriers to employment through training and rehabilitation, by making hours more flexible so that persons who cannot work the usual hours may be employed, and by providing part-time work for those who desire it. Expanding child-care facilities and transportation systems so that people are actually able to work are also obvious considerations. Only at this point, Nixon contends, could we assume that persons who are not working are doing so out of choice.

These four concepts of full employment could obviously encompass a variety of divergent proposals, including one made by Arthur F. Burns, when he was chairman of the Federal Reserve Board, that the government should become the employer of last resort "to anyone who is willing to work at somewhat below the Federal minimum wage."[10] At the other extreme, it could mean the concept as used in early versions of the Humphrey-Hawkins Bill, with government gearing its economic policies toward expanding private-sector employment but also acting as an employer of last resort by providing guaranteed jobs at prevailing wages for those otherwise unable to find jobs. Simultaneously, as in Nixon's fourth phase, programs designed to remove barriers to employment for those currently unable to work—such as child care, public transportation, training, and rehabilitation—are expanded. The fact that full employment means such different things to different people has broad policy implications that are an implicit part of debate on the topic.

Full employment is often defined as some rate of unemployment considered by the definer to be the minimum (or frictional) amount of unemployment the society is capable of achieving. Alternatively, it may simply represent some politically tolerable unemployment rate—the amount perceived to be low enough to keep social order—or it may represent a rate thought to be high enough to control inflation. (These concepts are discussed in greater detail in chapter 2.)

Defining full employment as a rate of unemployment raises the issues of whether that rate is really the lowest society can achieve and whether the unemployment rate itself is actually an accurate measure of the extent of joblessness. If full employment means jobs for all, who is included in the *all*? Does *all* include only those who are currently defined as unemployed? Are there some people not now considered unemployed who might be included? Thus measurement of unemployment and the significance of the unemployment rate become important issues in defining full employment. These are discussed in chapter 2. Since it is not possible to examine the various meanings of full employment without considering contrasting and evolving interpretations of unemployment, we now turn to these interpretations.

Unemployment in Economic Theory and in Practice

It is more than three centuries since the pioneering English economist, Sir William Petty, advocated a new and daring approach to the growing problem of unemployment. In contrast to actual practice in seventeenth-century England, Petty was convinced that the unemployed "ought neither to be starved, nor hanged, nor given away."[11] That idea seemed absurd to wealthy Englishmen at the onset of capitalism, as did his belief that lack of employment, rather than innate laziness, might be the real cause of the miserable condition of the unemployed.

Ironically, Petty was motived by hardheaded economic logic rather than humanitarianism. Reasoning that the unemployed represented an untapped source of labor available to enrich the nation, he suggested that they be publicly employed to build highways, plant trees, build bridges, and so forth—a proposal that is still controversial in the United States in the 1980s.

The lot of the unemployed poor was not a happy one in Petty's time or in subsequent centuries. The continued spread of poverty and unemployment in England during the initial transition to industrial capitalism convinced the upper classes that relief caused poverty by encouraging dependency. Therefore unemployed paupers were put to work. But this work was punishment rather than dignified employment—and the misery of the paupers continued unabated. The many workhouses that were established throughout England and later in America served as punitive institutions to discourage the poor from relying on relief. Historian Paul Mantoux observed that these workhouses were more like prisons than places of refuge. The fear they inspired served to frighten away all but those who had reached the last stage of destitution.[12]

Some of the "idle poor," mostly children, were provided with "real" jobs outside the workhouses—in the prisonlike textile factories that sprang up in England during the Industrial Revolution. As Mantoux tells it, the parishes, eager to get rid of their paupers, entered into regular bargains that were beneficial to both the Poor Law authorities and the spinners, though not to the children, "who were dealt with as mere merchandise." Poor children, as Mantoux put it, were supplied in lots of fifty, eighty, or a hundred and "sent like cattle to the factory where they remained imprisoned for many years."[13]

Even with the passing of the worst abuses of the Industrial Revolution, unemployment persisted. Indeed, bouts of unemployment recurred more or less periodically in all industrial-capitalist nations. Attempts to understand these phenomena have given us sharply different interpretations of the causes and significance of unemployment, and varied policy prescriptions. These interpretations have a long history in economic thought.

Classical and Neoclassical View

The Frenchman Jean Baptiste Say, the Englishman Alfred Marshall, and a long line of classicists and neoclassicists stretching from the late eighteenth century into the twentieth century stressed the transitory nature of unemployment.[14] Their theories denied or minimized the existence of involuntary unemployment, except perhaps as a transitory phenomenon that could be cured by lower wages. Belief in the self-regulating nature of capitalism is the core of these theories, and advocacy of laissez-faire flowed naturally from such a perspective. Even in times of high unemployment, the government was admonished to do nothing to reduce unemployment—to keep its hands off the economy. When actually faced with a recession or a depression, orthodox economists usually prescribed belt-tightening based on cutting wages and slashing government expenditures.

Marxian View

Another line of thought stems from socialist theorist Karl Marx. Writing in the nineteenth century, Marx considered depressions and unemployment inevitable under capitalism. The business cycle, with its alternating periods of expansion and contraction of the economy, is the normal means of capitalist development. Marx viewed the unemployed as an industrial reserve army vital to the functioning of the capitalist system. As a readily available supply of labor, the unemployed permit the system to expand during the boom phase. The reserve army then grows larger during periods of contraction when fewer workers are needed and as a by-product of labor-displacing technology introduced by capitalists to increase profit. Unemployment also helps to increase profit by holding down the wages of employed workers, who can always be replaced by the unemployed. Class struggle between capitalists and workers—another feature of capitalism, according to Marx—is also intensified by depressions and unemployment, which eventually contribute to the system's collapse. Out of the ashes, Marx predicted, socialism would arise—a rational and humane system without unemployment. To Marx and his followers, capitalism without unemployment was as unattainable as socialism with unemployment.

Pushed into what Robert Heilbroner has called the underworld of economics, Marxian analysis had little influence on most mainstream economists and even less on policymakers, for whom the implications could hardly be described as reassuring.[15] At the onset of the Great Depression of the 1930s, neoclassical economics still reigned supreme; but that depression shattered its commanding authority—as well as millions of lives. Far more than the stock market had collapsed. The economy was in near ruin. Poverty, mass unemployment, conflict, and chaos were everywhere. At the depression's worst, nearly 13 million people were out of work; miners earned $1.75 a day; soup kitchens and breadlines dotted the landscape; and labor was picketing, marching, demonstrating, and sitting-in.[16]

Keynesian View

The introduction of John Maynard Keynes's theory in 1936—in the midst of this catastrophic worldwide depression that left no capitalist nation unscathed—seemed to fill an obvious policy void. The influential British economist gave firm intellectual support for active government intervention in the economy. Keynesian or "new economic" theories eventually, though not immediately, gained widespread acceptance among policymakers and economists in most of the capitalist world.

Like Marx, Keynes acknowledged the chronic tendency of advanced capitalist economies to generate high levels of unemployment. Indeed, to Keynes, unemployment was the central problem of the capitalist system that he sought to preserve. The culprit, he claimed, was not wages that were too high but recurrent sagging demand in the private sector. Under such conditions the economy was unable to generate sufficient jobs. The end result would be unemployment—unless the government actively intervened in the economy and increased its expenditures during depressions. Given sufficient government expenditures and other policies designed to stimulate demand, Keynes was certain that a private-enterprise economy could be pushed to full employment. Keynesianism not only challenged neoclassical theory; but, by claiming to have found techniques for maintaining full employment under capitalism, also implicitly denied orthodox socialist thought about the inevitability of unemployment under capitalism.

Job-Creation Programs in the Great Depression

The Great Depression was a traumatic event and a turning point in U.S. history. There had always been unemployment, but never so massive or so persistent. Who could have known in 1929, when 3 percent of the work force was unemployed, that by 1933 unemployment would skyrocket to 25 percent? Who could have known that from 1931 to 1940 joblessness would never fall below 14 percent—and that in four of those years it would average more than 20 percent (see table 1-1)?

Politics and pragmatism, more than theory, determined New Deal policies. The New Deal strategy to end unemployment antedated the 1936 publications of Keynes's influential work, *The General Theory of Employment, Interest and Money*.[17] Nevertheless, New Deal policies bore a remarkable, though far from total, resemblance to those advocated by Keynes. With armies of the unemployed clamoring for jobs, laissez-faire was simply out of the question.

Pump Priming

The New Deal used indirect efforts to create private-sector employment through pump priming. A noted example is the Public Works Administration (PWA), which stimulated employment with publicly financed construction projects. Between 1933 and 1939 the PWA helped to build about 70 percent of the nation's new schools; 65 percent of its courthouses, city halls, and sewage plants; 35 percent of its hospitals and public-health facilities. The PWA helped to construct the Lincoln Tunnel and the Triborough

Table 1-1
Unemployment in the United States, 1929-1946

Year	Percentage Unemployed[a]	Year	Percentage Unemployed
1929	3.2	1938	19.0
1930	8.7	1939	17.2
1931	15.9	1940	14.6
1932	23.6	1941	9.9
1933	24.9	1942	4.7
1934	21.7	1943	1.9
1935	20.1	1944	1.2
1936	16.9	1945	1.9
1937	14.3	1946	3.9

Source: *Employment and Earnings* 19 (February 1973), Table A-1, p. 27.
[a]Unemployed as percentage of civilian labor force 14 years and over.

Bridge in New York; the port of Brownsville, Texas; the overseas highway between Key West, Florida, and the mainland; the library of the University of New Mexico; and Oregon's coastal highway. It made possible the electrification of the Pennsylvania Railroad's New York-Washington line and the completion of Philadelphia's 30th Street Station, to cite some examples.[18]

Direct Job Creation

There were also direct efforts at government job creation, such as the Civil Works Administration (CWA), the Works Progress Administration (WPA), and for young people the Civil Conservation Corps (CCC) and the National Youth Administration (NYA), among others.

The CWA was established in November 1933 by President Franklin D. Roosevelt at the urging of his advisor and friend, Harry Hopkins, then head of the Federal Emergency Relief Administration (FERA). Hopkins had witnessed the demoralization and hopelessness of men and women out of work for reasons beyond their control and forced to live on government handouts. Why not, he reasoned, offer useful jobs instead of the dole?[19]

Hopkins's objective was ambitious: to create 4 million jobs by mid-December 1933. Although that target date was not met, by mid-January 1934 more than 4 million Americans in every state were put to work at prevailing wages by the federal government. During the CWA's short existence, its workers did a tremendous variety of jobs. For example, they built or improved 500,000 miles of roads, 40,000 schools, 1,000 airports, and about 3,500 playgrounds and athletic fields. About 50,000 teachers taught in rural schools and in adult-education programs in cities. The CWA helped to develop parks, clear waterways, build swimming pools and sewers; it also employed 3,000 artists and writers, including opera singers who toured the Ozarks.[20]

Roosevelt, however, quickly succumbed to pressure from businessmen who opposed the CWA.[21] They attacked, among other things, its cost and its policy of paying regular wages, which low-wage employers viewed as a threat to their own ability to keep workers at these jobs. By April 1934 the CWA was out of existence.

The CCC served a total of 2.5 million young men in all and 500,000 at its peak in 1935.[22] With an emphasis on conservation, CCC workers planted trees on hillsides that were burned over or eroded and on mountain slopes that were denuded of timber. They thinned 4 million acres of trees; stocked nearly a billion fish; and built a network of fire lookout towers, roads, and trails. The CCC left a legacy of land, water, and forest preservation and restoration for future generations.

The NYA, in its seven years of existence, gave part-time employment to a total of more than 1.5 million high-school students and over 600,000 young people in college. It also aided more than 2.6 million out-of-school jobless youths.[23]

The WPA is perhaps the best remembered of all New Deal job programs—and was one of the most controversial. In 1935 President Roosevelt proposed a program to provide a job for every ablebodied unemployed person. The Emergency Relief Appropriation Act of 1935, which established the WPA, authorized the largest single appropriation in the history of the United States up to that time.[243] At its peak the WPA employed more than 3 million persons.[25] Unlike CWA, the WPA paid a so-called security wage—more than relief but less than the prevailing wage—in order to make these jobs less attractive than private employment. Nevertheless, this did not deter opposition. The most common charge against the WPA was that it was nothing more than leaf raking. Indeed, one of the major problems of the WPA was that it was not permitted to compete with private industry or to engage in regular government tasks. Despite these constraints, even a partial listing of its activities shows that the WPA literally changed the face of the nation.[26] To cite some examples, WPA workers not only built or reconstructed 617,000 miles of roads, 124,000 bridges and viaducts, and 120,000 public buildings; they also left the nation with thousands of new parks, playgrounds, and athletic fields. Moreover, they drained malarial swamps, exterminated rats in slums, organized nursery schools, and taught illiterate adults to read and write. Unemployed actors set up theaters throughout the land, often performing in remote towns and backwoods areas. WPA orchestras gave 6,000 live concerts. WPA artists produced murals, sculptures, and paintings that still adorn our public buildings. Even though it was a means-tested relief program, WPA helped sustain the talent of artists like Jackson Pollock, Ben Shahn, and Willim de Kooning, and of writers like Saul Bellow, Studs Terkel, and Richard Wright—as well as the dignity of millions of other people who would otherwise have been forced to remain idle.

Lessons from the New Deal

The WPA was never able to give jobs to all the unemployed. In fact, at its point of greatest impact, it employed only 31 percent of the jobless.[27] The WPA and other New Deal job programs did show, however, that, given the will, it was feasible for the federal government to undertake large-scale, socially useful, direct job creation. These experiences also revealed that extensive opposition to such programs, even in the midst of such a massive depression, could prevent their being fully utilized to end unemployment.

Indeed, New Deal policies on employment frequently wavered. The previously cited case of the CWA is just one example. Another important example occurred in 1937. Such improvements as had occurred in the economy by then had been achieved mostly through the government's deficit spending. In June 1937, however, Roosevelt, inordinately worried about inflation, cut government spending sharply.[28] The WPA rolls were drastically reduced, and the PWA's pump priming was turned off. Roosevelt's anxiety followed on the heels of the Federal Reserve Board's concern over the possibility of rising prices, which had led it to double the reserve requirements of member banks between August 1936 and May 1937.[29] The result of these actions was the birth of a depression within a depression, which threw another 2 million people out of work by the end of 1937. As table 1-1 shows, unemployment rose from 14.3 percent in 1937 to 19 percent in 1938. Thus, although the New Deal encompassed a great deal of Keynesianism in its approach, some of the old orthodoxy also remained.

World War II

Throughout the 1930s there was no dearth of opposition from conservative adherents of laissez-faire, who often attacked what they regarded as the grandiose scale of New Deal efforts. In fact, these efforts were not even massive enough to end unemployment, which still averaged 14.6 percent in 1940. It was still nearly 10 percent in 1941, and even that decline was largely due to the military buildup that had already begun in 1940.[30] Even though the United States did not officially enter World War II until December 1941, the Selective Service Act was passed in 1940. By late 1941, with the draft and voluntary enlistments, the size of the armed forces had already doubled to about 1.6 million. With rising military spending, defense-industry payrolls grew by 2.6 million, and government civilian payrolls shot up by 400,000 during 1941. In that year military expenditures were already 11 percent of gross national product (GNP).

Thus it took World War II to end the Great Depression. During the war the situation changed dramatically. From 1943 to 1945 unemployment stayed below 2 percent, hitting an all-time low of 1.2 percent in 1944. With some 11.5 million men and women eventually absorbed into the armed forces, and with millions of war jobs to fill, severe labor shortages developed. Now the shoe was on the other foot. People whose labor had previously been rejected, or who had been out of the labor force, were hired. The formerly unemployed, the young, the aged, and the disabled became valuable workers. Women were called out of the kitchen; Rosie the Riveter became the prototype of the new female worker whose labor was needed—especially in jobs that had traditionally been held by men—in order to win the war. Federal involvement in day-care centers expanded enormously in order to enable mothers to take jobs in defense industries, and care was provided for approximately 600,000 children.[31] Moreover, given the tight labor market plus the threat by black labor leader A. Philip Randolph of a protest march on Washington of 50,000 blacks against employment discrimination, President Roosevelt issued an executive order creating the first Fair Employment Practices Committee. As a result, Jim Crow hiring practices abated somewhat. Black workers thus scored some employment breakthroughs in industry, though mostly as manual workers.[32]

World War II proved to be the most extended period of full employment ever experienced by this nation, and it was a powerful weapon against poverty. Steady paychecks enabled millions of families to leave the ranks of the poor. Earnings and income inequalities declined.

Even a few years of wartime full employment were insufficient to erase the deep scar left by the depression of the 1930s. Fear of a postwar return of mass unemployment was pervasive, as was the strong feeling—especially in liberal and labor circles—that a nation capable of providing jobs for all during wartime could and should do no less during peacetime. The United States, it was thought, should not have to rely on war to solve its unemployment problem. This environment provided fertile soil for the emergence of full employment as a major policy issue.

In 1944, while the war still raged, Franklin Roosevelt formulated a Second Bill of Rights. First on the list was "the right for all to . . . useful and remunerative jobs." The Democratic party's 1944 platform promised to "guarantee full employment." In that year's election the issue seemed beyond controversy. Not only did Thomas Dewey, the Republican presidential nominee, support full employment; he even emphasized the government's obligation to intervene in the economy to provide sufficient jobs when necessary, to give "every man and woman a chance to earn a decent living."[33]

The Full Employment Bill of 1945

In reality, however, conflicting interests and philosophies had not vanished. By 1945 the political sentiment for full employment had entered the congressional arena, where liberal senators introduced the ill-fated Murray-Wagner Full Employment Bill, which called for a "national policy and program for assuring full employment." The bill, with an emphasis on human rights, had the support of numerous liberal, labor, social-welfare, and religious organizations. These included the American Federation of Labor (AFL), the Congress of Industrial Organizations (CIO), the National Association for the Advancement of Colored People (NAACP), the National Farmers' Union, the American Veterans Committee, the Young Women's

Christian Association, the National Catholic Welfare Conference, the National Council of Jewish Women, and the Union for Democratic Action (founded mainly to unite labor and liberal groups behind an antifascist foreign policy), to name a few.[34]

The Murray-Wagner bill was just as vehemently opposed by congressional conservatives and by organizations such as the National Association of Manufacturers, the Chamber of Commerce, and the American Farm Bureau Federation. In the spring of 1945 there was a hint of the intensity of the opposition to full employment that would soon occur on Capitol Hill. At the San Francisco United Nations Conference, Senators Arthur Vandenberg (R-Michigan) and Thomas Connally (D-Texas), leaders of the U.S. delegation, took violent exception to the use of the term *full employment* in the U.N. Charter. They threatened Senate rejection if "full employment" was used and pressed for substitution of "high and stable levels of employment." In the end, "full employment" was inserted in the charter and, through use of a face-saving device, the U.S. delegation finally accepted it.[35]

It is also interesting to recall that in 1944, when the bill was still in its embryonic state, only two organizations in the liberal-labor bloc supported it enthusiastically: The Union for Democratic Action and the National Farmers' Union. The bloc was far from a united one, and disunity prevailed in the house of labor. Less than a decade had passed since the expulsion of the CIO from the AFL; a deep chasm of bitterness, power struggles, and ideological differences still separated the two federations. Initially, the AFL suspected that the Full Employment Bill was CIO-inspired.[36] Some CIO and AFL leaders also feared that the bill was a pie-in-the-sky proposal that would drain energy from more immediate issues such as unemployment insurance and minimum wages.[37] Ultimately, however, labor leaders recognized that the bill could no longer be ignored and that stronger support for it was required. Attitudes changed for a variety of reasons: a substitute bill that had been anticipated never developed; rank and file support for the bill was growing, stimulated by direct efforts from Senator Wagner's staff; both the AFL and the CIO worried that the other might give the bill its strong support and thereby gain adherents; and attempts to bring together groups that had expressed support for the bill and to get them to work harder for its passage were bearing fruit. Roosevelt's death in April 1945 also shocked labor leaders into recognizing that obtaining future progressive legislation would require an uphill battle; and with the war rapidly coming to an end, the specter of widespread unemployment once again seemed close at hand.[38]

As for the bill itself, the goal of full employment meant that:

All Americans able to work and seeking work have the right to useful, remunerative, regular and full-time employment, and it is the policy of the

United States to assure the existence at all times of sufficient employment opportunities to enable all Americans who have finished their schooling and who do not have full-time housekeeping responsibilities to freely exercise this right.[39]

The bill spelled out the federal government's role in assuring full employment. The president was to transmit annually to the Congress a National Production and Employment Budget with estimates of the size of the labor force, the total national production required to provide jobs for that labor force, and total production in the absence of special measures by the federal government. If anticipated production was insufficient to provide jobs for the whole labor force, the federal government was to encourage enough additional nonfederal investment and expenditures to stimulate private-sector employment. If necessary, however, federal investment and expenditures were to be used to close any remaining gap to assure full employment. In sum, the bill was designed to apply Keynesian techniques to attain full employment.

On September 28, 1945, the more liberal Senate passed the Full Employment Bill by an overwhelming 71-10. In the amended version that passed, liberal pressures had succeeded in expanding the scope of the meaning of full employment so that persons with "full-time housekeeping responsibilities" were not excluded from the right to employment. (Their exclusion, not in the original draft, had been inserted before the bill was introduced in order to get more support.)

The bill was then debated in the House, where it faced a different destiny. By then the situation had changed. The expected postwar depression had not happened. The first wave of postwar strikes had started, fueling antilabor feeling. Conservative groups, especially big business, intensified their campaign against the bill. Also, some lukewarm supporters probably voted for the bill in the Senate because they knew it would not be passed in the House.

Testifying for the bill on behalf of the U.S. Conference of Mayors, Fiorello La Guardia—then mayor of New York but in the early 1930s a member of the House of Representatives—contrasted the situation in the two periods. Some of the very same businessmen, La Guardia recalled, who "came to President Roosevelt with hat in hand and tears in their eyes" at that time "are now coming before you saying the same thing that they were saying prior to the crash of 1929. . . ."[40]

A variety of arguments were used by opponents. Mainly they alleged that full employment cannot be guaranteed in a free society, that full employment means tyranny, that full employment would kill initiative, that government spending undermines business confidence, and that the necessary economic forecasting would be impossible. A few argued that full employment would lead to inflation or defended the need for a floating pool of unemployed—although for public-relations reasons the latter was not widely publicized. However, the Farm Bureau, representing big farmers, openly expressed fear of losing a cheap labor supply if the bill passed, a refrain echoed by many in the Congress.[41]

The Employment Act of 1946

The more conservative House thus defeated the Full Employment Bill and offered a substitute, which differed substantively from that passed by the Senate. The Employment Act of 1946 is the compromise that emerged from that struggle.

Differing markedly from the Full Employment Bill of 1945, the 1946 act no longer emphasized human rights. It rejected the full-employment goal and the federal obligation to intervene in the economy to guarantee jobs for all in favor of an obligation to create "conditions under which there will be afforded useful employment opportunities for those able, willing and seeking work, and to promote maximum employment, production and purchasing power."[42]

For full employment, the vaguer goal of "maximum employment" was substituted; the government commitment was limited to "all practical means consistent with the needs and obligations of national policy." Thus employment was no longer the unambiguous priority, and "impractical" means of attaining the act's goals did not have to be used. That phrase also left the door open to flexible interpretations, such as the assertion that attaining the employment goal would be inconsistent with the policy goal of stable prices. Other changes were consistent with these. Instead of the National Production and Employment Budget and the explicit pledge to use federal resources to assure full employment if the private sector failed to do so, the act simply required an Annual Economic Report of the president and the establishment of the Council of Economic Advisers and the Joint Economic Committee of Congress.

One could argue that the difference between "full employment" and "maximum employment" is insignificant. But in the context of the time, that was not the case. These were not mere semantic differences but represented important philosophical disagreements about the employment objective and the role and extent of government involvement in the economy. As the Conference Report of the Congress stated:

> The House substitute declared that . . . the function of Government is to promote and not to assure or guarantee employment. . . . [In the conference agreement] the term "full employment" is rejected, and the term

"maximum employment" is the objective . . . the words or terms "full,"
"guarantee," "assure," "investment," and "expenditures," do not occur
in the conference agreement. The goal is maximum or high levels of employment. The emphasis on expenditures and disbursements is omitted
from the conference agreement.[43]

As Senator Robert Taft (R-Ohio), who led the fight against the Full
Employment Bill, told the Senate in the final 1946 debate, "I do not think
any Republican need fear voting for the bill because of any apprehension
that there is a victory [for its proponents] in the passage of the full employment bill, because there is no full employment bill anymore."[44]

Nevertheless, the significance of the Employment Act of 1946 should
not be minimized. It was a landmark piece of legislation. Interpretations
continue to vary. Bertram Gross, who served as chief drafter of the original
Full Employment Bill and the Employment Act of 1946 feels that the purpose of the act was not to guarantee employment. It was, according to
Gross, then distinguished professor at Hunter College, to prevent the recur-
rence of a mass depression.[45] Others, however, continued to call it a full-
employment act.

Notes

1. P.L. 523, 95th Cong., 2d Sess. The description of this event is found
in "Carter Signs H.-H. at White House," *Full Employment Action News*
(Washington, D.C.: Full Employment Action Council, November 1978), p. 1.

2. "Carter Signs H.-H."

3. Ibid.

4. William H. Beveridge, *Full Employment in a Free Society* (London:
Allen & Unwin, 1944), p. 18.

5. Ibid., p. 18.

6. Ibid., p. 23.

7. Russell A. Nixon, "The Historical Development of the Conception
and Implementation of Full Employment as Economic Policy," in *Public
Service Employment: An Analysis of Its History, Problems, and Prospects*,
ed. Alan Gartner, Russell A. Nixon, and Frank Riessman (New York:
Praeger, 1973), pp. 13-14.

8. Ibid., p. 13.

9. Ibid., p. 14.

10. Arthur F. Burns, Address, University of Georgia, Athens, 19
September 1975, in U.S. Congress, Joint Economic Committee, *Hearings
on the Thirtieth Anniversary of the Employment Act of 1946—A National
Conference on Full Employment*, 94th Cong., 2d Sess., 1976, p. 153.

11. Sir William Petty, *A Discourse of Taxes and Contributions* (London, 1667) in *Poverty, Economics and Society*, ed. Helen Ginsburg

(Boston: Little, Brown, 1972; reprint ed., Washington, D.C.: University Press of America, 1981), pp. 12-14.

12. Paul Mantoux, *The Industrial Revolution in the Eighteenth Century* (1905), rev. ed. (New York: Harper Torchbooks, 1962), p. 432.

13. Ibid., pp. 410-411.

14. For a policy-oriented discussion of the economic theories of Marx, Say, Marshall, and Keynes, see, for instance, Daniel R. Fusfeld, *The Age of the Economist*, 3rd. ed. (Glenview, Ill.: Scott, Foresman, 1966); or E. Ray Canterbery, *The Making of Economics* (Belmont, Calif.: Wadsworth, 1978).

15. Robert L. Heilbroner, *The Worldly Philosophers*, 3rd ed. (New York: Simon and Schuster, 1977).

16. There is an abundant literature on the depression. See, for instance, Broadus Mitchell, *Depression Decade: The Economic History of the United States*, vol. 9 (New York: Holt, Rinehart and Winston, 1947). The impact on labor is in Joseph G. Rayback, *A History of American Labor* (New York: Free Press, 1966), chap. 22. Estimates of unemployment are found in ibid., p. 316. Miners' wages are cited in Clarence Pickett, "Children in the Coal Mining Towns," in *The Great Depression*, ed. David A. Shannon (Englewood Cliffs, N.J.: Prentice-Hall, 1960), pp. 53-54.

17. John Maynard Keynes, *The General Theory of Employment, Interest and Money* (New York: Harcourt, Brace and World, 1936).

18. William E. Leuchtenberg, *Franklin D. Roosevelt and the New Deal: 1932-1940* (New York: Harper Torchbooks, 1963), p. 133.

19. Arthur M. Schlesinger, Jr., *The Coming of the New Deal: The Age of Roosevelt* (Boston: Houghton Mifflin, 1959), pp. 268-271.

20. Schlesinger, *Coming of the New Deal*, p. 270; Leuchtenberg, *Franklin D. Roosevelt*, pp. 121-122.

21. These controversies are described in Schlesinger, *Coming of the New Deal*, pp. 274-277, and Leuchtenberg, *Franklin D. Roosevelt*, pp. 122-123.

22. Leuchtenberg, *Franklin D. Roosevelt*, p. 174.

23. Ibid., p. 129.

24. Ibid., p. 124.

25. Nixon, "Full Employment as Economic Policy," p. 19. A complete analysis of the WPA is given in Alden T. Briscoe, "Public Service Employment in the 1930s: the WPA," in *The Political Economy of Public Service Employment* ed. Harold L. Sheppard, Bennett Harrison, and William J. Spring (Lexington, Mass.: Lexington Books, D.C. Heath and Company, 1972), pp. 95-115.

26. Briscoe, "Public Service Employment, pp. 105-108; "WPA: It . Wasn't All Leaf-Raking," *Newsweek*, 20 January 1975, p. 57.

27. Briscoe, "Public Service Employment," p. 113.

28. Leuchtenberg, *Franklin D. Roosevelt*, pp. 243-245.

29. Charles H. Hession and Hyman Sardy, *Ascent to Affluence: A History of American Economic Development* (Boston: Allyn and Bacon, 1969), pp. 740-741.

30. Data on this military buildup are from Verle Johnston, "Summer of '41," Research Department, Federal Reserve Bank of San Francisco, *Weekly Letter*, 14 August 1981, pp. 1-3.

31. U.S. Congress, Congressional Budget Office, *Childcare and Preschool Options for Federal Support* (Washington, D.C.: U.S. Government Printing Office, 1978), p. 3.

32. For an overview of the black worker in World War II, see Ray Marshall, *The Negro Worker* (New York: Random House, 1967), pp. 120-123, and Arthur M. Ross, "The Negro in the American Economy," in *Employment, Race and Poverty*, ed. Arthur M. Ross and Herbert Hill (New York: Harcourt, Brace and World, 1967), pp. 16-18.

33. Quotes from Roosevelt, the Democratic party platform, and Dewey are from Stephen Kemp Bailey, *Congress Makes a Law* (New York: Vintage Books, 1960), pp. 41-43. Much of what follows relies heavily on Bailey's authoritative legislative history of the Employment Act of 1946.

34. Ibid., chaps. 3-6.

35. Ibid., pp. 102-103.

36. Ibid., p. 80.

37. Ibid., p. 82.

38. Ibid., p. 90.

39. S. 380, 79th Cong., 1st Sess., Sec 2(b), 1945.

40. Fiorello H. LaGuardia, quoted in Ginsburg, *Poverty, Economics and Society*, p. 122.

41. Bailey, *Congress Makes a Law*, Chaps. 7, 8.

42. P.L. 304, Employment Act of 1946, 79th Cong., 2d sess., sec. 2.

43. The House Conference Report on S. 380 is reprinted in U.S. Senate, Committee on Labor and Public Welfare, Subcommittee on Employment, Manpower and Poverty, *Comprehensive Manpower Reform Hearings*, pt. 5, 92d Cong., 2d Sess., 1972. Quote from pp. 2503-2504.

44. *Congressional Record*, 8 February 1946, quoted in Nixon, "Full Employment as Economic Policy," p. 27.

45. U.S. Congress, House, Subcommittee on Education and Labor, Hearing on H.R. 15476, *Equal Opportunity and Full Employment Act of 1976*, 93rd. Cong., 2d sess., 1974, p. 57. See also Bertram Gross, *Friendly Fascism: The New Face of Power in America* (New York: Evans, 1980), for other of his views.

2 Unemployment and the Unemployed

In the decades following passage of the Employment Act of 1946, mass depressions were averted. This very success helped to take away attention from the problem of unemployment. When unemployment was a mass affliction, it could not be ignored. Lower levels of unemployment made it easier to do so.

Recurrent recessions were not eliminated, however. Between passage of the Employment Act of 1946 and the Humphrey-Hawkins Full Employment and Balanced Growth Act of 1978, there were six recessions. The most severe one until then was in the mid-1970s. In 1975 the jobless rate was higher than it had been since the Great Depression. In 1975 it reached an annual rate of 8.5 percent, peaking at 8.9 percent in May (table 2-1). In 1980 there was another recession, quickly followed by one that started during the Reagan administration. As of August 1982 the unemployment rate of 9.8 percent had again broken all post-World War II records; with nearly 11 million people out of work, unemployment was still heading upward.

Even before the mini-depression of the 1970s, the average rate of joblessness was high and drifting upward. After 1948 it never dipped below 4 percent, except during the Korean and Vietnam wars. Large peacetime military expenditures also became a permanent part of the U.S. economy. For example, they made up 83 percent of federal purchases of goods and services in the cold-war year of 1960, 76 percent in the hot-war year of 1970, and 66 percent in 1980, before the Reagan administration began its military buildup.[1]

Actually, Keynes had recognized that an economy could be stimulated by "pyramid building, earthquakes, and even wars." Though personally favoring socially useful government expenditures, he sensed that there might be "political and practical difficulties" involved in expanding those kinds of expenditures to stabilize the economy.[2] His premonition was well justified. The huge military buildup in the post-World War II decades not only served the cold- and hot-war foreign-policy needs of the United States, but military expenditures also had become an integral part of the maintenance of aggregate demand. In the 1960s Marxian economists Paul A. Baran and Paul M. Sweezy pointed this out, as did iconoclast liberal John Kenneth Galbraith.[3] Despite the growth and massiveness of these expenditures, Galbraith noted a marked tendency among many economists to "minimize or ignore" their role in the economy.[4] Even with huge military expenditures,

21

Table 2-1
Unemployment in the United States, 1946-1981 and August 1982

| | Unemployed[a] | | | Unemployed | |
| | | *Number* | | | *Number* |
Year	*Percentage*	*(in thousands)*	*Year*	*Percentage*	*(in thousands)*
1946	3.9	2,270	1964	5.2	3,786
1947	3.9	2,311	1965	4.5	3,366
1948	3.8	2,276	1966	3.8	2,875
1949	5.9	3,637	1967	3.8	2,975
1950	5.3	3,288	1968	3.6	2,817
1951	3.3	2,055	1969	3.5	2,832
1952	3.0	1,883	1970	4.9	4,088
1953	2.9	1,834	1971	5.9	4,993
1954	5.5	3,532	1972	5.6	4,840
1955	4.4	2,852	1973	4.9	4,304
1956	4.1	2,750	1974	5.6	5,076
1957	4.3	2,859	1975	8.5	7,830
1958	6.8	4,602	1976	7.7	7,288
1959	5.5	3,740	1977	7.0	6,855
1960	5.5	3,852	1978	6.0	6,047
1961	6.7	4,714	1979	5.8	5,963
1962	5.5	3,911	1980	7.1	7,448
1963	5.7	4,070	1981	7.6	8,080
			August 1982[b]	9.8	10,805

Source: *Employment and Earnings* 21(January 1975):20, table A-1; *Employment and Earnings* 29(January 1982):9, table A-1; U.S. Department of Labor, Bureau of Labor Statistics, News Release, 3 September 1982. Unemployed as a percentage of the civilian labor force.

[a]Prior to 1947, persons 14 years and over; from 1947 on, persons 16 years and over.

[b]Seasonally adjusted. 1982 figures are based on 1980 Census Population Controls; 1981 and earlier figures are based on 1970 Census Controls.

however, unemployment did not disappear, not even during the Vietnam War. In 1969, for example, military expenditures amounted to 8.6 percent of GNP, and unemployment reached a low of 3.5 percent. However, that same year, many nations whose military expenditures made up smaller portions of GNP—such as Japan (0.8 percent), West Germany (3.5 percent), and Sweden (4.0 percent)—had significantly lower jobless rates—1.1, 0.8, and 1.9 percent, respectively.[5]

Inflation and Unemployment

Big business has always preferred some unemployment, though not major, system-threatening depressions. Unemployment gives business more control over workers, weakens unions, and helps hold down wages. Furthermore, as at present, it drives some smaller or weaker firms out of business and enables larger, stronger ones to buy some firms at bargain-basement prices. Even during the New Deal, restrictive government policies sometimes resulted in additional unemployment. Increasingly, however, economic theory helped to justify higher and higher levels of joblessness, all in the name of fighting inflation.

In the 1960s many economists and policymakers came to believe in the concept of the Phillips curve. In an influential article in 1958, A.W. Phillips reasoned that as unemployment falls, labor markets tighten and wages rise; conversely, as unemployment rises, labor markets loosen and wages rise slowly or not at all.[6] Using data from 1861 to 1957, Phillips concluded that, in the United Kingdom, the rate of *money-wage changes* could be explained by the level and change in unemployment. Soon, however, the concept came to mean an allegedly *inevitable* trade-off between unemployment and *price changes*. This shift assumed that prices are determined by wage costs and that nonwage components of prices (such as profits, rent, interest, and materials) rise and fall proportionately with wages. It also assumed that wage changes lead to price changes, not the other way around.

The original Keynesian theory did not consider inflation a problem in an economy at less than full employment. The trade-off theory, however, reasoned that the lower the unemployment rate, the higher the inflation, and the higher the unemployment rate, the lower the inflation.[7] This implied, in the most conservative interpretation, that full employment was too inflationary—and thus *unattainable* or even *undesirable*—and even that low unemployment was always inflationary. Each country was also said to have its own unemployment-inflation trade-off. Otherwise it would have been difficult to explain how Germany had both the lowest jobless *and* the lowest inflation rates among major Western industrial nations during much of this period.[8]

The idea that there is some supposedly "natural" rate of unemployment also gained acceptance among some economists. In his presidential address at the 1967 convention of the American Economic Association, conservative, economist Milton Friedman contended that policymakers cannot lower unemployment for more than very limited time periods because there is only one rate of unemployment consistent with a constant rate of inflation—the so-called natural rate of unemployment.[9] Friedman also warned that attempts by policymakers to shoot for unemployment that is too low—that is, below the "natural" rate—would lead to continuously accelerating inflation. Although other models of the natural rate were subsequently developed, all of them implied that unemployment rates are sometimes *too low*—that is, below the natural rate—and thus are not sustainable, except in the short run. The conservative policy implications are not hard to discern. One of them asks: Why try to lower unemployment and risk inflation when it probably won't even help to reduce joblessness? Another goes even further:

Why not take steps to *increase* unemployment so that it rises to its natural level? Interpretations of what the natural rate is have varied among adherents and, over the years, they have risen along with increases in the actual jobless rate.[10]

These theories helped to pave the way for a different meaning of full employment. At one time, as in the case of Beveridge's definition and in the spirit of the Full Employment Bill of 1945, it had focused on human beings. It meant that all those who wanted work could find it. Later the focus shifted from people to prices. Regardless of whether the relationship was even valid, in many circles full employment came to mean some unemployment rate consistent with the degree of price stability desired by policymakers, businessmen, economists, or others—or simply some rate of unemployment perceived to be politically tolerable.

There can be little doubt that the rate of unemployment considered tolerable rose during the postwar decades. The establishment's so-called full-employment unemployment rate climbed from 2 or 3 percent, to 4 percent, to 5 and 6 percent—and it did not stop there. In 1977 Herbert Stein, who had been head of President Richard Nixon's Council of Economic Advisers, called 7 percent unemployment, the official rate at that time, full employment.[11] Almost 7 million people were then officially jobless, and millions more were not included in the official figures.

Acceptance of higher and higher levels of unemployment was helped along by numerous factors. Racism, sexism, a divided working class, ignorance of the true extent of unemployment all played a role, as did apathy and an "I'm all right Jack" attitude. To these must be added the relative weakness of organized labor, the low degree of unionization, and the absence of any significant labor or political left. The remnants of the latter had been vitiated by the cold war, McCarthyism, and witch hunts, as well as by the expulsion from the CIO in the late 1940s of left-wing unions such as the United Electrical, Radio and Machine Workers (UE).

It is not surprising that, in this social and political climate, trade-off analysis appealed to conservative policymakers facing inflation. It has since become commonplace to see *open advocacy* of the use of economic policy to increase unemployment and to help hasten the advent of recessions, but this was less common in the 1960s. In 1968, with prices rising and unemployment at 3.6 percent, the Business Council, an influential federal advisory group of top corporate executives, urged the next president to push unemployment up to 5.5 percent, if necessary, to curb inflation.[12] (That round of inflation was the result of the escalating cost of the Vietnam War and President Lyndon Johnson's fear of raising taxes, lest such a move arouse further opposition to the war.) Soon afterward, the Nixon administration pursued policies that helped to drive unemployment up from 3.5 percent in 1969 to 5.9 percent in 1971, leaving about 2 million more workers jobless.[13] Planning recessions, to prod along the contraction phase of the business cycle, became an important part of the policy toolbox.

The recession that the Nixon administration helped to create led to more unemployment. But inflation persisted. *Stagflation* soon became the popular term to describe the coexistence of inflation and higher unemployment—something that trade-off analysis had not predicted.

One of the consequences of stagflation was the upward redefinition of full employment, mentioned previously. The official reason the Nixon administration gave for this redefinition—one that became very influential—is the structural hypothesis. This reasoning is based on the fact that the structure of the labor force had changed, over several decades, with women and young people making up a larger proportion than in the past. As the 1974 *Economic Report of the President* described it, the "maximum employment" goal of the Employment Act was met in 1973, "even though the average unemployment rate was 4.9 percent rather than 4.0 percent, which conventionally defines full employment."[14] This was justified because of the large increase in the labor force since 1956 in the proportion of "women and young workers of both sexes, two groups whose unemployment rates are substantially higher than the national average."[15]

A more recent example of this pervasive logic appeared in a 1978 Special Report of the National Commission for Manpower Policy, which stated that: "The 4 percent interim full employment goal of the 1960s must be translated because of the changing composition of the labor force—more young people and women—into a 5.5 percent level in the mid-1970s."[16]

Wellesley College economist Carolyn Shaw Bell, formerly head of the Committee on the Status of Women in the Economics Profession of the American Economic Association, has called that kind of reasoning "the economics of might have been." It is, she has said, "irrelevant to what exists here and now. Since it is the actual conditions of employment that warrant policy formulations, economists' energy must focus on actuality."[17]

In reality, the structural hypothesis was often simply used to redefine a problem out of existence, to minimize its seriousness, to accustom the nation to permanently higher jobless rates, and to blame the unemployed for unemployment. As the late Robert Aaron Gorden, subsequently president of the American Economic Association, told a congressional committee in 1972, according to this argument, "the new troublemakers are women and teenagers."[18]

Why was the U.S. economy generating inflation and unemployment? Some explanations offered during the years when stagflation became a household word made little headway in influencing public policy—even when findings came out of congressional committees or were supported by other evidence. All of them stressed the need for structural changes in the economy or changes in power relationships. Examples of interpretations that were put on the back burner are corporate power, the growth of multi-national corporations, and massive peacetime military expenditures.

The late John Blair pointed to the increasing concentration of U.S. in-dustry. Former chief economist of the Senate Antitrust Committee, Blair, in detailed studies of pricing practices during the 1970 recession, showed that firms in highly concentrated industries had a strong tendency to increase rather than to cut prices.[19] Thus, with more economic concentration, planned recessions that added to unemployment and reduced demand would not necessarily even cure inflation—unless they were very deep and long lasting. Howard Wachtel and Peter Adelsheim reported similar findings in a study for the Joint Economic Committee.[20] As long ago as 1973, Peter Gilpin's study for the Senate Committee on Labor and Public Welfare suggested that the export of jobs by multinational corporations was adding to the un-employment problem.[21] The rise of corporate power and multinational cor-porations as factors exacerbating stagflation were, understandably, not popular subjects among businessmen nor conservatives.

In 1974, the Joint Economic Committee raised the issue of the rela-tionship between *peacetime* military expenditures and inflation—something that later came into the limelight with the Reagan administration's huge military budget. According to the committee, such expenditures are inher-ently inflationary because

> Defense goods and services cannot be consumed by the public, and to the extent that they are employed by the military they are unavailable for civilian purposes. The removal of goods and services from the civilian economy may contribute to shortages. Defense programs inject expendi-tures into the economy but they do not produce goods and services to satisfy consumer needs. Arms are not sold to the public.[22]

Despite the fact that the committee felt that this was a neglected part of economic research, it found the Council of Economic Advisers unwilling to conduct research on the topic.[23]

Even at that time, however, the topic had not been neglected entirely. For example, Seymour Melman, professor of industrial engineering at Columbia University, had long been investigating the role of military expenditures in the U.S. economy. Melman not only concurred with the committee's view that the permanent war economy was highly inflationary; he also observed that it was causing dislocations in the civilian sector of the economy, robbing it of its vitality, and leading to the neglect of civilian technology. As Melman ex-plained it, the Pentagon, by gobbling up about three-quarters of federal research-and-development dollars, dominated and channeled the nation's re-search-and-development efforts. He warned that this was contributing to the erosion of the U.S. industrial base. The country was becoming less competi-tive with nations such as Japan, which concentrated on developing civilian technology, unencumbered by a huge military budget. Challenging the conventional wisdom that military expenditures create employment, Melman noted that *unemployment* as well as inflation is exacerbated by military expenditures because they generate fewer jobs than equivalent civilian expenditures.[24] Numerous studies have shown this to be the case. One of them, done by economist Marion Anderson for the Michigan Public Interest Research group, found that between 1970 and 1974, every time the military budget rose by $1 billion, it meant a loss of 11,600 jobs from the economy. Thus, during those years, with annual defense budgets averaging $78 billion, Anderson estimated a net loss of 907,000 jobs, which contributed to stagflation.[25]

Inflation in the 1970s was also stimulated at various times by many other factors, such as rising energy costs; the worldwide increase in the demand for U.S. farm products, which, along with the growth of agribusiness, helped to push food prices up; two devaluations of the dollar, which made imports dearer; rapidly rising health-care costs; and high interest rates. The last of these were used to slow down the economy but helped to push up prices, especially of housing.

Unlike the 1960s, the 1970s were years of stagnating real wages. Between 1970 and 1979, for example, gross average hourly earnings in the private sector, adjusted for inflation, rose by only five cents. By the beginning of the 1980s real wages had actually declined below the 1970 level.[26] Most workers were not winners in this inflation. Yet as Garth Mangum concluded in a study for the National Commission on Manpower Policy, inappropriate trade-off analysis was used to justify the go-slow recovery policy from the 1975 recession. In 1976, with 7 million still officially out of work, Mangum noted that "labor markets were being held in ransom to fears of an inflation to which they had not contributed."[27]

The point is that alternative policies to control inflation without adding to unemployment were always available. Those who stressed the goal of full employment, *and* the need to control inflation, advocated such alternatives. Several important examples will be cited.

Economist Leslie Nulty, in a 1977 study of the "new inflation" for the Exploratory Project for Economic Alternatives, confirmed what millions of ordinary Americans had already felt: that inflation was particularly severe in the necessities of life. What was needed, said Nulty, was not a general reduction in economic activity but an anti-inflation policy targeted to control the specific causes of inflation in each sector affecting the necessities. Thus separate policies were required to get at the structural roots of inflation in energy, food, medical care, and housing.[28]

Others advocated antirecessionary policies, partly on the grounds that recessions can actually add to inflation. Since recessions mean idle workers and unused capacity, there is less rather than more output. Furthermore, using plants at less than optimum capacity pushes up unit cost of production.[29]

Controls were another possibility. In 1975 Robert Lekachman, distinguished professor of economics at Lehman College, was one of those who argued that full employment without inflation was possible. He felt, however, that attaining it would require, among other things, an incomes policy with permanent but equitable controls focused on large corporations, unions, and professional societies. The last of these was meant to curb the fees of physicians, dentists, and other professionals.[30] That same year, in a report entitled *Full Employment without Inflation*, prepared for the Task Force of the National Committee for Full Employment, Leon Keyserling presented a broad approach incorporating many of these ideas, as well as recommendations for selective credit and interest-rate policies. Keyserling contended that, contrary to the trade-off idea, empirical evidence from the previous two decades demonstrated that improved economic health reduces inflation and vice versa. Nevertheless, he proposed, "serious consideration should be given to direct controls to deal with prices, wages, dividends, and interest, accompanied by an excess profits tax."[31]

As already noted, Melman and others talked of curbs on military expenditures as a way of reducing inflationary pressures on the economy, along with planned conversion away from a permanent war economy.

Inflation is a complex affair. The Phillips curve focused on just two factors and assumed that one inevitably caused the other. This deflected attention from other possible causes of inflation and from the variety of possible policies that might prevent or curb inflation, depending on the specific situation. Interestingly, by 1974, Nobel Laureate Paul Samuelson, who had earlier done an influential study (with Robert Solow) of the Phillips relationship that helped to popularize the idea of the trade-off in the United States, rejected the idea that contemporary inflation could be explained in that way. "I believe," said Samuelson, "that no monistic [single factor] theory can be validly maintained."[32]

Nevertheless, the idea that unemployment is needed to fight inflation persisted and continued to influence public policy. Whether the underlying reasoning was based on the concept of an inevitable trade-off or on the idea that there is some natural rate of unemployment, it made little difference to those who suffered unemployment as a consequence of such policies.

Ronald Reagan generated political support by presenting supply-side economics as a new way to reduce both inflation and unemployment. This approach, however, was simply an attempt to legitimize a traditional conservative measure: tax cuts going disproportionately to the rich and to corporations. This, along with deregulation, was supposed to act as an economic stimulus that would generate additional revenues to the government and would reduce inflation, unemployment, and the budget deficit. The trickle-down approach resulted in, among other things, escalating unemployment. With the continued pursuit of a high-interest-rate policy and the refusal of the administration to take measures to reduce unemployment, the Reaganomics jobless began to resemble others who had been sacrificed in the name of fighting inflation, or for other purposes. Although some thought that Reaganomics was not working, it would be more accurate to say that some of these policies were actually working as planned.[33] The use of deliberate unemployment was successfully weakening unions, disciplining workers, and holding down wages. Inflation was abating. The price was steep, however—a record number of farm and business bankruptcies; many industries, especially housing, construction, steel, and auto manufacture, in a state of depression; and massive unemployment.

Official Unemployment: The Tip of an Iceberg

The official jobless rate released monthly and annually by the Labor Department is extremely useful for many purposes, especially in analyzing cyclical trends in the economy. High as it often is, however, the official rate masks much of the problem of joblessness.

In 1981 official unemployment averaged 7.6 percent, representing an annual *average* of 8.1 million persons.[34] But 23.4 million people were jobless at one time or another during the course of the year.[35] Consider the 1981 annual average figures once more. In addition to the 8.1 million persons officially jobless, there were 4.7 million who wanted full-time jobs but had to settle for part-time work. They were not counted as unemployed because those who work for one or more hours for pay or profit during a survey week are counted as employed, even if they want full-time employment. Another 1.1 million workers wanted jobs but were so discouraged about employment prospects that they had stopped looking for work. They were not counted as jobless because, to be included in that category, a person must have sought work during the previous four weeks. Thus an average of 13.9 million people were either partly or fully unemployed, if discouraged workers (among whom blacks, younger, and older workers are all overrepresented) and involuntary part-time workers (among whom women, blacks, and younger workers are overrepresented) are included.

In addition to discouraged workers, millions of others outside the civilian labor force (which includes the employed and the official unemployed 16 years and over) would probably take jobs if they were available. In 1981, 60 million persons in the noninstitutionalized population were not in the civilian labor force. Most of them were housewives, retirees, students, and the ill and disabled.

Labor-force figures are based on a monthly sample survey of all households. Persons do not classify themselves as employed, unemployed, out of the labor force, or discouraged workers—the latter considered to be out of the labor force. That is done on the basis of respondents' answers to various questions, using official criteria. Thus, of the 5.7 million persons who wanted a job but were not looking for work, only 1.1 million were categorized as discouraged workers—only those who stated that they were not looking for work because they thought they could not find it. It is likely, however, that at least some of the 54.3 million persons who were out of the labor force but did not state that they wanted a job would respond positively if there actually were employment opportunities or necessary services such as day care or transportation for the disabled.

It is important to realize that all labor-force figures exclude the institutionalized population. Thus inmates of prisons are not counted in any labor-force category—neither employed, nor unemployed, nor out of the labor force. An unemployed person who commits a crime and is sent to prison disappears from the jobless figures. Therefore, a reduction in the prison population would require more jobs if ex-offenders are to become productive members of society. Similarly, one should note that unemployment figures relate only to the civilian labor force. A jobless young person who enlists in the armed forces is no longer counted as unemployed.

Consider those civilians who are not in the labor force. Some of them are prevented from taking jobs by circumstances that are amenable to change. A 1981 study by the U.S. Civil Rights Commission, for example, found that lack of child care or inadequate child care prevents many mothers from taking jobs.[36] Some of the disabled may be deterred from coming into the labor force because of heavy labor-market discrimination or lack of transportation, specially adapted jobs, or specially adapted hours that would enable them to work. During recessions, more disabled and older workers who lose their jobs give up and apply for Social Security disability or old-age pensions.[37] Their status then becomes "disabled" or "retired." These are just a few examples of nonparticipants who might not even say they want a job but who, nevertheless, might welcome the opportunity to work. Indeed, the National Commission on Employment and Unemployment Statistics, which was set up to examine the nation's labor-force statistics, pointed out that during the upswing of the business cycle, when opportunities for work increases, many nonparticipants who are not classified as discouraged workers also enter the labor force.[38] Ironically, that was one reason why the commission did *not* recommend inclusion of discouraged workers in the official jobless count. A substantial minority of the commissioners, however—four out of nine—voted to include them.[39] (It is also paradoxical that many of the disabled who cannot work and who receive disability insurance under Social Security are being terminated at a time when unprecedented numbers of the ablebodied cannot find work. This is a result of provisions in the Social Security law enacted in 1980 and its exceptionally harsh implementation by the Reagan administration.[40])

Labor-force participation rates, which show the proportion of a group or a subgroup that is in the labor force, often provide useful information to supplement the figures already discussed. Sometimes a low labor-force participation rate is a form of hidden unemployment. For example, in every age group, relatively fewer black than white men are in the labor force.[41] This reflects poor economic opportunities for black men as well as their greater incidence of disability. The mere fact that people are not in the labor force seeking work does not mean there is no serious social problem. Indeed, it may be indicative of a more critical problem than official unemployment, especially among working-age men. Those who are pushed out of the labor force by lack of steady, decent-paying jobs may turn to crime, hustling, and similar pursuits; and many of the men who are listed as out of the labor force are doubtless more alienated than the official unemployed.

How many people would actually work if employment opportunities and services were available to all? Short of actually providing the opportunities, no precise answer can be given because of the myriad variables involved and the fact that the U.S. economy does not normally operate at a level even reasonably close to these conditions. But the number is surely large. During World War II the civilian labor force expanded enormously when jobs became available. The potential labor supply was much greater than the jobless figures of previous years suggested. Bertram Gross, who was also a major architect of the original versions of the Humphrey-Hawkins Act (before its watering down, as discussed in chapter 3), has long contended that the official labor-force concept, since it only includes people who have jobs or are actively seeking them in a four-week period, seriously underestimates the number of persons for whom jobs would have to be planned for in a real full-employment economy. In his view, the concept bears little relationship to people's willingness to work.[42] Gross estimates that "the total number of persons not working for pay but able and willing to work has generally been at least three times the number of reported jobseekers—even between recessions." In 1978, when official unemployment averaged 6 million, he estimated that there were about 18 million people who would be able and willing to work.[43]

Similarly, Eli Ginzberg, when he was chairman of the National Commission for Manpower Policy, acknowledged that there are vast numbers of people on the periphery of the labor force who want to come in but do not have the chance. In 1977 Ginzberg estimated that as many as 24 million potential job seekers would welcome the opportunity to work—more than triple the 7 million official unemployed at the time.[44] As he noted, whenever there are plenty of decent jobs available, "millions of people come out of the woodwork" to take them.[45] Unlike Gross, Ginzberg rejects the idea that government policy should be geared to enabling all potential job seekers to work because he feels that goal is too ambitious.[46] This view reinforces the finding of sociologists Frank F. Furstenberg, Jr., and Charles A. Thrall that a chronic shortage of jobs has given rise to a job-rationing ideology in which a set of norms and beliefs has developed for allocating the limited supply of jobs. In effect, many of those outside the labor force have been told by society that they have no right to a job. Internalizing the dominant value system, these low priority outsiders—such as mothers or older persons—may not seek jobs to which they do not feel they are entitled.[47]

The AFL-CIO and the National Urban League (NUL), both concerned with the devastating impact of unemployment, also believe that the official rate understates the actual amount of joblessness. They periodically recalculate the official rates using different concepts. In 1981, when the official jobless rate was 7.6 percent, the AFL-CIO estimate, which includes discouraged workers and half of the involuntary part-time workers, was 10.7 percent; the NUL estimate was 14.2 percent. The NUL estimate of black unemployment was 29.1 percent, compared with the official 14.3 percent.[48] The main conceptual difference between the AFL-CIO and the NUL estimates stems from the latter's counting as jobless *all* persons who state that they "want a job now," rather than including only those who are officially recorded as discouraged workers.

The Labor Department now also issues a range of seven jobless measures, based on varying definitions of unemployment and the labor force. The most expansive one, U-7, is somewhat similar to the AFL-CIO measure; the most restrictive, U-1, counts only those who are jobless for fifteen or more weeks. Obviously, disagreements about the meaning of unemployment figures are not purely technical matters. They also reflect different conceptualizations, value judgments, and goals.

Despite the evidence presented that there are layers of unemployment hidden beneath the official figures, the idea that the problem of unemployment is overstated became very influential during the 1970s. It is argued, for example, that unemployment is no longer a hardship (this is analyzed in detail in chapter 4) or that unemployment insurance gives workers an incentive to remain jobless. Actually, a majority of the jobless do not even collect unemployment benefits. But according to a Bureau of Labor Statistics study, those who collect them do tend to be out of work longer than others. This same study also found, however, that beneficiaries are older (and face more age discrimination) and that they also looked for jobs further from home and were willing to commute longer distances than others.[49] Moreover, it is interesting to realize that, as shown in chapter 6, although its jobless benefits are relatively more generous than those in the United States, Sweden has a much lower incidence of unemployment.

Another charge is that the underground or irregular economy provides off-the-books work for the jobless.[50] Although such an economy exists, the actual number of persons working in it who are recorded as jobless is not known. Furthermore, such work is itself often symptomatic of an unemployment problem. For example, in a field study of the irregular economy in nine Detroit neighborhoods, Louis Ferman and his associates at the University of Michigan's Institute of Industrial Relations found that those who supplemented their unemployment benefits with irregular income did not view these pursuits as an alternative to regular work, with its predictability and fringe benefits. They were simply trying to make ends meet while out of work. In fact, the Ferman team recommended that the need for this extra income should be recognized and that those collecting unemployment benefits should be allowed to earn a certain amount of additional money.[51]

Perhaps the most important reason given is one that has already been mentioned: the structural hypothesis, which came into vogue in the early 1970s. Because women and youth, who have higher than average jobless rates, make up a larger proportion of the labor force than they did several decades ago, it has been reasoned that unemployment is less important than it used to be. An unusually candid interpretation was given in 1972 by John Connally, then secretary of the treasury. Connally's testimony before the Joint Economic Committee also included a large dose of racism, which, along with sexism, has often been part of this reasoning—though seldom so openly expressed. As Connally said:

> It is significant that compared to the 5.9 percent rate for total employment, about 17 percent was the rate for young people and about 10 percent was the rate for blacks. . . . If you take the unemployment rate of male adults, heads of families, you get down to an unemployment figure of 3 percent. So we can't be carried away by an unemployment figure of say, 6 percent.[52]

Using Connally's logic, the only unemployment that really matters is that of adult males who are heads of households, preferably white. Such official indifference has played an important role in shaping public policy at various times. As Robert Solow of the Massachusetts Institute of Technology (MIT) and one-time staff economist for John Kennedy's Council of Economic Advisers put it in 1973, "to officials and politicians . . . women and young people are less real members of the labor force"; their attitude is, "why take chances to create it [work] for them." Solow added that this was not his own view, "but I think that one can practically hear that thought going around in the backs of Washington minds."[53] Attempting to convince favored groups that unemployment is someone else's problem has, of course, made it immeasurably easier to maintain divisions among workers—and then to increase unemployment among all groups.

A decade after Connally wished away the seriousness of a 5.9-percent unemployment rate, President Reagan used a remarkably similar approach to wish away an 8.9-percent rate. The recession, Reagan claimed in April 1982, was not as deep or serious as the jobless rate indicated, partly because of the large number of women in the labor market.[54] At the time, 17 million persons were fully or partly unemployed, including 10 million official jobless, 1.3 million discouraged workers, and 5.7 million involuntary part-time workers.

Interestingly, in the early 1970s, when the structural hypothesis first became popular, similar facts were interpreted differently. Robert E. Hall of MIT, for example, demonstrated that reducing the unemployment rates of women and blacks to the overall level of white males would have reduced the overall jobless rate by between 1.0 and 1.5 percentage points. Such a trend toward equality, he pointed out, would also decrease inflationary pressures stemming from the labor market. Otherwise, as overall unemployment drops, potentially inflationary labor shortages and high unemployment among subgroups could persist side by side.[55]

That hardly describes the early 1980s, with high overall unemployment and surplus labor in almost every occupation. It does, however, point out that, as an economy moves toward full employment, vigorous efforts to abolish discrimination, to eliminate separate labor markets for men and women and blacks and whites, and to remove other impediments to equality are no luxuries. Indeed, they are necessary—though not sufficient—ingredients in any program for real full employment with less inflation.

The Composition of Unemployment

As John Connally already mentioned—but for a quite different purpose—a striking fact about unemployment is its uneven distribution. It usually hits hardest at certain groups, especially those subject to the most discrimination and with the least status and power. Thus, throughout the post-World War II period, prosperity for some groups has coexisted with recession- or depressionlike unemployment for others. It is important, however, to realize that although unemployment hits minorities hardest, it is not simply a minority problem. Most of the jobless—more than three out of four—are white. Nor is unemployment simply a women's problem. Although their jobless rate has usually been higher than that of men, a majority of the jobless are men. Nor is it simply a youth problem. Although teenagers 16-19 years old have the highest jobless rates, nearly four out of five of those without work are adults 20 years and over.

The 1981 figures for those groups are given in table 2-2. Although the national jobless rate was 7.6 percent, the rate was 14.3 percent for blacks but 6.7 percent for whites; and it was 7.4 percent for men but 7.9 for women; among adults 20 years and over, it was 6.3 percent for men but 6.8 percent for women; among 16-19 year olds it was 19.6 percent.

Table 2-2
Unemployment among Selected Groups, 1981

	Percentage Unemployed	Number Unemployed (in thousands)
Overall	7.6	8,080
All men	7.4	4.465
All women	7.9	3.615
White	6.7	6.246
Black and other nonwhites[a]	14.3	1,833
16-19 years	19.6	1,733
20 years and over		
Men	6.3	3,521
Women	6.8	2,826

Source: *Employment and Earnings* 29(January 1982):154, table 6.
[a]For an explanation of "black and other nonwhites," see footnote to table 2-4.

Numerous other groups have above-average jobless rates. For example, in 1981 the rate for Hispanics (mostly classified as white) was 10.5 percent, more than that for whites but less than the rate for blacks. Among Hispanics, however, it varied from 9.0 percent among those of Cuban origin to 10.5 percent among those of Mexican origin, reaching 13.7 percent among those of Puerto Rican origin.

The risk of unemployment also varies with occupation. Rates tend to be higher at the low end and lower at the high end of the occupational structure. Although the 1981 rates were 4.0 percent for white-collar compared to 10.3 percent for blue-collar workers, these broad classifications conceal extremes. Within the blue collar category, for example, unemployment was 14.7 percent among nonfarm laborers. Among white-collar workers, 2.8 percent of professional and technical workers were jobless, compared with 5.7 percent of clerical workers.

Considerable variation exists among industries. In recent years, workers in construction and manufacturing have been especially hard hit. In 1981 unemployment was 15.7 percent in construction and 8.2 percent in manufacturing. Within manufacturing the rates were considerably higher in some sectors: for example, 14.6 percent in autos, 12.5 percent in lumber and wood products, and 11.4 percent in apparel.

In mid-1982, with the rapid escalation of unemployment, all the rates rose even higher. For example, about half of all black teenagers in the labor force were out of work, and among blue-collar workers unemployment was 14.2 percent. Some of these rates are shown in table 2-3. Although these are clearly disastrous, it is important to understand that

Table 2-3
Unemployment Rates, Selected Groups, August 1982

Group	Unemployment Rate (Seasonally Adjusted)
Overall, national rate	9.8
All men, 16 and over	10.0
All women, 16 and over	9.5
White	8.6
Black and other nonwhites[a]	17.5
Black (excluding other nonwhites)	18.8
Hispanic origin	14.6
All 16 to 19-year-olds	24.0
16 to 19-year-olds, white	20.6
16 to 19-year-olds, black and other[a]	47.4
16 to 19-year-olds, black, excluding other nonwhites	51.6
All persons 20 and over	
Men	8.9
Women	8.2
White-collar workers, all	4.8
Professional and technical workers	3.1
Clerical workers	6.7
Blue-collar workers	14.2
Nonfarm laborers	17.4
Construction-industry workers	20.3
Manufacturing-industry workers	12.1

Source: U.S. Department of Labor, Bureau of Labor Statistics, "The Employment Situation: August 1982," news release, 3 September 1982.

[a]For explanation of "black and other nonwhites" see footnote to table 2-4.

for many groups there were severe problems even before this sharp rise in joblessness. A few examples are provided.

Blacks

Official black unemployment has been about double the white rate for decades (see table 2-4). Moreover, due to recurrent recessions, black unemployment was exceedingly high throughout the 1970s. It averaged 10 percent in the decade. The mid-1970s recession hit blacks particularly hard, with little recovery. From 1975 through 1979, black unemployment ranged from 11 to 14 percent. Clearly, the 1970s were years of deep depression for blacks, even without considering the vast amount of hidden unemployment in the form of discouraged and involuntary part-time workers. Consider also that the labor-force participation rate of black men, already lower than that for white men, fell sharply. In 1970, 80 percent of white men and 77 percent of black men were in the civilian labor force, compared with 78

Table 2-4

Unemployment Rates, by Race, 1948-1981 and August 1982

Year	National Rate, All Workers (%)	Black and Other (%)[a]	White (%)	Ratio, Black and Other to White[a]
1948	3.8	5.9	3.5	1.7:1
1949	5.9	8.9	5.6	1.6
1950	5.3	9.0	4.9	1.8
1951	3.3	5.3	3.1	1.7
1952	3.0	5.4	2.8	1.9
1953	2.9	4.5	2.7	1.7
1954	5.5	9.9	5.0	2.0
1955	4.4	8.7	3.9	2.2
1956	4.1	8.3	3.6	2.3
1957	4.3	7.9	3.8	2.1
1958	6.8	12.6	6.1	2.1
1959	5.5	10.7	4.8	2.2
1960	5.5	10.2	4.9	2.1
1961	6.7	12.4	6.0	2.1
1962	5.5	10.9	4.9	2.2
1963	5.7	10.8	5.0	2.2
1964	5.2	9.6	4.6	2.1
1965	4.5	8.1	4.1	2.0
1966	3.8	7.3	3.3	2.2
1967	3.8	7.4	3.4	2.2
1968	3.6	6.7	3.2	2.1
1969	3.5	6.4	3.1	2.1
1970	4.9	8.2	4.5	1.8
1971	5.9	9.9	5.4	1.8
1972	5.6	10.0	5.0	2.0
1973	4.9	8.9	4.3	2.1
1974	5.6	9.9	5.0	2.0
1975	8.5	13.9	7.8	1.8
1976	7.7	13.1	7.0	1.9
1977	7.0	13.1	6.2	2.1
1978	6.0	11.9	5.2	2.3
1979	5.8	11.3	5.1	2.2
1980	7.1	13.2	6.3	2.1
1981	7.6	14.3	6.7	2.1
1982, August[b]	9.8	17.5	8.6	2.0

Source: From, and calculated from, U.S. Bureau of the Census, *Current Population Reports,* Special Studies, series P-23, no. 80, *The Social and Economic Status of the Black Population in the United States: An Historical View, 1790-1978* (Washington, D.C.: U.S. Government Printing Office, n.d.), table 47, p. 69; *Economic Report of the President, January 1976* (Washington, D.C.: U.S. Government Printing Office, 1976), table B-22, p. 196; and *Monthly Labor Review,* table 4, various issues.

Note: *Unemployment rate* is the percentage of the civilian labor force that is unemployed.

[a]*Black and other* refers to blacks and all other nonwhites. Generally, national statistics for black and other reflect the condition of the black population, since blacks make up about 90 percent of the nonwhite population. Persons of Asian origin, Native American Indians, Alaskan natives, and Pacific Islanders are classified as nonwhite. Most of the Hispanic-origin population is classified as white—at the time of the 1970 census, approximately 96 percent.

[b]Seasonally adjusted. 1982 figures are based on 1980 census population controls; others are based on 1970 census controls.

percent and 71 percent, respectively, in 1980.[56] Moreover, for blacks, these declines took place at all ages, including the prime working years, whereas for whites they were most pronounced among middle-aged and older workers, and the participation rates of those under 24 years actually rose.

It would be a mistake to conclude that there has been no black progress in the labor market. Spurred by the economic expansion of the 1960s; by the protests that led to passage of the Civil Rights Act of 1964 and the establishment of the Equal Employment Opportunity Commission; and by positive government action against discrimination in various areas of society, the occupational structure of blacks has improved favorably. Even so, it is still very different from that of whites, with underrepresentation in white-collar jobs, especially in professional and managerial work, and overrepresentation in blue-collar and service occupations, as well as on the lower rungs of the occupational ladder within broad occupational groupings. Movement up the occupational scale was slower in the 1970s, however. According to a Bureau of Labor Statistics economist, "the number of black professional and craft workers increased only about half as fast as during the 1960s. Clearly, economic disruptions affected the occupational advancement not only of blacks, but of all workers as well."[57]

Black income is still substantially lower than white income. In 1980 the weekly earnings of black men who worked full time were only about 75 percent those of white men, whereas black women who worked full time earned about 92 percent as much per week as white women.[58] It has been easier for this racial earnings gap to narrow for women because women of both races are concentrated in low-wage jobs. These figures, however, are for *weekly earnings for those working full time. The fact that blacks are unemployed, involuntarily working part-time, and out of the labor force more often than whites substantially reduces annual earnings.*

When income rather than earnings is considered, the situation looks considerably worse. The annual *income* gap between blacks and whites *increased* during the 1970s. During the 1970s black income declined from 61 percent to 57 percent of white income.[59] Not surprisingly, poverty, which has been rising among all groups since the late 1970s, plagues the black community. In 1980 one-third of blacks, compared with one-tenth of whites, had incomes below the official (already unrealistically low) poverty level.[60] To a greater extent than whites, working-age blacks are dependent on the welfare system and other income-transfer programs, whereas poverty among whites is more concentrated among the aged.

The need for steady, decent-paying jobs is essential for black progress. Blacks have been tremendously hurt by recessions. Housing discrimination and low incomes have also kept them overly concentrated in inner cities with the highest unemployment rates. Even in suburban areas, however, black jobless rates are much higher than those for whites. Blacks are also more prone to unemployment than whites because of their concentration in blue-collar and service occupations and in industries such as manufacturing, all with above-average unemployment. To make matters worse, even within the same occupation, blacks suffer more joblessness than whites.[61] Often they are last hired, first fired. Whereas lack of seniority makes many vulnerable to job loss, others are disproportionately found in menial, low-wage jobs in the secondary labor market, where seniority frequently means little. Regardless of education, blacks also have a higher incidence of unemployment. Finally, discrimination, whether in the job market or institutionalized in other areas of society—for instance, housing and education—still plays an important role in black employment and unemployment problems.

The economic disaster facing blacks in the early 1980s thus should not obscure the fact that substantial black progress requires more than a return to the 1970s.

Young People

Unemployment among young people, though considerably worsened by the near depression of the early 1980s, is not simply its by-product. Double-digit unemployment has been the norm for 16- to 19-year-olds since 1954 (see table 2-5). Even though differences in skill and experience are less pronounced among young people than among adults, there is no equality. The black-white gap is wider than for adults, and it has worsened. Between 1954 and 1980 the jobless rate for white 16- to 19-year-olds rose from 12.1 percent to 17.8 percent, whereas for blacks it rose from 14.8 percent to 35.8 percent.

Hidden unemployment is especially severe among young blacks and is getting worse. Between 1970 and 1980 civilian labor-force participation rates rose sharply for young white men and women but only slightly for young black women—and actually fell for young black men. In 1980, among 16- and 17-year-olds, 47 percent of white compared to only 26 percent of black women were in the labor force; for males the figures were 54 percent and 32 percent, respectively. Among 18- and 19-year-olds, 65 percent of white and 46 percent of black females were in the labor force; for males the figure was 74 percent for whites, compared with only 56 percent for blacks.

Sometimes youth unemployment is erroneously considered simply a problem of high-school students. Many American youngsters start their working lives right after high school. In 1979 nearly 90 percent of 16- and 17-year-olds were still in school, but only 45 percent of 18- and 19-year-olds and 22 percent of 20- to 24-year-olds.[62] Although soaring tuitions and cuts

Table 2-5
Youth Unemployment, by Race, 1948-1981 and August 1982

Year	16 Years and Over (%)	16 to 19 Years (%)		
		Total	White	Black and Other[a]
1948	3.8	9.2	NA	NA
1949	5.9	13.4	NA	NA
1950	5.3	12.2	NA	NA
1951	3.3	8.2	NA	NA
1952	3.0	8.5	NA	NA
1953	2.9	7.6	NA	NA
1954	5.6	12.6	12.1	16.6
1955	4.4	11.0	10.4	15.6
1956	4.1	11.1	10.1	18.1
1957	4.3	11.6	10.6	19.1
1958	6.8	15.9	14.4	27.4
1959	5.5	14.6	13.1	26.1
1960	5.5	14.7	13.5	24.3
1961	6.7	16.8	15.3	27.7
1962	5.5	14.7	13.3	25.3
1963	5.7	17.2	15.5	30.3
1964	5.2	16.2	14.8	27.3
1965	4.5	14.8	13.4	26.5
1966	3.8	12.8	11.2	25.4
1967	3.8	12.9	11.0	26.3
1968	3.6	12.7	11.0	24.9
1969	3.5	12.2	10.7	24.1
1970	4.9	15.2	13.5	29.1
1971	5.9	16.9	15.1	31.7
1972	5.6	16.2	14.2	33.5
1973	4.9	14.5	12.6	30.3
1974	5.6	16.0	14.0	32.9
1975	8.5	19.9	17.9	36.9
1976	7.7	19.0	16.9	37.1
1977	7.0	17.7	15.4	38.3
1978	6.0	16.3	13.9	36.3
1979	5.8	16.1	13.9	33.5
1980	7.1	17.7	14.8	35.8
1981	7.6	19.6	17.3	39.5
1982, August[b]	9.8	24.0	20.6	47.4

Source: *Employment and Earnings* 29(January 1982):154, and 19(February 1973):179-180, 186, and 190; *Monthly Labor Review,* table 4, various issues; and U.S. Department of Labor, Bureau of Labor Statistics, "The Employment Situation: August 1982," News Release, 3 September 1982.

Note: The unemployment rate is the percentage of the civilian labor force that is unemployed. NA = not available.

[a]For an explanation of *black and other,* see note a to table 2-4.

[b]Seasonally adjusted. Based on 1980 census population controls; all other figures based on 1970 census controls.

in student aid will make it even harder for many students to remain in college, work has long been a necessity for many college students. Further, some high-school students, especially those from low-income and working-class families, require the income, aside from the valuable experience, work habits, and self-esteem gained from employment.

A great deal of unemployment afflicts out-of-school youngsters, however. Although a majority of jobless 16- and 17-year-olds are still in school, it is important to realize that three out of four jobless 18- and 19-year-olds and seven out of eight jobless 20- to 24-year-olds in 1980 *were no longer students*. Unemployment rates are consistently higher among out-of-school youth. The problem is especially severe among black youngsters, but it cannot simply be attributed to lack of education or skill deficiencies because white youngsters with less schooling have considerably lower unemployment rates than blacks with much more schooling. For example, in 1980, among 16- to 24-year-olds, 51 percent of black high-school graduates were unemployed, compared with 27 percent of white high-school dropouts. White high-school dropouts have lower unemployment rates than black youths with some college and about the same rates as black college graduates.[63] According to the Labor Department's National Longitudinal Survey, black youngsters are also out of work longer and earn less than their white counterparts with similar or lower abilities, training, and background.[64]

In 1980 the Vice-President's (then Walter Mondale) Task Force on Youth Unemployment released a comprehensive three-volume study showing that, by almost any measure, the severity of youth unemployment had increased and that those with the most severe problems are an absolutely and relatively increasing proportion of the problem; that racial disparities, already noted, are increasing; and that youths from poor families are becoming worse off relative to those from rich families. Long-term joblessness among youth, who are often out of work for only short periods of time, is on the rise. Myriad reasons for youth unemployment have been given. It is significant that the task force not only acknowledged many of them but also acknowledged that, for minority youngsters, discrimination, lack of jobs, and lack of access to jobs are large parts of the problem.[65]

According to the task force:

Those who would explain away youth unemployment and particularly minority youth unemployment, by high turnover, volatility, seasonality of employment, or lack of values are hard-pressed to support this claim for more than the tail of the severity gradient. Where jobs are available, youth fill them. Many of the alleged supply-side shortfalls such as lack of dependability or awareness of job mores are simply the cumulation of stunted past opportunities. Supply variables affect the rationing of opportunities much more than the level. In the central cities and poverty areas, the problem is not basically the inadequacy of individuals but the shortage of opportunities.[66]

The task force was not optimistic. Despite the slowing down of the growth of the youth population, it did not think the problem would recede without action. As for the minority population, the task force dismally concluded, the educational gains of the last decade have not improved the situation of minority youth:

> Increased equality for minority adults has not "trickled down" to minority youth. Private sector employment has grown rapidly in the last several years but the expansion of public programs provided most of the jobs for minority teenagers; the recession ahead looms as a depression for disadvantaged youth.[67]

The Reagan administration's solution to the youth-unemployment problem is a subminimum wage for youth. It is important to realize that the real value of the minimum wage has actually eroded because the minimum wage is not indexed for inflation. Furthermore, there is little evidence that a youth subminimum would solve the problem.[68] Studies of the Work in America Institute and data from the National Longitudinal Survey suggest that a majority of employed youngsters are already paid less than the minimum wage. Moreover, it is a fact that a legal subminimum wage already exists under *current* law, although a majority of exempt businesses do not fully utilize it; according to Robert Hill, formerly NUL research director, an expansion of the subminimum would not benefit black youth and would probably lead to a displacement of black adults from jobs. He believes that proponents of a youth subminimum may actually be more interested in eliminating or severely undermining the minimum wage for adults.[69] The AFL-CIO also opposes a youth subminimum on the valid grounds that it would weaken labor standards.

It is difficult to escape the conclusion that urban ghettos are a catastrophe for youth. The NUL hidden-unemployment index for 1980 showed 59 percent of black teenagers jobless nationally but estimated that in some specific inner cities the figure might be closer to 80 or 90 percent.[70]

Unfortunately, as table 2-6 shows for 1981 figures, although jobless rates decline with age, unemployment remains at astronomical levels for minorities even at ages 20-24—with nearly one out of four *officially* jobless. Double-digit unemployment even persists in the 25- to 35-year-old group. Such an environment nourishes crime, alienation, and welfare dependency. Stable family formation is severely threatened during these formative years.

It would be a mistake to think that youth unemployment has never been a cause of national concern. Indeed, the Vice-President's Task Force found

Table 2-6
Unemployment Rates, by Age, Race, and Sex, 1981

	Percentage Unemployed[a]			
	Male		Female	
Age	White	Black and Other[b]	White	Black and Other[b]
16 and over	6.5	14.3	6.9	14.4
16-19	17.9	38.3	15.3	38.6
20-24	11.6	24.9	9.1	24.5
25-34	6.2	13.0	5.5	14.0
35-44	4.1	8.7	5.1	9.1
45-54	3.6	7.2	4.2	6.7
55-64	3.4	6.1	3.6	4.5
65 and over	2.4	8.1	3.4	5.8

Source: *Employment and Earnings* 29(January 1982):151-152, table 4.
[a]Unemployed as a percentage of the civilian labor force.
[b]For explanation of *black and other,* see note a to table 2-4.

a knowledge overload, with more data available on the issue than on almost any other social-welfare subject. It also found that no strategy worked for everyone but that employment, training, and education programs did work. "Many of the shortcomings of the programs are straightforward but ignored in seeking 'panaceas'," it observed. For instance, "employment and training programs suffer extraordinarily from instability"; yet we fail to eliminate that instability because we only "fund them from year-to-year."[71] This statement was made before the Reagan administration's devastating program cuts and pursuit of deliberately high overall unemployment rates and weakened commitment to equal employment opportunities.

Also *before* the Reagan administration's recession, the NUL warned that the nation is producing generations of young people who may reach adulthood without ever holding a regular job, and that, "if the experience of their parents is any indication, there is no guarantee that they will secure stable employment as adults, either."[72] Thus a real full-employment program rather than a return to the 1970s appears to be a necessity if all young people who wish to work are to get jobs that will enable them to start to build productive lives.

Women

In recent decades, American women have entered the labor market in record numbers. Between 1970 and 1980 the civilian labor force grew by about 35 million, of whom 21 million—some 60 percent—were women. At the beginning of this period, women represented 33 percent of the civilian labor force, compared with 43 percent by 1980. Whereas the civilian labor-force participation rate of men fell during these years from 84 percent to 78 percent, women's rose from 38 percent to 52 percent. Thus more than half of women are now in the labor force, although they still participate to a lesser extent than men.

The most dramatic change has been the large-scale entrance of married women and mothers of young children into the civilian labor force. As recently as 1960, only 30 percent of married women were in the civilian labor force, compared with 50 percent in 1980. During that same period, the proportion of married women with children under 6 years old more than doubled, from 19 percent to 45 percent. In just one decade, from 1970 to 1980, the proportion of children under 18 with mothers in the labor force rose from 39 percent to 53 percent. Thus, more than half of all children under 18 have mothers who are in the labor force.

During these decades the incidence of unemployment has nearly always been higher for women than for men, although these differences are not as large as the racial differences. (The traditional gap is currently declining and even reversing—not because the unemployment situation is getting better for women but because it is deteriorating faster for men. This reflects the fact that men are more concentrated in heavy industry and construction, which have had staggering rates of unemployment in recent years. Thus in August 1982, as table 2-3 shows, the unemployment rate was actually higher for men than for women.) During the 1970s women's rates averaged about 30 percent higher than men's.[73] The true gap is understated, however, because there is more hidden unemployment among women. They are much more likely than men to drop out of the labor force when out of work, are overrepresented among discouraged and involuntary part-time workers, and are often deterred from coming into the labor force because of lack of child care and for related reasons.

Women's traditionally higher unemployment rates are related to many factors, including discriminatory hiring practices, although the problem is not simply outright discrimination. The pervasiveness of sex-tagged jobs cuts down women's options, as does women's role in the family. For example, the husband's place of employment usually determines where a couple will live. In an area with few traditionally female jobs, a wife who wants to work may be unemployed or have to drop out of the labor force. Some employers are reluctant to hire mothers, who may stay home from work when their children are ill. Mothers often can only work certain hours because of their child-care responsibilities. Women often leave the labor force to have children and may reenter the labor force at a later time. These factors partly explain why women are more likely than men to be new entrants or reentrants into the labor market. Women are less likely than men to work in the most cyclically sensitive industries or to be blue-collar workers, which should make them less vulnerable to unemployment; but their lack of seniority adds to their vulnerability when there are layoffs. In most occupations and industries, women have a higher incidence of unemployment than men.[74]

Although some attribute great importance to women's higher turnover rates, it should be noted that these are also characteristic of other groups, such as blacks and youth, with poor labor-market prospects. As labor economist Lloyd Ulman observes, "people don't quit good high-wage jobs as frequently as they quit low-wage dead-end jobs, or for the same reasons."[75] Economist Isabel Sawhill has found that women are more likely to be employed in industries and occupations in which both men and women leave jobs frequently.[76] According to economist Barbara Bergmann, occupational discrimination is a major reason for women's typically higher unemployment rates. Women are segregated into relatively few fields compared with men, and this oversupply, Bergmann feels, helps to push up their unemployment and hold down their wages—factors she believes also affect blacks.[77]

Neither the women's movement nor women's entrance into the labor market has brought about labor-market equality. The Equal Pay Act of 1963 made it illegal to pay women less than men for equal work, though not for work of comparable value, which has emerged as a major issue. And Title VII of the Civil Rights Act of 1964, as amended, prohibits sex discrimination in employment practices as well as discrimination based on color, religion, or national origin. These and other laws, executive orders, and court decisions have helped to reduce discrimination against women in various areas of society. Some women have made considerable headway with these changes. Between 1972 and 1979, for example, the proportion of lawyers and judges who were women rose from 3.8 percent to 12.4 percent; in accounting, the gain was from 21.7 to 32.9 percent; among telephone installers, the change was from 1.9 to 9.9 percent. The proportion of women graduating in some professional fields also rose enormously. For example, in 1970 women made up only 8.4 percent of those who received medical degrees and 5.4 percent of those who received law degrees. By 1978 the figures had risen to 21.5 percent in medicine and 26 percent in law.[78] Similar breakthroughs can be cited in other fields. For the bulk of women, however, there has been little or no change. As a National Research Council study concluded, the central fact is that men and women hold different jobs. This study also found that the work women do pays less than the work men do and that "the more an occupation is dominated by women, the less it pays."[79] Thus in 1970 women were 99.1 percent of all secretaries, the same as in 1979; for typists the figures were 96.1 percent and 96.7 percent; and for registered nurses, they were 97.6 percent and 96.7 percent. In 1979 more than three out of five women were still in clerical, sales, or service jobs.

A Labor Department report summarizes some disconcerting facts about women's earnings:

> At the beginning of the 1980s, working women were in the same position they were in at the outset of the 1970s regarding full-time wages and salaries. They averaged about $6 for every $10 earned by men. While earnings parity with men was nearly achieved in some of the comparatively newer fields—computer science, for instance—most women were still in the lower end of the pay scale.[80]

Women are also less unionized than men, another factor that holds down their wages. Consider, too, that wage disparities are the rule, regardless of education. The National Research Council study, which also took race into account, has shown that among full-time, year-round workers, women and black men at all levels of education earn less than white men; for example, both blacks and white women who are college graduates earn less than white men with eighth-grade educations.[81] Thus women's unemployment problems are greatly compounded by their low earning power, even when they are working.

Women, as well as men, often do have valid noneconomic reasons for working. It is a sign of inequality and lack of acceptance of the idea of a right to a job, however, that women's motives for working, but not men's, are still questioned at all. Contrary to a prevalent myth, most women are not working for pin money. They have compelling economic reasons for working, and their unemployment can cause financial hardship or worse. In 1980, 19.6 million of the 43 million women in the labor force worked to support themselves—that is, they were either single, widowed, divorced, or separated—and millions of married women were working to help their families maintain decent living standards. Most women—nearly seven out of ten—work full time. Among married women, about three out of ten work part time, mostly by choice and often because of child-care or home responsibilities, but sometimes because they cannot find full-time work.[82]

A growing number of women head families and must support not only themselves but also their children. For these women, steady jobs at *decent wages*, with adequate, affordable child-care facilities, are a necessity if they and their children are to avoid poverty and welfare—which is too often their fate. (In 1980 just over half of the 11.5 million children under the age of 18 who were living in families maintained by women had incomes under the official poverty level.)[83] These women are actually most prone to joblessness, and the racial disparities make the situation even worse for black women. Consider, for example, the figures for March 1978, when the national jobless rate for all workers was 6.2 percent. At that time the jobless rate for black women with children under 18 who had never been married was 25.4 percent, compared with 16.8 percent for their white counterparts. For married women with children that age, unemployment was 9.2 percent for blacks, compared with 5.8 percent for whites.[84]

For the poor and for women who head families, child care is a necessity. Indeed, child care is important for all mothers who work. Yet no national policy on child care adequately recognizes that need. Richard Nixon vetoed a comprehensive child-care bill. Tax credits for child care enacted since then have been grossly inadequate, and publicly funded child-care facilities are being hurt by budget cuts.[85] Any real full-employment policy would have to include an adequate child-care policy as well as more labor-market equality and decent-paying jobs for all women who want to work, as well as for men. Women may have come a long way. As with the failure to win ratification of the Equal Rights Amendment, however, even a glance at labor-market conditions as well as other societal and family conditions shows how far they still have to go.

Other Groups and Areas

These brief descriptions illustrate some chronic unemployment problems that have been with us for a long time. They are not meant to be exhaustive studies of these groups, which would be beyond the scope of this book, nor do they exhaust the universe of groups with persistent problems. Other examples include but are not limited to Native Americans, who have the highest incidence of unemployment but for whom fewer data are available,[86] Hispanics, a growing proportion of the nation's population; older workers, less likely to lose their jobs but with tremendous problems should they become unemployed;[87] displaced homemakers—older women who, because of divorce, widowhood, separation, or for other reasons, must enter the labor force for the first time or reenter after a prolonged absence; ex-offenders, low on any employer's list; the disabled, who have been demanding equal rights in all areas of society;[88] some Vietnam-era veterans; welfare mothers; and so on.

Many groups also suffer from low wages when they do work, and that has been a continuing problem. Even in the best of times as far as unemployment goes—in 1967, with the national unemployment rate less than 4 percent—a Labor Department survey found that from one-quarter to nearly half of the residents of urban slums were subemployed—that is, they were officially unemployed, discouraged workers, involuntary part-time workers, *or* heads of households working full-time but earning less than $60 a week (the poverty level at that time).[89] Poor people, even those on welfare—as Leonard Goodwin has shown in a Brookings Institution study—are committed to the work ethic and have the same aspirations as middle-class persons.[90] But for many, even hard work does not enable them to live in decency. The problem of low wages is compounded by the failure of the economy to produce full employment and by the particularly high levels of unemployment among unskilled workers and minorities, resulting from continuing recessions—and high levels of unemployment in the intervening years—since the 1970s. The task is also made more difficult by the fact that illegal aliens, who themselves come from countries with desperate conditions, are often forced to work under conditions of superexploitation that violate labor standards and pay below the minimum wage. Thus a deteriorating economy and the existence of an underclass of undocumented workers, who have few legal rights and live in constant fear of being deported, make it more difficult to upgrade low-wage work.[91]

At various times, unemployment problems of varying degrees of severity have also hit groups not considered disadvantaged or especially prone to unemployment. In recent recessions, white-collar and professional workers have experienced more unemployment than in the past. Even in the absence of recessions, some others have experienced difficulties. For example, during the 1970s schoolteachers and even college professors were laid off because of declining enrollments or budget cuts, and highly skilled engineers and others employed in military industries were affected by changes in weapons systems. In the latter case it is important to realize that, although a transfer of funds from military to civilian purposes would produce more jobs, planned conversion of the economy would be necessary in order to provide new, socially productive work for displaced workers; retraining might sometimes be needed for engineers and for other highly skilled and professional workers feeling the impact of all kinds of shifts in the economy.

Structural and locational shifts in employment have also been a problem. Many cities have experienced a substantial loss of jobs to the suburbs. Encouraged by federal housing and transportation policies, large segments of the middle class fled from inner cities, often leaving blacks locked into major cities with declining or slow job growth. High unemployment in inner cities compared with suburbs partly reflects this. Unemployment varies considerably not only between cities and suburbs, but also between poor and middle-class or affluent sections within cities.

Jobs have also gone from one region to another, especially from the so-called Snowbelt to the Sunbelt. Jobs have gone out of the country altogether, often nurtured by policies that give tax write-offs to corporations that abandon old plants and tax breaks to those that invest overseas. Plant closings, as Barry Bluestone, Bennett Harrison, and Lawrence Baker show in their study of corporate flight, affected millions of U.S. workers during the 1970s. The dislocation was particularly severe in the Snowbelt.

These authors found, however, that there were also many plant closings in the Sunbelt, especially in industries such as textiles. They feel that to a large extent capital has been running away from unions in the north to locations in the relatively union-free environment of the south, and that multinational corporations are trying to reorganize the international division of labor "in order to play off workers in one nation against those of another."[92] In some cases, workers in low-wage countries are prevented from unionizing by repressive regimes that are maintained in power, in part, through the support of the U.S. government.

There is, of course, a regional dimension to unemployment, but the Snowbelt-Sunbelt dichotomy is an oversimplification. In August 1982, with the deepening recession, twenty states and the District of Columbia reported unemployment rates of 10.0 percent or more. Michigan topped the list with 14.5 percent. The whole industrial heartland of the United States was devastated with Pennsylvania, Ohio, Illinois, Indiana, and Wisconsin on the list. Even the south was not immune, with Mississippi, Louisiana, Alabama, South Carolina, Tennessee, Kentucky, Delaware, and West Virginia also part of the club. In the west, California, Washington, Oregon, Arizona, Nevada, and New Mexico had double-digit unemployment. Numerous individual cities were experiencing much higher unemployment, reminiscent of the Great Depression, with Youngstown, Ohio, scoring nearly 21 percent.[93]

Many of the unemployed lived in areas not usually hard hit by unemployment, and some of the jobless were experiencing a situation new to them. Even when the recession ends, many parts of the country will have substantial problems remaining. In the interim, an unresponsive government was doing nothing to lower unemployment.

Employment and Training Programs

Although an increasing level of politically tolerable unemployment has been characteristic of the post-World War II decades, it would be incorrect to conclude that U.S. society has ignored unemployment. Indeed, as a political issue, it helped John Kennedy and Jimmy Carter get elected. Many federal policies, including employment and training programs, were explicitly or implicitly designed to help the jobless.[94]

The GI Bill of Rights enabled nearly 8 million World War II veterans to attend college or to receive other kinds of education or training, but the first training programs explicitly or implicitly for the unemployed were established in the 1960s. The first one that was national in scope was the Manpower Development and Training Act of 1962 (MDTA). Initially its emphasis was not on the economically or racially disadvantaged. Its aim was to retrain mature, experienced, predominantly white workers who had been displaced by technological change. As overall unemployment declined in the 1960s, however, especially among white male family heads, the program's focus shifted to those who usually lacked experience and skills.

The Economic Opportunity Act of 1964 (EOA) and the War on Poverty led to new programs, mostly for the poor and minorities; the 1960s, of course, were years of black protest, urban riots, and passage of significant civil-rights legislation. The Neighborhood Youth Corps provided work experience for youngsters in school and for those who had left school. New Careers and Operation Mainstream provided skill and work experience for poor adults. The Job Corps provided intensive skill training for disadvantaged youth, usually in a residential setting. By the late 1960s there were myriad federally administered categorical programs, as well as charges of fragmentation and duplication. These programs mainly aimed at helping the poor gain skills, rather than engaging in direct job creation. The premise was that the skills would improve individuals' earning power and that jobs would be available in the tight labor markets of the time. But dual-labor-market theorists such as Peter Doeringer, Michael Piore, and Bennett Harrison contended that the poor were often trained for menial, dead-end, low-wage jobs in the secondary labor market.[95] Studying the period 1960 to 1975, however, Garth Mangum concluded that manpower programs (as employment and training programs were then called) did work. That is, those who went through them were better off in terms of income and employment stability. Mangum added, though, in a book written at the request of the National Commission for Manpower Policy, that the average gain was only "from well down in the poverty ranks to its upper levels" because these programs had little impact on the way that labor markets work. In fact, he concluded that during those years only civil-rights and equal-employment-opportunity policies had a significant impact on the way labor markets work.[96]

The Emergency Employment Act (EEA), the first major job-creation program since the New Deal, was passed during the recession year of 1971, when the jobless rate was 5.9 percent. (Recall that between 1969 and 1971 the Nixon administration's policies had helped to increase the number of persons officially unemployed by about 2 million).[97] By 1971 about 5 million persons were officially out of work, so the program was actually quite small. It created 150,000 public service employment jobs—about one for every thirty-three of the unemployed, or, from another perspective, only one job for every thirteen *additional* persons added to the official unemployment count. Thus much more was taken away than was given back. The program was authorized for two years, after which the Nixon administration strongly opposed continuation of federally funded jobs and battled congressional Democrats on the issue. In line with Nixon's philosophies of general revenue sharing and "new federalism," the administration preferred shifting responsibilities for programs away from the federal government and supported local control of "manpower" programs.[98]

The Comprehensive Employment and Training Act of 1973 (CETA)—the major employment and training legislation of the post-World War II era—was a compromise that subsumed in one act the "manpower" programs of the MDTA, EOA, and EEA. CETA's dominant themes were decentralization and decategorization. Instead of federal program administrators, states and local communities were designated as prime sponsors (decentralization) and had a great deal of discretion in the use of funds (decategorization).

CETA was keyed to the economically disadvantaged, unemployed, and underemployed. It authorized a full range of services, such as classroom and on-the-job training, work experience, basic and remedial education, counseling and orientation, job-search assistance, supportive services, and public service employment—originally meant to provide transitional employment for the hard-core jobless.

Shortly after CETA's birth, the escalating unemployment of the mid-1970s recession led Congress to add a countercyclical public service employment program. Those with chronic unemployment problems were soon competing with the newly unemployed for CETA jobs, and many of those who were hired were not disadvantaged. Indeed, some were very well educated; if not for the recession, they could have qualified for regular, unsubsidized employment. The theme was to repeat itself over and over again. In fact, unemployed "regular" workers were pitted against the disadvantaged and poor, competing for an inadequate number of public service employment jobs in an economy that did not supply enough jobs for either group.

The 1978 CETA reauthorization targeted the program largely to the economically disadvantaged and low-income persons, with eligibility criteria for most parts of CETA based on both low income and employment status. Low wage restrictions were also put on the public jobs. After implementation of the new rules, nearly all the participants were economically disadvantaged (see table 2-7). The definition of economically disadvantaged is shown in footnote b to table 2-7. Table 2-7 shows, for fiscal 1980, the characteristics of CETA participants in public service employment programs (Titles II D and VI), as well as those in upgrading, retraining, and other services for the disadvantaged (Titles II B and C). The reauthorization also added a Private Sector Initiative Program (PSIP) aimed at involving the private sector more actively in these programs.

Like most U.S. job programs, CETA suffered from a bad press. There were many criticisms of public service employment. Paramount among these was "substitution"—the charge that CETA workers would have been hired anyway. Estimates of substitution varied in different studies, with

Table 2-7

Percentage Distribution of Characteristics of Participants in Selected CETA Programs, Fiscal 1980

Characteristic	Title II B and C	Title IID	Title VI
Total	100.0	100.0	100.0
Male	47.0	49.6	55.2
Female	53.0	50.4	44.8
Age			
Under 22	47.9	36.1	24.0
22-44	45.7	61.5	62.8
45-54	4.1	7.5	7.6
55 and over	2.4	5.0	5.5
Education			
High-school student	19.6	2.9	2.8
High-school dropout	29.4	29.9	27.9
12 years and over	51.0	67.1	69.3
Economic status			
AFDC recipient	20.8	19.0	14.9
Public-assistance recipient	27.0	27.7	22.0
OMB poverty level[a]	95.1	90.9	80.0
Economically disadvantaged[b]	98.2	96.0	89.5
Race/ethnic group			
White	50.7	50.8	51.1
Black	33.3	33.7	33.0
Hispanic	11.6	12.2	13.0
Other	4.4	3.3	2.9
Limited English-speaking ability	5.0	5.1	4.3
Migrant or seasonal farm worker	.9	.9	1.1
Veteran group:			
Total	7.9	13.6	15.3
Vietnam-era[c]	3.4	5.0	5.7
Special disabled[d]	.6	.7	.9
Handicapped	8.5	6.1	4.7
Offender	8.6	6.7	6.0
Labor-force status			
Underemployed	3.3	1.1	1.1
Unemployed	73.1	86.7	89.8
Other	23.7	12.2	9.1
Unemployment-insurance claimant	5.3	8.6	11.0
Median hourly wage:			
Preenrollment	$3.11	$3.17	$3.36
Postenrollment (unsubsidized)	$3.77	$4.01	$4.26

Source: U.S. Department of Labor, Employment and Training Administration, *Employment and Training Report of the President, 1981,* table F-8, p. 265.

Note: Title IIB and C: Ungrading, retraining and other services for the disadvantaged; Title IID: Transitional public-service employment for the disadvantaged; Title VI: Countercyclical public service employment.

[a]For a nonfarm family of four in 1980, the poverty level was $7,450.

Table 2-7 *(continued)*

[b]A person who is either (1) a member of a family that receives public assistance; (2) a member of a family whose income during the previous six months on a annualized basis was such that the family would have qualified for public assistance if it had applied or did not exceed the poverty level or did not exceed 70 percent of the Bureau of Labor Statistics lower-living-standard income level ($12,585 for a family of four in 1979); (3) a foster child on whose behalf state-or local-government payments are made; or (4) a client of a sheltered workshop; a handicapped person; a person residing in a prison, hospital, or other institution or facility providing twenty-four-hour care; or a regular outpatient of a mental hospital or rehabilitation or similar facility, where such status presents a significant barrier to employment.

[c]Served between 5 August 1964 and 7 May 1975, and under age 35.

[d]Served in Indochinese or Korean theater of operations between August 1964 and May 1975.

critics generally finding more than supporters.[99] Fraud and mismanagement were other charges. Few would deny that CETA has had problems. However, as Paul Bullock of the University of California at Los Angeles noted in his study of CETA, the press by its very nature concentrates on scandalous events, which may or may not reflect the worth of a law.[100] The 1978 amendments introduced tighter regulations designed to overcome these problems.

It is fair to say that CETA provided employment, training, and services to many of the jobless, especially those with very low incomes, and that CETA workers performed many useful jobs for both public and nonprofit employers throughout the nation. Programs for youth and young adults were also incorporated into the act (Title IV), as well as special national programs for target groups such as Indians and other Native Americans, migrant and seasonal farm workers, ex-offenders, older workers, displaced homemakers, women, and the handicapped (Title III).

Actually, CETA was too small to serve all who might have benefited from it. In 1977, when there were about 7 million officially jobless, the Carter administration authorized an expansion of public service employment, and the number of these job slots grew from about 300,000 to a peak of 725,000 in 1978, when there were still 6 million officially and many more unofficially jobless.[101] Afterward, these jobs were again cut back sharply by the Carter administration, even though unemployment rose again in 1980. One might also note that, compared with GNP, CETA expenditures were rather modest. They were highest in fiscal 1977, when total expenditures on CETA were at a maximum of $12.8 billion, which represented about 0.7 percent of GNP; in most years, CETA funding was half or less of that proportion of GNP.[102]

CETA public service employment was eliminated by the Reagan administration at the end of fiscal 1981. As of this writing, the rest of CETA is slated to be eliminated at the end of fiscal 1982. Replacement programs under the Reagan administration will probably be even smaller, will be more private-sector oriented, and will not restore public service employment.

CETA was not the only employment program. For example, the Work Incentive Program (WIN) is for recipients of relief under the Aid to Families with Dependent Children (AFDC) program, but registration is mandatory for certain categories of recipients. The Reagan administration, however, has proposed terminating this program at the end of 1982. Instead, it has proposed forcing states to establish workfare programs that would require AFDC recipients to work enough hours at public-sector minimum-wage jobs to offset their welfare benefits, without providing them with regular jobs.[103] Another program is the Targeted Jobs Tax Credit (TJTC), a relatively new program that partially subsidizes wages of disadvantaged workers to encourage their employment. The extent to which it does so has been seriously questioned, however.[104] Indeed, civil-rights, equal-opportunity-employment, general education, health, vocational-rehabilitation, transportation, housing, urban, regional, foreign-trade, fiscal, and monetary policies—to name only a few—may directly or indirectly affect employment, as well as its distribution. The impact can be either positive or negative.

Jobs programs like CETA were often working in a general environment that precluded maximum effectiveness. There would have been a greater impact if more jobs had been created. Graduates of these programs would have had more opportunities if there had been a full-employment economy, with tight labor markets pushing up low wages. More unionization of workers, especially low-wage workers, would also have helped. Finally, their impact would have been much stronger if all government policies had been geared toward full employment and equal opportunity. Instead, government policies often helped to make millions of persons jobless and then created a few hundred thousand jobs for the victims. Jobs and training programs could be an integral part of any real full-employment policy—indeed, they would have to be. However, neither CETA nor any other government policy yet implemented has had full employment as its aim. No policy has been *part* of an overall full-employment strategy designed to provide *jobs at decent wages* to everyone willing to work. Still, the dream of jobs for all did reemerge in the 1970s. We now turn to that struggle for full employment.

Notes

1. *Economic Report of the President*, Transmitted to the Congress, February 1982 (Washington, D.C.: U.S. Government Printing Office, 1982), derived from table B-1, p. 233.

2. John Maynard Keynes, *The General Theory of Employment, Interest and Money* (New York: Harcourt, Brace and World, 1936), p. 129.

3. Ibid.

4. Paul A. Baran and Paul M. Sweezy, *Monopoly Capital: An Essay on the American Economic and Social Order* (New York: Monthly Review Press, 1966), chap. 7, and John Kenneth Galbraith, *The New Industrial State* (New York: Signet, 1967), esp. chaps. 20, 24.

5. Galbraith, *New Industrial State,* p. 239.

6. A.W. Phillips, "The Relation between Unemployment and the Rate of Change of Money Wage Rates in the United Kingdom, 1862-1957," *Economica* 25 (November 1958):283-299.

7. For a comparison of the Keynesian and Phillips-curve approaches from a liberal viewpoint, see James Tobin, "Inflation and Unemployment," Presidential address, American Economic Association, *American Economic Review* 62 (March 1972):1-18. A good brief review of some theoretical issues is in Erich Spitaller, "Prices and Unemployment in Selected Industrial Countries," *IMF Staff Papers* 18 (November 1971), esp. pp. 528-537.

8. See Helen Ginsburg, *Unemployment, Subemployment, and Public Policy* (New York: New York University Center for Studies in Income Maintenance Policy, 1975), p. 24.

9. Milton Friedman, "The Role of Monetary Policy," Presidential address, American Economic Association, *American Economic Review* 58 (March 1968):1-17.

10. For a critical analysis of the natural rate of unemployment approach that examines ideological and theoretical aspects of the various models, see Robert Cherry, "What Is So Natural about the Natural Rate of Unemployment?" *Journal of Economic Issues* 15 (September 1981):729-743.

11. Herbert Stein, "Full Employment at Last?" *The Wall Street Journal,* 14 September 1977.

12. Eileen Shanahan, "Executives Back Job Cut in a Split with President," *The New York Times,* 21 October 1968, p. 1.

13. For a description and critique of the process, see Edmund S. Phelps, "Unreasonable Price Stability—the Pyrrhic Victory over Inflation," in *The Battle against Unemployment,* ed. Arthur M. Okun (New York: Norton, 1972), pp. 214-223.

14. *Economic Report of the President,* transmitted to the Congress, February 1974 (Washington, D.C.: U.S. Government Printing Office, 1974), p. 58.

15. Ibid., p. 61.

16. National Commission for Manpower Policy, *The Need to Disaggregate the Full Employment Goal,* by R.A. Gordon, Special Report no. 17 (Washington, D.C.: U.S. Government Printing Office, 1978), p. 2.

17. Carolyn Shaw Bell, "The Economics of Might Have Been," *Monthly Labor Review* 97 (November 1974):42.

18. U.S. Congress, Joint Economic Committee, *The 1972 Economic Report of the President*, Hearings, pt. 4, 92d Cong., 2d Sess., 1972, p. 704.

19. John M. Blair, *Economic Concentration, Structure, Behavior and Public Policy* (New York: Harcourt, Brace and World, 1972), pp. 544-549.

20. Summaried in Howard M. Wachtel and Peter D. Adelsheim, "How Recessions Feed Inflation: Price Markups in a Concentrated Economy," *Challenge* 20 (September-October 1973):6-13.

21. U.S. Senate, Committee on Labor and Public Welfare, *The Multinational Corporation and the National Interest* (report submitted by Robert Gilpin), 93d Cong., 1st Sess., 1973, pp. 13-19.

22. U.S. Congress, Joint Economic Committee, *Report on the 1974 Economic Report of the President*, 93rd Cong., 2d Sess., 1974, p. 64.

23. Ibid.

24. Seymour Melman, "Inflation and Unemployment as Products of War Economy: The Trade Union Stake in Economic Conversion," Speech, annual convention of the United Electrical Workers, Cleveland, Ohio, 1976. See also other books by Melman, especially *The Permanent War Economy* (New York: Simon and Shuster, 1974).

25. Marion Anderson, "The Empty Pork Barrel: Unemployment and the Pentagon Budget, 1978 Edition" (Lansing, Mich.: Public Interest Research Group, 1978), pp. 1-3, mimeo.

26. U.S. Bureau of the Census, *Statistical Abstract of the United States: 1980* (Washington, D.C.: U.S. Government Printing Office, 1980), derived from table 699, p. 421.

27. Garth L. Mangum, *Employability, Employment and Income: A Reassessment of Manpower Policy* (Salt Lake City, Utah: Olympus, 1976), p. 113.

28. Leslie Ann Nulty, *Understanding the New Inflation: The Importance of the Basic Necessities* (Washington, D.C.: Exploratory Project for Economic Alternatives, 1977).

29. See, for example, Ray Marshall, "Full Employment: The Inflation Myth," *AFL-CIO American Federationist* (August 1976):3-10.

30. Robert Lekachman, "Managing Inflation in a Full Employment Society," *The Annals* 418 (March 1975):85-93. The entire issue, edited by Stanley Moses, is devoted to *Planning for Full Employment*.

31. Leon H. Keyserling (with help from the Task Force), *Full Employment without Inflation*, prepared for the Task Force of the Committee on Full Employment (Washington, D.C.: Conference on Economic Progress, 1975), pp. 1-2.

32. Paul A. Samuelson, "Worldwide Stagflation," *Morgan Guaranty Survey*, June 1974, p. 9.

33. A full critique of Reaganomics is found in Robert Lekachman, *Greed Is Not Enough: Reaganomics* (New York: Pantheon, 1982).

34. Unless otherwise specified, all data for 1981 in this chapter are taken or derived from official Labor Department data found in *Employment and Earnings* 29 (January 1982). For a full description of how unemployment is measured, see U.S. Department of Labor, Bureau of Labor Statistics, *How the Government Measures Unemployment*, Report 505 (Washington, D.C.: U.S. Government Printing Office, 1977).

35. "One in Five Persons in Labor Force Experienced Some Unemployment during 1981," News Release, U.S. Department of Labor, Bureau of Labor Statistics, 20 July 1982, p. 1.

36. U.S. Commission on Civil Rights, *Child Care and Equal Opportunity for Women*, Clearinghouse Publication no. 67 (Washington, D.C.: Commission on Civil Rights, 1981).

37. See, for instance, Nancy H. Teeters, "Built in Flexibility of Federal Expenditures," *Brookings Papers on Economic Activity* 3 (1971):626-629, and Mordechai E. Landon, Malcolm B. Coate, and Ruth Kraus, "Disability Applications and the Economy," *Social Security Bulletin* 43 (October 1979):3-10.

38. National Commission on Employment and Unemployment Statistics, *Counting the Labor Force* (Washington, D.C.: U.S. Government Printing Office, 1979), p. 45. This volume and its *Appendix*, vol. 1, *Concepts and Data Needs* (1979), are devoted to measurement concepts and problems.

39. Commission on Employment, *Counting the Labor Force*, p. 56.

40. "The Disability Insurance Bill," Update 18, 11 May 1982 (New York: Study Group on Social Security), p. 1, mimeo.

41. See, for instance, U.S. Department of Labor, *Employment and Training Report of the President*, transmitted to the Congress, 1981 (Washington, D.C.: U.S. Government Printing Office, 1979), table A-5, pp. 127-128.

42. Bertram Gross, *Friendly Fascism* (New York: Evans, 1980), p. 145. See also Bertram Gross and Stanley Moses, "How Many Jobs, for Whom?" in *Public Service Employment: An Analysis of Its History, Problems and Prospects*, ed. Alan Gartner, Russell A. Nixon, and Frank Riessman (New York: Praeger, 1973), pp. 28-36, and, for an analysis of the development of the labor-force concept, Stanley Moses, "Labor Force Concepts: The Political Economy of Conceptual Changes," *The Annals* 418 (March 1975):85-93.

43. Gross, *Friendly Fascism*, p. 145.

44. Eli Ginzberg, "The Job Problem," *Scientific American*, November 1977, p. 43.

45. Quoted in A.H. Raskin, "The Changing Face of the Labor Force," *The New York Times*, 15 February 1976, sect. 4, p. 5.

46. Ginzberg, "Job Problem," pp. 49-50.

47. Frank F. Furstenberg, Jr. and Charles A. Thrall, "Counting the Jobless: The Impact of Job Rationing on the Measurement of Unemployment," *The Annals*, 418 (March 1975):45-59.

48. AFL-CIO, Department of Economic Research, Washington, D.C., unpublished data. For the methodology, see Markley Roberts, "Good Policy Needs Good Figures," *AFL-CIO American Federationist*, September 1978, esp. pp. 18-19; and National Urban League, Research Department, Washington, D.C., unpublished data. For the methodology, see "Computation of Quarterly NUL Hidden Unemployment Index," National Urban League, Research Department, n.d., mimeo.

49. Anne McDougall Young, "Job Search of Recipients of Unemployment Insurance," *Monthly Labor Review* 102 (February 1979):49-54.

50. See, for instance, Peter M. Guttmann, "The Grand Unemployment Illusion," *Journal of the Institute for Socioeconomic Studies* 4 (Summer 1979), esp. pp. 25-26. This article summarizes the view that unemployment is overstated. Additional material is found in various parts of the volumes of the National Commission on Employment and Unemployment Statistics.

51. Louis Ferman, Louise Berndt, and Elaine Selo, "Analysis of the Irregular Economy: Cash Flow in the Informal Sector," report to the Bureau of Employment and Training, Michigan Department of Labor (University of Michigan-Wayne State University, Institute of Labor and Industrial Relations, March 1978), pp. 4.13-4.14.

52. *1972 Economic Report of the President, Hearings*, pt. 2, p. 323.

53. Robert M. Solow, "What Happened to Full Employment?" *Quarterly Review of Economics and Business* 13 (Summer 1973):17.

54. "Jobless Rate Tied to Big Work Force," *The New York Times*, 18 April 1982, p. 37.

55. Robert E. Hall, "Prospects for Shifting the Phillips Curve through Manpower Policy," *Brookings Papers on Economic Activity* 3 (1971):701.

56. Unless otherwise specified, all data in this chapter for 1980, as well as comparisons between 1980 and earlier years, are taken or derived from U.S. Department of Labor, Employment and Training Administration, *Employment and Training Report of the President, 1981* (Washington, D.C.: U.S. Government Printing Office, 1981).

57. Diana Nilsen Westcott, "Blacks in the 1970s: Did They Scale the Job Ladder?" *Monthly Labor Review* 105 (June 1982):29.

58. Ibid., p. 36.

59. Robert B. Hill, "The Economic Status of Black Americans," in *The State of Black America, 1981*, ed. James D. Williams (National Urban League, 1981), p. 32.

60. U.S. Bureau of the Census, *Consumer Population Reports*, series P-60, no. 130, *Money Income and Poverty Status of Families and Persons*

in the United States: 1980 (Advance Data from the March 1981 Current Population Survey) (Washington, D.C.: U.S. Government Printing Office, 1981), table B, p. 4.

61. Ginsburg, *Unemployment,* appendix table 4-F, p. 93.

62. *Statistical Abstract of the United States, 1980,* table 230, p. 145.

63. Robert B. Hill, "Discrimination and Minority Youth Unemployment" p. 11, in U.S. Department of Labor, Employment and Training Administration, Vice-President's Task Force on Youth Unemployment, *A Review of Youth Employment Problems, Programs and Policies,* vol. 2, *Special Needs and Concentrated Problems* (Washington, D.C.: U.S. Government Printing Office, 1980).

64. Cited in ibid., pp. 15-17.

65. "Overview", in Task Force, *Youth Employment,* vol. 2, pp. 1-7.

66. Ibid., p. 4.

67. Ibid., p. 3.

68. Information on the minimum wage in this paragraph draws heavily from Hill, "Economic Status," pp. 16-20.

69. Ibid., p. 20.

70. Ibid., p. 10.

71. "Overview," in Task Force, *Youth Unemployment,* p. 6.

72. Hill, "Economic Status," p. 10.

73. Calculated from data in *Employment and Training Report of the President, 1981,* table A-30, p. 166.

74. See, for instance, *Employment and Earnings* 29 (January 1982):158, tables 11, 12.

75. Lloyd Ulman, "Labor Markets and Manpower Policies," *Monthly Labor Review* 95 (September 1972):25.

76. Cited in Barbara R. Bergmann, "Curing High Unemployment among Blacks and Women," in *The Economics of Women and Work,* ed. Alice H. Amsden (New York: St. Martin's Press, 1980), p. 354. See also other articles in this anthology, especially in parts II and III. A useful source of information about female workers is U.S. Department of Labor, Womens Bureau, *1975 Handbook on Women Workers,* Bulletin 297 (Washington, D.C.: U.S. Government Printing Office, 1976).

77. Bergmann, "Curing High Unemployment," pp. 350-356.

78. Data in this section for 1978 and 1979 and comparisons of 1979 with other years are from Census Bureau, *Statistical Abstract: 1980.*

79. National Research Council, *Women, Work and Wages,* ed. Donald J. Treiman and Heidi I. Hartmann (Washington, D.C.: National Academy Press, 1981) p. 28.

80. U.S. Department of Labor, Bureau of Labor Statistics, *Employment in Perspective: Working Women, 1979 Summary,* Report no. 587 (Washington, D.C.: U.S. Government Printing Office), p. 1.

81. Research Council, *Women, Work and Wages,* p. 13.

82. Data are for 1981 and are derived from *Employment and Earnings,* January 1982, table 35, p. 176.

83. Bureau of Census, *Consumer Population Reports,* series P-60, no. 130, table 18, p. 30.

84. U.S. Department of Labor, Bureau of Labor Statistics, *Marital and Family Characteristics of Workers, 1970 to 1978,* Special Labor Force Report 219 (Washington, D.C.: U.S. Government Printing Office, 1979), table F, pp. A-24, A-25.

85. See, for instance, Jill Norgren and Sheila Cole, "Heaven Help The Working Mother: Child Care Tax Credit," *The Nation,* 23 January, 1982, pp. 77-79, and Commission on Civil Rights, *Child Care.*

86. See, for instance, Mary Ellen Ayres, "Federal Indian Policy and Labor Statistics—A Review Essay," *Monthly Labor Review* 101(April 1978):22-27, and U.S. Department of the Interior, Bureau of Indian Affairs, *Local Estimates of Residents: Indian Population and Labor Force, April 1979* (Bureau of Indian Affairs, Financial Management, July 1980). The traditional concept of the labor force and unemployment have been considered especially inappropriate for Indians on reservations. Some idea of the magnitude of the problem can be gleaned from 1970 census figures, which showed that 74 percent of all men, but only 56 percent of all Indian men, were working. See Ayres, "Federal Indian Policy," p. 24; table 1, p. 25.

87. U.S. Department of Labor, Employment and Training Administration, *Employment Related Problems: A Research Strategy.* R&D Monograph no. 73, by Harold Sheppard (Washington, D.C.: U.S. Government Printing Office, 1979).

88. See Sar A. Levitan and Robert Taggart, *Jobs for the Disabled* (Baltimore, Md.: Johns Hopkins University Press, 1977).

89. U.S. Department of Labor, "A Sharper Look at Unemployment in U.S. Cities and Slums," (Washington, D.C.: U.S. Government Printing Office, 1967). See also Ginsburg, *Unemployment,* Chap. 5 for other studies and for further discussion of subemployment.

90. Leonard Goodwin, *Do the Poor Want to Work?* (Washington, D.C.: Brookings Institution, 1972). See also Goodwin's critical discussion of workfare, "Can Workfare Work?" *Public Welfare* 39 (Fall 1981):19-25.

91. See, for example, National Commission for Manpower Policy, *Manpower and Immigration Policies in the United States,* Special Report no. 20, by David North and Allen LeBel (Washington, D.C.: U.S. Government Printing Office, 1978), chap. V, and U.S. Commission on Civil Rights, *Documented and Undocumented Persons in New York City,* Report of the New York State Advisory Committee to the U.S. Commission on Civil Rights (Washington, D.C.: U.S. Government Printing Office, 1982), esp. pts. 2, 3B.

92. Barry Bluestone, Bennett Harrison, and Lawrence Baker, *Corporate Flight: The Causes and Consequences of Economic Dislocation* (Washington, D.C.: Progressive Alliance, 1981), p. 55. See also Barry Bluestone and Bennett Harrison, *The Deindustrialization of America* (New York: Basic Books, 1982).

93. The source of all data for August 1982 is U.S. Department of Labor, Bureau of Labor Statistics, "State and Metropolitan Area Unemployment, August 1982," Press Release 82-371, Washington, D.C., 19 October 1982.

94. This section draws heavily from Illona Rashkow, *Comprehensive Employment and Training Act,* Library of Congress, Congressional Research Service Report no. 81-56 EPW, 27 February 1981 (Washington, D.C.: Congressional Research Service), pp. 1-8.

95. Peter B. Doeringer and Michael J. Piore, *Internal Labor Markets and Manpower Analysis* (Lexington, Mass.: Lexington Books, D.C. Heath and Company, 1971), pp. 105-106; Bennett Harrison, "Institutions on the Periphery," in *Problems in Political Economy: An Urban Perspective,* 2nd ed., ed. David M. Gordon, (Lexington, Mass.: D.C. Heath and Company, 1977), pp. 201-202.

96. Mangum, *Employability,* p. 76. Mangum's book surveys and reassesses twenty-five years of employment and training policy in the United States.

97. A full treatment of the Emergency Employment Act is found in Sar A. Levitan and Robert Taggart, *The Emergency Employment Act: The PEP Generation* (Salt Lake City, Utah: Olympus, 1974).

98. Paul Bullock, *CETA at the Crossroads: Employment Policy and Politics* (Los Angeles: University of California: Institute of Industrial Relations, 1981), p. 5. The section on CETA draws heavily on Bullock's work.

99. The evidence on substitution is summarized in Bullock, *CETA,* chap. 5.

100. Bullock, *CETA,* chap. 5.

101. Bullock, *CETA,* p. 12.

102. Author's calculation's based on fiscal-year funding (Rashkow, *Comprehensive Employment and Training Act,* appendix table B, pp. 38-39) as a percentage of calendar-year GNP.

103. "Reaganomics: The Second Dose," *AFL-CIO American Federationist,* February 1982, pp. 15, 23. For a critical view of workfare, see Leonard Goodwin, "Can Workfare Work?" *Public Welfare* 39 (Fall 1981):19-25.

104. See John Fish, *The Economic Rationale for the Targeted Tax Credit,* Library of Congress, Congressional Reference Service, Report no. 80-196E, 6 November 1980 (Washington, D.C.: Congressional Research Service). The Targeted Jobs Tax Credit (TJTC), enacted in 1978, allows

firms a tax credit, counted as taxable income. (50 percent of first-year wages and 25 percent of second-year wages up to $6,000 for workers) in several targeted groups such as economically disadvantaged youth, welfare recipients, handicapped persons in vocational-rehabilitation programs, economically disadvantaged ex-convicts, economically disadvantaed students in cooperative-education programs, and economically disadvantaged Vietnam War veterans. TJTC has been criticized, first, because it was little used; second, because of extensive substitution—most workers would have been hired anyway; and third, because it was a tremendous windfall for employers. Retroactive certifications accounted for two-thirds of tax credits awarded in the program's first eighteen months, and some firms made a business of advising other companies how to get certificates for persons already on the payroll; a large proportion of youngsters were cooperative-education students who were not economically disadvantaged (they now must be economically disadvantaged, and certification can no longer be retroactive). See "Targeted Jobs Tax Incentives Program Creates Windfall for Some Firms, But Not Much New Employment," *Daily Labor Report,* no. 77 (Washington, D.C.: Bureau of National Affairs, 22 April 1981), pp. C-1–C-6.

3

The Struggle for the Humphrey-Hawkins Full Employment Act

Despite the persistence of unemployment in the postwar years, not until the mid-1970s did full employment again emerge as a major policy issue. The main attempt to commit the federal government to a policy of full employment centered on the struggle that culminated in the passage of the Humphrey-Hawkins Full Employment and Balanced Growth Act of 1978.

Background

This legislation was first introduced into the Congress in June 1974 by Representative Augustus Hawkins (D-California), an influential member of the Congressional Black Caucus from the Watts district of Los Angeles. Hawkins was deeply committed to equality for all people and to a broad interpretation of full employment as a human right, in the spirit of the Full Employment Bill of 1945. He did not conceive of the bill as simply an antirecession measure or as just another jobs program. Indeed, when the legislation was in the formative stage, the economy was not in a recession. In the first half of 1974 unemployment averaged just under 5.2 percent, and in 1973 it had been 4.9 percent.

Hawkins, however, representing a ghetto district plagued even in so-called good times by endemic poverty and depression levels of unemployment, had a two-pronged, long-term strategy: to provide jobs for all Americans who want to work, and to fill unmet social needs by using the untapped labor of the unemployed and the underemployed. Full employment was to be the key to reducing poverty, inequality, discrimination, crime, welfare, alienation, and human misery—and to improving the living standards and quality of life of Americans. Hawkins's original bill was cosponsored in the House by Henry Reuss (D-Wisconsin), and soon thereafter Hubert Humphrey (D-Minnesota) sponsored an identical bill in the Senate.[1]

The bill was meant to be a focal point for raising consciousness over the issue of full employment. As such, it was oriented to the future. Hoping to gain time to build support for the idea of full employment, Hawkins called it the Equal Opportunity and Full Employment Act of 1976. Addressing a Full Employment Conference at Columbia University in March 1974, before the Hawkins-Reuss bill was introduced into the Congress, he predicted that the 1974 election was not likely to produce a Congress that would be sufficiently interested in full employment to pass the kind of legislation he was proposing, unless it was watered down and stripped of its most essential parts. Nevertheless, Hawkins felt that the political trends were veering toward liberalism, and he expected the election of a liberal Democratic president and Congress in 1976. Thus his strategy at that time was to give the issue enough visibility to encourage a national debate so that a commitment to full employment might become part of the 1976 Democratic party platform, thereby positioning the bill for passage in 1977.[2]

Even before Jimmy Carter became president, several variants of H.R. 50 and S. 50, as they came to be numbered—all building on the Employment Act of 1946—were introduced. But along the way, the goal shrank from jobs for all to jobs for some.[3]

First Version, June 1974: The Vision

The goal of the first, June 1974, version was a job for everyone who wanted and was able to work. It called for a national policy and nationwide machinery for guaranteeing all adult Americans 16 years of age or more who were willing and able to work equal opportunities for useful employment at fair rates of compensation. *All* meant just that—women; older people; younger people; members of racial, ethnic, national, or religious minorities; veterans; the physically and mentally handicapped; former drug addicts; and released convicts, among others.

Federal economic policies were to be geared toward increasing the overall demand for labor; most of the jobs were to be created that way. To help ensure that the economy generated jobs, certain procedures were stipulated. The president, for example, was required to submit to Congress annually a long- and a short-run full-employment and production plan. The Congressional Joint Economic Committee was to review the needed appropriations.

An integral backup measure obligated the federal government itself to create enough jobs to employ *everyone* still out of work. Federally financed reservoirs of public and private projects to meet community needs were to be developed by local planning councils in every labor market. Job seekers were to be referred by local Job Guarantee Offices to suitable private or public employment or, if necessary, to temporary, paid assignments in a Standby Job Corps.

The bill, as its title promised, was strongly oriented toward equal opportunity. It recognized that those with special problems would need extra assistance, since anyone who applied for work at a Job Office, even if handicapped, was to be considered "prima facie 'willing and able' to work," including persons with "impairments of sight, hearing, movement, coordination, mental retardation or other handicaps." Finally, there was an enforceable, legal right to employment—the most controversial part of the bill. Individuals who felt unfairly deprived of their job rights were entitled to an administrative appeal and, if necessary, could sue the government. No numerical rate of unemployment was set as a target because the goal was simply to have jobs for everyone willing and able to work, *including those not in the labor force as customarily measured.* Full implementation was scheduled to take five years. Five years, however, can seem like a millenium when one faces an immediate crisis. In June 1974 Hawkins did not know that the economy was about to nosedive, with millions of newcomers soon to join the army of the unemployed.

Second Version, March 1975: Response to an Immediate Crisis

In March 1975, when the second version of H.R. 50 was unveiled, nearly 8 million were officially jobless—3.2 million more than when the original version was presented only nine months earlier.[4] Unemployment had jumped from 5.2 to 8.7 percent and was still climbing. In those circumstances the bill needed more credibility. It had to seem like more than pie in the sky to those who were caught in the immediate crisis. Thus an *interim* target was set. Unemployment was to be slashed to 3 percent within eighteen months, without altering the final goal of real full employment or the underlying philosophy.

The bill's list of national priorities was greatly expanded. Among them were adequate housing, health care, child care, education for all, expansion of mass transit, conservation of resources, environmental improvement, the development of cultural and recreational activities, and the elimination of poverty within ten years. Employment was to be geared toward meeting a variety of socially useful needs. For the first time national defense also appeared as a priority, but a section on the conversion of the military industry to civilian pursuits was retained from the original bill.

The bill also had more specific measures to ensure consistency between fiscal and monetary policies, including those of the Federal Reserve System, and the full-employment goal, as well as policies to curb inflation without sacrificing that goal.

The bill was clearly designed to capture the imagination and support of persons concerned with social justice and similar issues that had sparked so much activity in the 1960s. By April 1975 the list of House cosponsors had grown to more than eighty. The 1960s, however, were over. The political climate had already become much more conservative, a fact that hardly assured serious political support or even attention. The full-employment goal and most of the bill's priorities, with the exception of defense, were neither on the national agenda nor on that of the Democrats. Moreover, with escalating unemployment, more and more workers were pitted against each other for scarce jobs. The unemployed themselves were remarkably passive, as were unions. The largest labor-sponsored protest was a Jobs Now rally held in Washington, D.C., on April 26, 1975.[5] In contrast to the Solidarity Day protest against Reagan's economic policies on September 19, 1981, which drew an estimated 250,000-400,000 demonstrators from labor and other organizations, the Jobs Now rally was attended by only about 60,000 union members.[6] Moreover, the 1975 rally did not even have the full support of the AFL-CIO, since it was sponsored only by its Industrial Union Department (IUD). In this atmosphere, few Americans, particularly those who would benefit most from it, grasped the concept of full employment and the right to a job or had even heard of the Humphrey-Hawkins bill.

Building Support

Nevertheless, some limited support and consciousness was building around the full-employment issue and the bill. In 1975 the Hawkins Subcommittee on Equal Opportunities held hearings on the bill in eight cities, and Humphrey's Joint Economic Committee stirred up interest by holding hearings on unemployment and full employment. During this period, groups had also been formed to work for full employment. The National Committee for Full Employment was established in June 1974 and soon set up a legislative arm, the Full Employment Action Council.[7] Both organizations were and still are cochaired by Coretta Scott King, widow of Martin Luther King, and Murray Finley, head of the Amalgamated Clothing and Textile Workers Union. These coalitions brought together leaders from labor, liberal, religious, civil-rights, black, ethnic, women's, senior citizens' and other organizations with a stake in full employment or a belief that this was a major need. The organizations from which these leaders were drawn from an impressive list, including the National Council of Churches, the United Church Board for Homeland Ministries, the Union of American Hebrew Congregations, the U.S. Catholic Conference, the Synagogue Council of America, and the American Jewish Committee; the National Women's Political Caucus, the National Organization for Women, and the League of Women Voters; the National Council of Negro Women, the National Urban League, the National Association for the Advancement of Colored

People, the Martin Luther King Center for Social Change, and the National Urban Coalition; the Industrial Union Department of the AFL-CIO; the American Federation of State, County, and Municipal Workers; the United Automobile Workers; the United Farm Workers; the International Association of Machinists; the Building Trades Department of the AFL-CIO; the United Steel Workers of America; the American Federation of Teachers; Americans for Democratic Action, the National Council of Senior Citizens, the National Farmers' Union, Americans for Indian Opportunity, and the National Center for Urban Ethnic Affairs—to name only a few. Environmentalists were not involved in these coalitions originally, although they came in later. In 1975 they had formed their own organization, Environmentalists for Full Employment. At that time much of organized labor regarded environmental concerns with suspicion, as being likely to lead to reductions in employment and loss of jobs for their members.

Labor

Throughout this period, H.R. 50 itself lacked support from the AFL-CIO. Without such endorsement the bill had practically no chance in Congress. The AFL-CIO strongly opposed the legally enforceable right to a job, calling it impractical and unnecessary. Two independent unions, the United Electrical Workers and the United Auto Workers (UAW) (not affiliated with the AFL-CIO at that time), did support the bill and the legal guarantee.[8] In the opinion of the UAW legal department, without the private right to sue, the rights in the act would be unenforceable. In its view the administrative appeals scheme was similar to that created by many federal and state acts, particularly those covering unemployment insurance.[9] There was some speculation about other possible reasons for the AFL-CIO's nonsupport, none of it verified. Some felt it was based on a fear that the labor market would be flooded with job seekers, who would then compete with union members for work; or that full employment was simply not a high priority because the AFL-CIO's main concerns were with matters more directly affecting their members, most of whom were employed. Whatever actual additional reasons, there may have been for nonsupport, union members were not immune to unemployment. As the recession deepened, there was growing pressure within the federation to do something. On December 8, 1975, George Meany, AFL-CIO president, made public a policy statement on the "Principles of Full Employment Legislation," adopted a few days before by the Economic Policy Committee of the AFL-CIO, chaired by I.W. Abel, president of the United Steelworkers of America.[10] The statement called for a reduction of unemployment to 3 percent and support for a full-employment act, which it felt it imperative that the next session of Congress consider.[11] On December 11, 1975, George Meany and other AFL-CIO officials met with members of the Congressional Black Caucus to discuss efforts to secure passage of full-employment legislation. At at time when relations between blacks and the AFL-CIO had often been strained as a result of the racist practices of some unions, especially in the building trades, and with minorities pushing for affirmative action, this seemed to be a significant event. At last the AFL-CIO had decided to give full employment a high spot on its 1976 agenda and had promised all-out support for a more realistic and practical bill.

The Democrats

With a presidential election not far off and unemployment becoming more of a political issue, the House Democratic leadership also became more interested. They promised the Congressional Black Caucus, which was pushing for legislation, that a redrafted bill, one able to attract broader support, would get top priority. The bill was to be passed and placed on President Gerald Ford's desk by the end of May. Ford was sure to veto it; and since the veto could not be overridden, H.R. 50 would become the main campaign issue of the Democrats. Humphrey hoped to use a more acceptable version of the bill to help him gain the presidency.[12]

Thus the version introduced in March 1976 was heavily influenced by Humphrey and by the AFL-CIO, which gave it "support without reservation."[13]

Third Version, March 1976: The Influence of the AFL-CIO and Senator Humphrey

The bill now had a new title, "The Full Employment and Balanced Act of 1976,"[14] and adopted some features of an earlier planning bill sponsored by Humphrey and Senator Jacob Javits (R-New York).[15] It therefore had a much more elaborate economic-planning mechanism than its predecessors, but it was weaker in its ability to make the Federal Reserve System conform to the full-employment goal. It was also more comprehensive, calling for the development of policies such as countercyclical grants to state and local governments, special financial assistance to depressed areas and inner cities, youth-employment programs, and additional anti-inflation tools. Although the means were more elaborate, however, the aims were far more modest.

As expected, the right to sue for a job—and thus the job guarantee— was gone. Also gone was the provision covering workers with special obstacles. The stated goal was a 3 percent adult unemployment rate within four years, but *adult* was not defined. Thus it was not clear whether that rate included 16- to 19-year-olds, as in the second version. If not, that was equivalent to about a 4-percent unemployment-rate goal, only about 1 percentage point less than the Ford administration's projection at that time of a 4.9-percent unemployment rate by 1981. (The actual unemployment rate in 1981 averaged 7.6 percent.) Supporters who wanted the bill strengthened pointed out that even if the goal was 3-percent unemployment and even if it was attained, substantial joblessness might persist among some groups such as blacks, women, and youths. Certain areas, especially inner-city slums, could have substantial unemployment, as was true even in the late 1960s, when unemployment was less than 4 percent. Discouraged workers and some others who were out of the labor force and not counted as unemployed might still have tough employment problems or might require services to enable them to work—some of the disabled, mothers requiring child care, and ex-offenders, for example.[16] In this version, unlike the second version, the 3-percent unemployment rate represented a final rather than an interim goal, suggesting that many of the problems cited earlier might continue and that no further efforts would be made to solve them once unemployment dropped to 3 percent.

This version of the bill also reflected the long-standing bias against direct job creation by reducing the role of the government as employer of last resort. Job reservoirs would come into being only when it seemed likely that other measures would not reduce unemployment to 3 percent within four years. The result would be to postpone for the longest time job creation for those with the most severe employment problems—those least likely to get regular employment through expansion of the economy.

Limiting the size of the last-resort jobs program was another important change. This was necessary, since the goal was no longer a job for everyone who wanted one. Thus criteria, including a means test, were set up for job eligibility. Women's groups protested the discrimination against married women implied by the criterion "number of employed persons in the household."[17] This helped to dampen the enthusiasm of the National Organization for Women, one of the first organizations to support the original Hawkins-Reuss bill.[18] Other supporters were dismayed to see another new clause: a job applicant who knowingly provided false information, probably out of desperation for work coupled with knowledge that he or she did not meet the criteria, was to be subject to criminal penalties.[19] These changes indicated that, however worthy the bill might be in other respects, the philosophical underpinnings of the original bill had changed. Indeed, according to economist Carolyn Shaw Bell, the introduction of eligibility criteria conflicted with the bill's own stated goal of the right to employment of all adult Americans able, willing, and seeking to work. "The bill is no longer talking about providing work to anyone able and willing to work," Bell told a Senate committee. "The right to a job in Title I becomes a privilege in Title II."[20]

Also in this version of H.R. 50, priorities were reduced from nineteen to five. National defense was retained, but mention of conversion of some military resources to civilian uses was dropped. This reflected the greater influence of the AFL-CIO and of Senator Humphrey, both strong supporters of U.S. foreign policy and a large military budget.

Many original supporters of the bill from outside the ranks of organized labor, such as those from religious, women's, and civil-rights groups, were extremely disappointed by the extent of the changes, which came as a result of negotiations in which they had not participated. Though recognizing that compromise would be needed to pass the bill, some thought that too much had been given away too soon. There seemed to be few bargaining points left as the bill started its journey through the Congress. Tension between some elements in labor and some other groups in the full-employment coalition, though not publicly stated, was exacerbated.[21]

Inflation and Last-Resort Jobs

Despite these changes, this and subsequent versions of the bill were to have rough sailing. There was opposition from big business, conservatives, and many Republicans. Much more than in 1945, some Democrats also lacked enthusiasm for the bill. The bill was criticized for various reasons: it was too costly; it had unrealistic goals about reducing unemployment and thus would create false hopes; it would lead to make-work jobs; it required too much government planning; it would put a burden on the private sector. Above all, it was attacked as inflationary.[22] A whole section of the March 1976 version was devoted to anti-inflationary policies, but the inflation charges persisted.

The bill specified that anti-inflationary policies were to be set forth annually in the President's Economic Report. Among other things, they were to include a system of monitoring sectoral trends to avert potentially inflationary bottlenecks in the economy; of gearing monetary and fiscal policy to the capabilities of a full-employment economy; of increasing the supply of goods, services, labor, and capital in structurally tight markets, with particular emphasis on increasing the supply of food and energy; and of stockpiling food and other critical materials for emergencies and to help maintain price stability. There were also recommendations to strengthen and enforce antitrust laws and other means of increasing private-sector competition, and recommendations for administrative legislative actions to promote reasonable price stability if price stability were seriously threatened. There was, however, no requirement for mandatory wage-price controls, and no mention of the possibility that military expenditures might under certain circumstances exacerbate inflation.

Crucial testimony against the March 1976 version of the Humphrey-Hawkins bill came from economist Charles Schultze of the Brookings Institution, later head of the Council of Economic Advisers under President Carter. Interestingly, according to Paul Lewis of *The New York Times,* Schultze had once been involved in the Johnson administration's effort to cover up the rapidly escalating costs of the Vietnam War, which proved to be highly inflationary.

In this Senate testimony on Humphrey-Hawkins, reprinted as an op-ed piece in the influential *Washington Post,* Schultze stated that the bill was highly inflationary; he claimed that an unemployment rate below 5.5 percent, because of the composition of the labor force, is inflationary in itself. He singled out the last-resort jobs as the bill's main spur to inflation, partly because they had to pay prevailing wages. In an example cited by Schultze, low-wage workers making around $2.50 an hour would leave private industry in droves to take $3.50- or $4.50-an-hour jobs, thereby driving up low wages in the private sector.[23]

Labor economist Ray Marshall, also soon to join the Carter administration as secretary of labor, responded to Schultze's analysis (in a piece inserted in the *Congressional Record* months after Schultze's testimony). Marshall noted that there was scant evidence to support the theory of a trade-off between unemployment and inflation. He contended that unemployment is inflationary because it means, among other things, lost output and rising expenditures on income-maintenance programs. He questioned the implicit assumption that recent inflation had its origin in labor markets, citing causes such as rising energy prices, among others. He said that paying the prevailing wages would not necessarily be inflationary, since the bill would be a stimulus to create better as well as more jobs. Raising the wages of marginal workers, according to Marshall, would not be an inevitable outcome. Even if it was, that would not necessarily be either inflationary or undesirable. Low-wage employers, he claimed, would have a greater incentive to use labor more efficiently and to improve job quality as the pool of workers forced to work at these jobs diminished. Marshall's view did not prevail.[24]

Political Factors

The basics of the third H.R. 50 became part of the Democratic party platform, but Senator Humphrey had dropped out of the 1976 primary because of failing health. Some leading primary candidates such as Morris Udall and Fred Harris were early supporters of the Humphrey-Hawkins bill. Only after some reluctance did Jimmy Carter endorse the goals of the bill in the spring of 1976. Once Carter gained the nomination, the Democrats were left with a candidate who lacked enthusiasm for the bill and had a strong orientation toward the private sector. Congressional enthusiasm also waned. Although the bill reported out of the House Labor Committee, it never got out of committee in the Senate. Inflation had become a more important national issue by 1976. In midsummer, freshman Democrats asked the House leadership not to put the bill to a vote, lest it hurt their chances for reelection.[25] It was said that many members of Congress reported little pressure from their constituents for H.R. 50. Carter preferred to have the bill revised before giving it his approval. This was done prior to the election, as will be described next.

Fourth Version, September 1976: Again Rewritten, for Carter's Approval

Once again H.R. 50 was rewritten extensively, this time to get Carter's approval and to meet the objections of Schultze and others. It was approved by the House Labor Committee in September 1976.[26] Most of the changes reflected the absence of a strong counterpressure in the country calling for strengthening the bill.

The new goal was a 3-percent jobless rate within four years for adults 20 years and over—equivalent to an overall 4-percent jobless rate. The young were covered by separate programs but without timetable for reducing their unemployment. For the first time there was an inflation goal.

Although inflation was a concern of groups affiliated with the Full Employment Action Council, there was a fear that a specific numerical goal could lead to a sacrifice of the priority to reduce unemployment, regardless of the cause of the inflationary pressures.[27] Ending unemployment was viewed as an absolute priority. Another factor was the AFL-CIO's opposition to mandatory wage-price controls because of its negative experience during Richard Nixon's presidency. Wages had been controlled far better than prices and profits. One member of the Nixon control team later admitted that the controls had been designed to "zap" labor.[28] The target in this version was an inflation rate no more than that existing at the time of enactment but to be attained without sacrificing the employment goal or timetable.

In this version of Humphrey-Hawkins the planning mechanism was weakened, as was the jobs reservoir. These jobs were to be created only as a last resort—and not before two years after enactment. They were to be designed so that they would not draw workers from private employment. They were to be mainly in the lower range of skills and pay, with the eligibility criteria limited even further. The prevailing wage no longer applied, although the jobs still had to pay at least the federal minimum wage.

Many of these features were retained in the final Humphrey-Hawkins Act as enacted. Carter endorsed this version in October 1976 but scarcely mentioned it during the campaign. Although full employment was not a campaign issue, unemployment was an important issue, especially among Carter's black supporters, who were impressed when the candidate sometimes called jobs the number-one priority.

The Subsequent Fate of Humphrey-Hawkins

Despite Carter's endorsement of a further eviscerated Humphrey-Hawkins, the bill languished after he entered the White House. Pressure from Humphrey, labor, black leaders, and Speaker of the House of Representatives Thomas (Tip) O'Neill (D-Massachusetts) finally got the bill back on the agenda.[29] After Senator Humphrey's death in January 1978, there was also a feeling among some Democrats that the bill should be enacted as a tribute to the late senator. His widow, Senator Muriel Humphrey (D-Minnesota), appointed to his vacated seat, continued to press for its passage.

From November 1977—when still another Carter-endorsed version was introduced—until its final passage in October 1978, the bill was under continual attack. As the recession abated, inflation became more and more of an issue. As Harvey L. Schantz and Richard H. Schmidt show, the legislative strategy used by opponents was to alter the bill by adding on additional specific goals. There was great difficulty in maintaining full employment as the purpose of the bill.[30] Although there were many issues, government spending and inflation were the main ones. For example, a goal of 0-percent inflation by 1983 and a balanced budget by the same year made strong headway in the Senate, as did Senator William Proxmire's (D-Wisconsin) amendment (not in the act as passed) to limit the federal budget to 21 percent by fiscal 1981 and to 20 percent by fiscal 1983. Adoption of inflation goals of 3 percent by 1983 and 0 percent by 1988 helped clear the way for passage on 15 October 1978. As seen in chapter 1, President Carter signed the bill into law on October 27, 1978.

The Humphrey-Hawkins Full Employment and Balanced Growth Act of 1978

The Humphrey-Hawkins Full Employment and Balanced Growth Act of 1978 is very different from the original bill introduced by Hawkins into the Congress in 1974, just as the Employment Act of 1946 was very different from the Full Employment Bill of 1945.[31] What is actually contained in this very complicated law? Some of its features follow.

Contents of the Humphrey-Hawkins Act

It is significant that the stated purpose of the act is "to translate into practical reality the right of all Americans who are able, willing and seeking to work to full opportunity for useful paid employment at fair rates of compensation." Also, the federal government is given the responsibility to gear "its policies and programs to promote full employment, production, and real income, balanced growth, adequate productivity growth, proper attention to national priorities, and reasonable price stability."

Despite the multiplicity of goals, the only numerical targets are for unemployment and inflation. Unemployment was to be reduced to 4 percent within five years after enactment—by 1983. It is not widely recognized that this was clearly stated as an *interim* rather than a final goal. After reducing unemployment to 4 percent, the goal is to achieve and maintain full employment (and a balanced budget). Thus, although the law nowhere defines full employment, it implicitly rejects the notion that 4-percent unemployment is full employment. Other significant longer-range employment goals include reduction and ultimate removal of the gap between the unemployment rates of certain groups such as teenagers, women, and minorities and the overall rate, and calls for structural programs targeted to disadvantaged groups. As already mentioned, inflation was to be reduced to 3 percent by 1983 and 0 percent by 1988.

Though vague and confusing in many respects, and with possibly conflicting goals, the act clearly states the primacy of the objective of reducing unemployment, since "policies and programs for reducing the rate of inflation shall be designed so as not to impede achievement of the goals and timetables for reducing unemployment."

The act establishes a process of planning and coordination involving the president, the Congress, and the Federal Reserve Board. The president is required to submit to the Congress, every year, short- and medium-term numerical goals for employment, unemployment, and production; real income; productivity; and prices for the next five years. These are to be consistent with the goals of full employment and production and an improved trade balance—but also with those of a balanced budget and federal outlays at the lowest percentage share of the GNP that is practical. The latter two goals reflect the curious amalgamation of broad social concerns about unemployment of the bills initial sponsors and the fiscal conservatism included to secure enactment.

The act emphasizes private job creation, as the order of priority shows: (1) expansion of conventional private jobs through general economic and structural policies; (2) expansion of private employment through federal assistance; (3) expansion of regular public employment; and, finally, (4) federally subsidized job reservoirs, which were clearly meant only as a last resort. They were not to be put into action until at least two years after the act's passage, and then only after the president had informed the Congress that other means were not yielding enough jobs to be consistent with the goals and timetables. Moreover, those involving new programs rather than expansion of existing ones require congressional authorization and funding. There is no automatic trigger to bring them into being when, for example, joblessness for the nation, an area, or a group rises above a given level. These last-resort jobs must draw no workers from private employment and are to be mainly low-skill and low-paying jobs, but they must pay at least the federal minimum wage. This section reflects many of Schultze's original objections, already incorporated into previous versions.

A few other features of the act will be mentioned briefly. A section on anti-inflation policies is similar to one in the March 1976 version, as are sections on countercyclical, regional, and structural employment policies, and on youth-unemployment policies, all of which require prior presidential recommendations and congressional action, since Humphrey-Hawkins is basically a process law. That is, it sets forth procedures for coordinating economic policymaking toward specific goals and requires further implementation in order to be effective.

As part of the process, the Federal Reserve System must explain to Congress semiannually how it is gearing its policies to furthering the unemployment and inflation goals. A procedure is also established for congressional review of the goals, programs, and policies recommended by the president in the Economic Report. If the president postpones the unemployment timetable, Congress may express its own opinion but is not required to do so. Congress could, in theory (although it has not happened in practice) prevent the president from altering the timetable for reducing unemployment.

Implementation

As in 1946, when opinions varied about the meaning of the Employment Act, so opinions about the Humphrey-Hawkins Act varied among supporters of full employment. These views ranged from negative to Representative Hawkins's optimistic assertion that the act was "one of the most important pieces of economic and social legislation enacted during the past generation, and certainly by far the most important piece related to the subject of full employment."[32]

Before long, however, it was obvious that little had changed and that economic policies were not about to be redirected toward meeting the act's modest employment goal. In January 1979, when Jimmy Carter transmitted his Economic Report to Congress, inflation was his paramount concern. Although unemployment at the time was 5.8 percent, goals of 6.2 percent were projected for 1979 and 1980.[33] A Democratic Congress did not challenge the president by setting different goals. Hawkins soon charged the administration and the Congress with eleven violations of the act.[34] By 1980 another recession had pushed unemployment up to an annual rate of 7.1 percent. By the end of 1981, with Ronald Reagan at the helm, the country was in still another recession. Nevertheless, Murray Weidenbaum, head of the Council of Economic Advisers, referring to the slight drop in the inflation rate, stated that the president's economic program was "already working."[35] The recession with its rising unemployment was seen simply as an unfortunate consequence of falling inflation. In December 1981 unemployment was up to 8.8 percent, and in January 1982 it was still 8.5 percent. In February 1982, when Reagan unveiled his budget proposals, he called for additional drastic cuts in social programs and a continued buildup of the Pentagon budget. The economic projections, actually underestimates, showed an unprecedented $91.5-billion deficit for the coming year and indicated that the jobless were going to have to wait a long time for *their* recovery.[36] Shortly thereafter, the President's Economic Report transmitted to the Congress gave the unemployment-rate goals for the next five years as:[37]

1982	8.9 percent
1983	7.9 percent
1984	7.1 percent
1985	6.4 percent
1986	5.8 percent
1987	5.3 percent

Nominally the law of the land, the Humphrey-Hawkins Act had no impact at all. Implementation of the mandate to reduce unemployment to 4 percent and to make the fight against unemployment a national priority had vanished.

The Reasons

Why, after another struggle for full-employment legislation, was the act that finally emerged so weak? Moreover, why was even that law ignored?

An impressive list of organizations supported the act, but the strength of the movement for full employment was never equal to the task that had to be done or to the resistance or lack of enthusiasm encountered even in a

Democratic Congress, by a Democratic president, and even by some who considered themselves liberals. Furthermore, endorsement of a concept or of a piece of legislation by a national organization or its leaders does not automatically bring with it the activity needed to create and sustain a movement or even to do day-to-day political work.

At the founding meeting of the National Committee for Full Employment, Leonard Woodcock, then head of the UAW, called for formation of a committee of one hundred to establish a committee of one million to work for full employment. The committee of one million was never established.[38] Instead, the National Committee for Full Employment remained, for the most part, a Washington-based organization bringing together leaders of various groups. For several years, the committee did little to encourage local organization. Grass-roots organizing on the issue eventually did take place, with the major stimulus coming from the National Council of Churches. Starting in 1976, the council held conferences, first at the national level and then at the regional level in Kansas City, Boston, Chicago, Detroit, San Francisco, Denver, Buffalo, Sioux City, Des Moines, Omaha, and elsewhere. Local full-employment coalitions then came into being in numerous cities and brought together—or attempted to bring together—individuals from religious, labor, civil-rights, and other groups, as well as those not affiliated with any group, including the unemployed themselves. However, full employment was a difficult issue on which to organize. The problems included the lack of interest of the employed, the apathy and feeling of powerlessness and alienation of the unemployed, and strains between groups unaccustomed to working with each other—for example, sometimes between unions and jobless blacks, or between unions that supported building nuclear power plants and environmentalists.

Support for full employment stemmed from pragmatic concern about unemployment. But much of it was based on a moral issue—the right to a job as a human right. Despite formal endorsement, the progressive weakening of the legislation in Washington made it more difficult to sustain the enthusiasm of some supporters. To the extent that full employment was perceived of only as "full employment for my group," or a "job for me," declining unemployment after 1976 may have had a similar impact.

Nevertheless, there was grass-roots activity, and it did exert some pressure. Coordinated activities such as Full Employment Week in September 1977 were officially supported by various organizations associated with the coalition, including the AFL-CIO; and groups across the country attempted to focus attention on full employment through parades, rallies, and the like.[39].

Full employment would require a vast restructuring of the U.S. economy and shifts in political power, which rarely have been accomplished without major effort. The labor movement of the 1930s and the civil-rights and antiwar movements of the 1960s are a few examples of movements that helped to accomplish major change. The full-employment movement, however, never attained their dynamism nor scale. There were no mass demonstrations in Washington to focus national attention on the issue and to put pressure on the Congress and the president. There was no significant counterpressure for a stronger law comparable to the Townsend movement, which helped to get the Social Security Act passed by demanding an unrealistic (for the 1930s) $200 a month for all persons, starting at age 60.

The struggle over Humphrey-Hawkins, its watering down, and its subsequent neglect thus mirror in part the weakness of the movement for full employment. Obviously, this cannot be separated from the larger political climate, which showed a growing conservatism. Moreover, politicians need not appeal to the interests of those who do not register or vote, and the unemployed are far less likely than the employed to do either. In 1978 only 44 percent of the unemployed, compared with 63 percent of the employed, had registered; only 27 percent of the jobless, but 47 percent of the employed, voted.[40]

Controversies

Full employment has always been controversial. The struggle over Humphrey-Hawkins spotlighted attention on some of the controversies, whereas others remained beneath the surface. A few will be mentioned here.

Inflation, as has already been shown, was a major controversial issue, even though unemployment and inflation often went hand in hand in the 1970s. The controversy over the wage standard for the last-resort jobs seemed to be related to the inflation issue. There was another important underlying issue, however. Full employment with decent wages implies restructuring of low-wage labor markets and a redistribution of income and status to the poor, rather than simply a transformation of the jobless or the welfare poor into the working poor. In line with this, economist Robert Lekachman attributes part of the general opposition to full employment to the benefits unemployment bestows on the more prosperous. Among these, he contends, is the availability of a low-wage pool of labor to do dead-end jobs such as those in laundries, restaurant kitchens, and filling stations.[41]

Full employment also raises the issue of the relative size of the military and social budgets. Low unemployment has been associated with wars, and military expenditures contributed to the demand for labor in the postwar decades. As mentioned in chapter 2, however, military expenditures create fewer jobs than equivalent civilian expenditures. Nevertheless, the presence of job insecurity and the lack of guaranteed jobs have made it more difficult to generate the needed support for reordering priorities.

The AFL-CIO's traditional support for large military budgets was undoubtedly one reason that, after endorsing Humphrey-Hawkins, the issue was rarely mentioned. But in August 1981, the impact of the first Reagan budget caused the executive council of the AFL-CIO to state that "our support for national defense is not, however, to be taken as a blank check for the Pentagon." It then called on Congress to subject the administration's defense budget "to the closest scrutiny."[42]

Similarly, although full employment raises the issue of the source of energy for long-run job growth, it does not imply that nuclear power is the only alternative. Solar energy, conservation, and other methods could be used effectively at lower cost and with greater ability to generate jobs. Nor does job growth necessarily entail degradation of the environment. In fact, job growth could actually be used to clean up the environment. Environmentalists helped to clarify many of these issues.[43] Indeed, Lane Kirkland, head of the AFL-CIO, invited the nation's environmental community to participate in Solidarity Day in 1981—something that could not have occurred less than a decade before.[44]

It is clear that in the absence of full employment and the existence of job insecurity and unemployment pose clear threats to the environment, since the threat of a corporation to leave an area if too many environmental demands are made is a real one to the workers and towns involved. Similarly, occupational health and safety standards are easier to erode when unemployment or the threat of it exists.

Although corporations may oppose full employment because it tilts power toward labor, that does not adequately explain why many Americans without corporate interests have failed to respond to the issue. Ray Marshall, when he was secretary of labor, attributed much of the opposition or indifference to myths about unemployment. Among those that he mentioned is that inflation is necessary to curb unemployment; another is that meaningful jobs cannot be created.[45] Several decades ago John Kenneth Galbraith stated that the United States is characterized by private affluence and public squalor.[46] Since Galbraith made that statement, public squalor has become more firmly entrenched in U.S. society. Not only have budget cuts wrought havoc with human services, but even before the budget cuts there were vast unmet social needs for child care; services for the aged, disabled, and ill; and so on. Moreover, not only the human services have unmet needs. Much of the United States' physical infrastructure is so deteriorated that *Business Week* reports that it could jeopardize business investment. For example, 200,000 bridges—two-fifths of the nation's total—need replacement or rehabilitation; more than 8,000 miles of the interstate highway system need rebuilding; and sewer, water, and mass-transit systems need replacement, expansion, or repair in many parts of the country.[47]

Marshall also mentions the pervasiveness of another important myth—that the reason for unemployment is not a lack of jobs but the fact that many people do not want to work. In Marshall's experience, the fact that there were always many more applicants than jobs—even for low-wage public-service jobs funded by the Labor Department—contradicts this myth.[48] In line with Marshall's view, a *New York Times*/CBS poll taken in 1981 found that 43 percent of whites but only 7 percent of blacks thought that laziness was a major cause of black unemployment.[49] No figures were given for views about the cause of white unemployment.

From time to time the large number of applicants for available jobs even breaks into the newspapers. For example:

> In Atlanta in 1975, 3,000 job seekers, many waiting all night in the rain, lined up for 225 city jobs paying from $114 to $174 a week.[50]

> In Detroit in 1977, 30,000 persons applied for 1,800 jobs at a new hotel before it even opened.[51]

> In New York in 1977, unspecified thousands lined up to apply for 2,700 CETA jobs, slated to last for three weeks and paying $150 to $190 a week.[52]

> In Baltimore in 1981, 26,000 persons stood in line to apply for 70 jobs paying $7,690 for clerical work and $11,500 for warehouse work. The opening had been announced in churches and in a black newspaper.[53]

But evidence of this sort has not been enough to generate adequate support for full employment.

Notes

1. H.R. 15476, 93d Cong., 2d sess. (1974), and S. 3947, 93d Cong., 2d sess. (1974).

2. Augustus F. Hawkins, "Full Employment is the Key," Address, Conference on Full Employment Policy, Columbia University, New York, 1 March 1974.

3. A history of this bill, from its origin through the summer of 1976, is provided by Nancy Sullivan, "Planning for Employment—Not a New Idea," *Public Interest Economic Review,* 15 September 1976, p. 4. The entire issue is devoted to *Full Employment and the Hawkins-Humphrey Bill* and contains statements by supporters and opponents of H.R. 50/S. 50, as well as information about the full-employment coalition. Another history, from the origin to the fourth version of September 1976, is Helen Ginsburg, "Jobs for All: Congressional Will-o'-the Wisp," *The Nation,* 5 February 1977, pp. 138-143, from which this chapter draws heavily. For coverage from the

origin to the passage, see Harvey L. Schantz and Richard H. Schmidt, "Politics and Policy: The Humphrey Hawkins Story," in *Employment and Labor Relations Policy,* ed. Charles Bulmer and John L. Carmichael, Jr. (Lexington, Mass.: Lexington Books, D.C. Heath and Company, 1980), pp. 25-29. Two indispensable publications on the history of the Humphrey-Hawkins full-employment legislation and the issues are *A Full Employment Policy for America,* ed. Paul Bullock (Los Angeles: University of California Institute of Industrial Relations, 1974); and *Goals For Full Employment,* ed. Paul Bullock (Los Angeles: University of California Institute of Industrial Relations, 1978). Another analysis of many of the issues by a supporter of Humphrey-Hawkins full-employment legislation is Andrew Levison, *The Full Employment Alternative* (New York: Coward, McCann and Geoghegan, 1980).

4. H.R. 50, 94th Cong., 1st sess. (1975). Committee on Education and Labor, Subcommittee on Equal Opportunities, Subcommittee Print with Amendments, 20 March 1975.

5. For coverage and demands of the Jobs Now IUD rally, see "A Program for Jobs: Opportunities Exist for Full Employment," *Viewpoint: An IUD Quarterly,* 5 (Second Quarter 1975):16-19.

6. *The New York Times,* 20 September 1981, reported 250,000; the AFL-CIO reported 400,000. For AFL-CIO coverage of Solidarity Day, see *AFL-CIO American Federationist,* October 1981, entire issue.

7. The National Committee for Full Employment is located at 707 D Street, S.E., Washington, D.C. 20003. The Full Employment Action Council is located at 815 16th Street, N.W., Washington, D.C. 20006.

8. The United Electrical Workers supported the Humphrey-Hawkins bill as early as 1974. See United Electrical, Radio and Machine Workers of America, *General Officers Report, 41st International Convention, Cleveland, 1976* (New York: UE Publication no. 558, 1976), p. 38. Irving Bluestone (then vice-president of the UAW), testimony, in U.S. Congress, House Committee on Education, Subcommittee on Equal Opportunities, *Equal Opportunities and Full Employment, Hearings on H.R. 50, Part 3,* March and April 1975, 94th Cong., 1st sess., 1975, pp. 57-76.

9. Ibid., pp. 76-79.

10. AFL-CIO, Department of Public Relations, press release, 8 December 1975.

11. AFL-CIO Economic Policy Committee, "Statement on Principles for Full Employment Legislation," 5 December 1975, p. 3, mimeo.

12. "Hubert Humphrey's Springboard for '76," *Business Week,* 15 December 1975, pp. 68-70.

13. "New Full Employment Bill to Be Introduced March 16," *Daily Labor Report,* 12 March 1976, p. A-12 (Washington, D.C.: Bureau of National Affairs). For AFL-CIO testimony for this version of the bill, see, for instance, statement of Andrew J. Biemiller, director of legislation of the

AFL-CIO, in U.S. Senate, Committee on Labor and Public Welfare, *Full Employment and Balanced Growth Act, 1976, Hearings on S. 50 and S. 472.* 94th Cong., 2d sess., May 1976, pp. 357-369.

14. H.R. 50, 94th Con., 2d sess. (1976). Committee on Education and Labor, Subcommittee on Equal Opportunities, Subcommittee Print with Amendments, 10 March 1976.

15. S. 50, 94th Con., 1st sess. (1975).

16. See, for instance, the testimony of Helen Ginsburg on behalf of the Friends Committee on National Legislation, the Commission on Social Action of Reformed Judaism, and the Center for Social Action of the United Church of Christ, in U.S. Senate, *Hearings on S. 50 and S. 472,* pp. 704-723, for a discussion of these and other issues from the perspective of strengthening the bill.

17. See, for instance, in ibid., the statements of Elaine Day Latourell, legislative vice-president, National Organization for Women, p. 580; Carol Burris, president, Women's Lobby, Inc., p. 618; Coretta King, cochairperson, Full Employment Action Council, p. 641; Representative Bella Abzug, p. 648; Carolyn Shaw Bell, Coman Professor of Economics, Wellesley College, and then also chair, Federal Advisory Council on Unemployment Insurance, pp. 380-381; and Helen Ginsburg, p. 716.

18. Sara Nelson (ed.), "The Challenge before Us: Full Employment and the Economy," *Do It Now* (National Organization for Women), December 1976, special insert, p. 1.

19. Bella Abzug, *U.S. Senate, Hearings on S. 50 and S. 472,* p. 651, and Helen Ginsburg, ibid., p. 716.

20. Carolyn Shaw Bell, ibid., p. 380.

21. For a short time in 1976, there was an attempt to form another coalition, the National Coalition for Full Employment, by several groups that wanted to exert more pressure to strengthen the bill.

22. Testimony of Carl Madden, chief economist, U.S. Chamber of Commerce, in U.S. Senate, Hearings on S. 50 and S. 472. See also in ibid., the testimony of Herbert Stein, pp. 369-376, and William Kolberg, pp. 323-356, among others.

23. Testimony of Charles Schultze in ibid., pp. 141-165. The excerpt appeared in *The Washington Post* on 7 June 1976. See also Paul Lewis, "Schultze of the C.E.A.," *The New York Times,* 9 January 1977, Business Section, p. 7.

24. Marshall's analysis was in the *Congressional Record,* 26 July 1976.

25. *The Washington Post,* 6 August 1976. Cited in Sullivan, "Planning for Employment," p. 4.

26. H.R. 50, 94th Cong., 2d sess. (1976), Committee Print. Text of revised substitute amendment to H.R. 50, as reported by the Education and Labor Committee on 14 May 1976, said revised substitute approved by the Education and Labor Committee on 16 September 1976.

27. "What Do President Carter, the AFL-CIO, the National Association of Manufacturers and the U.S. House of Representatives Have in Common?" [pamphlet about inflation target] (Washington, D.C.: Full Employment Action Council, n.d.).

28. Arnold Weber, quoted in Sumner Rosen, "Healing Our Economic Ills," *Journal of Current Social Issues* (Spring 1976):5.

29. See, for instance, Ron Sarro and Lance Gay, "Jobs Bill Expected to Reverse Carter 'Slippage'" among Blacks," *Washington Star*, 11 November 1977, p. A-2; Edward Cowan, "Carter Endorses Modified Version of Humphrey-Hawkins Jobs Bill," *The New York Times*, 15 November 1977, p. 1; and Schantz and Schmidt, "Politics and Policy," pp. 31-32.

30. Schantz and Schmidt, "Politics and Policy," pp. 32-35.

31. P.L. 523, 95th Cong., 2d sess. (1978).

32. Augustus F. Hawkins, "Economic and Social Gains in the 'Full Employment and Balanced Growth Act of 1978' and Analysis of Major Provisions of the Act," 1978, p. 1, mimeo.

33. *Economic Report of the President, Transmitted to Congress, January 1979* (Washington, D.C.: U.S. Government Printing Office, 1979), table 2.2, p. 109.

34. "This Is How the Humphrey-Hawkins Act Is Being Violated," in "Optimum Growth and Price Stability and Full Employment: A Joint Venture," Paper Issued by Office of Representative Augustus Hawkins, Washington, D.C., 1979.

35. "Weidenbaum Sees More Joblessness," *The New York Times*, 16 November 1981, section 4, p. D.1.

36. Executive Office of the President, Office of Management and Budget, *The United States Budget in Brief, Fiscal Year 1983* (Washington, D.C.: U.S. Government Printing Office, 1982).

37. *Economic Report of the President, Transmitted to the Congress, February 1982* (Washington, D.C.: U.S. Government Printing Office, 1982), table 214, p. 214.

38. Speech at Conference on Full Employment, New York, 14 June 1974. The conference was cosponsored by the Martin Luther King Center for Social Change and the National Conference on Public Service Employment. The National Committee for Full Employment grew out of this meeting.

39. See, for example, "National Coalition Begins Full Employment Week: Action Planned in 75 Cities September 4-10," *Full Employment Advocate* (Washington, D.C.: National Committee for Full Employment, Labor Day, 1977), p. 1, and "Millions Turn Out for Full Employment Week," *Full Employment Advocate*, October 1977, p. 1.

40. U.S. Bureau of the Census, *Statistical Abstract of the United States, 1980* (Washington, D.C.: U.S. Government Printing Office, 1980), table 857, p. 520. This is based on a Current Population Survey.

41. Robert Lekachman, "The Specter of Full Employment," *Harper's,* February 1977, p. 36.

42. *Statements Adopted by the AFL-CIO Executive Council, Chicago, August 3-5, 1981* (Washington, D.C.: AFL-CIO, 1981), pp. 10, 11.

43. See, for instance, Patrick Heffernan, "Jobs and the Environment," *Sierra Club Bulletin,* April 1975; Richard Grossman and Gail Daneker, *Energy, Jobs and the Economy* (Boston: Alyson Publications, 1979); and Richard Kazis and Richard Grossman, *Fear at Work* (New York: Pilgrim Press, 1982).

44. Letter from Lane Kirkland to environmentalists [inviting them to participate in Solidarity Day], 12 August 1981. For an early attempt to bring together environmentalists, labor, and other groups, see *Summary of Conference Proceedings, Working for Environmental and Economic Justice and Jobs,* National Action Conference, 2-6 May 1976, at the Walter and May Reuther UAW Family Education Center, Onaway, Michigan. The UAW, the Communication Workers of America, and the United Steelworkers, as well as some environmental groups, foundations, and churches, funded the conference, which was sponsored by more than a hundred organizations, including some international unions affiliated with the AFL-CIO. The AFL-CIO itself was not a sponsor.

45. Ray Marshall, address to the International Labor Press Association, 14 April 1977, excerpted in *Full Employment Advocate* (National Committee for Full Employment), Labor Day, 1977, pp. 2,7.

46. John Kenneth Galbraith, *The Affluent Society* (New York: Mentor, New American Library, 1963).

47. "Infrastructure: A National Need to Build and Repair," in *State and Local Government in Trouble,* Special Report, *Business Week,* 26 October 1981, pp. 138-141.

48. Marshall, address to Labor Press, p. 2.

49. Adam Clymer, "Polls Find Black-White Gaps on Variety of Issues," *The New York Times*, 28 August 1981.

50. B. Drummond Ayres, Jr., "3,000 Seek Jobs in Atlanta Melee," *The New York Times,* 10 January 1975.

51. *Detroit News,* 25 October 1976, cited in *Full Employment Advocate* (National Committee for Full Employment), Labor Day, 1977, p. 3.

52. Joseph Fried, "Plan to Temporarily Employ 2,700 Begins in Chaos," *The New York Times,* 9 February 1977, section 2, p. B.3.

53. Gus Tyler, "26,000 Apply for 75 openings: Long Lines of Job Applicants Show Fallacy of Welfare Myth," *AFL-CIO News,* 10 October 1980, p. 4, and "10,000 Line Up in Baltimore Seeking 70 Federal Jobs," *The New York Times,* 16 September 1980, p. A.17. (This report was for the first day after the announcement; Tyler reported 26,000 applicants by the end of that week.)

4

The Hidden Costs of Unemployment

It is often said that full employment is expensive. In truth, it is unemployment that is costly. This fact is not often appreciated since many of the costs of unemployment are hidden. There are both economic and human costs, but there is considerable overlap between the categories, and one kind of cost often gives rise to the other.

Economic Costs of Unemployment

Lost Output

One of the biggest losses caused by unemployment is foregone output. In plain language, jobless workers do not produce goods and services. Unused plant capacity does not turn out the products that could be used to enhance the standard of living of the country. Houses that are not built, urban transit systems that are not produced, and child- and health-care workers who are not hired cannot meet the housing, mass-transit, and human-service needs of Americans.

The magnitude of this loss is not trivial. In 1975 alone, the Senate Budget Committee estimated that the recession cost the nation $200 billion in lost production—nearly $1,000 for every man, woman, and child.[1] In that year the annual jobless rate was higher than at any time since the Great Depression. It shot up to an annual average of 8.5 percent from 5.6 percent the previous year. This estimate shows how much production was lost as a result of the *increased* unemployment. It does not give us any idea of the size of the loss attributable to the failure of the economy to attain full employment, unless one considers 1974 to have been a year of full employment. Moreover, it does not show the extent of foregone output over a long period of time, since pervasive unemployment persists even in times of so-called prosperity. Several estimates of this sort are available.

The Swedish economist Erik Lundberg has studied the performance of a number of advanced capitalist economies, including that of the United States, from the early post-World War II years through the mid-1960s. Lundberg wanted to measure the actual performance of each nation against its potential output, had there been full employment. How should full employment be defined for this study? Searching for a reasonable benchmark, he assumed a

2-percent unemployment rate. Coming from a country in which unemployment was usually at or below 2 percent, he did not consider this unreasonable or unfeasible. To the contrary, defining full employment as 4-percent unemployment—as the U.S. government did in the mid-1960s—was rejected as unreasonable.[2] Using it would have implied overfull employment for most other countries, though not for the United States, for the period from 1950 to 1965. Lundberg found no compelling evidence that the United States was any less capable of attaining lower unemployment than were numerous other nations. Still, Lundberg observed, during those years U.S. unemployment remained considerably above any reasonable definition of full employment, and the economy was operating below its potential. This was true even during peak periods of the business cycle.[3] The final conclusion was that over a fifteen-year span these shortfalls in U.S. production amounted to about one year's GNP.[4]

A decade later, University of California economist Steven Sheffrin again documented the fact that unemployment significantly reduces the living standards of Americans. Sheffrin measured the cumulative costs of continued employment from 1956 to 1976. His initial assumption was much more modest than Lundberg's. Suppose that unemployment had simply been maintained during this period at the 4.1-percent rate that existed in 1956, a peacetime year during the Eisenhower administration. His calculations show that the failure of the U.S. economy to maintain even that rate of unemployment cost the nation $2.3 trillion (in 1976 dollars) in lost production over that twenty-year period.[5] The sheer size of that figure boggles the imagination. To gain some perspective, consider that in 1976 alone this lost output was equivalent to about 17 percent of that year's total production of goods and services—GNP—in the United States.

Another question also intrigued Sheffrin: What if U.S. unemployment had been brought down to the low rates existing during that period in other industrial capitalist countries? He used the examples of Great Britain, France, Australia, Sweden, Japan, and West Germany. Although unemployment in most of these countries was higher in 1976 than in 1956, unemployment averages (adjusted to U.S. methods of measurement) were all in the 1- to 3-percent range for the period as a whole.

Assume now, said Sheffrin, that U.S. unemployment had been reduced from 4.1 percent in 1956 to what he dubbed a European range of 2 percent by 1962—and assume also that it had been maintained at that rate through 1976. In that case the people of the United States could have enjoyed $3.8 trillion more in GNP during those years. That additional GNP, in turn, would have generated an additional $750 billion in federal tax revenues. In 1976 alone, according to Sheffrin's estimate, these federal tax revenues would have been nearly $100 billion above what they actually were.[6]

There is, of course, no assurance that the extra GNP would have been socially useful. More alcohol, bombs, and cigarettes? Or services for the aged, libraries, and housing? Similarly, extra federal tax revenues could have been used in a variety of ways. Gar Alperovitz and Jeff Faux, codirectors of the Exploratory Project for Economic Alternatives (for whom Sheffrin's study was undertaken) speculate on how the extra $100 billion in tax revenues might have been used by the federal government. The extra $100 billion could have financed *all* of the following:

It could have brought the entire poor population at least up to the government's official poverty-line income at an estimated cost of $16 billion *and* established a national health-insurance program along the lines of the Kennedy-Corman bill for an additional $64 billion *and* also increased public antipollution expenditures by another $18 billion a year to clean up the environment by 1985.[7] Obviously, numerous other alternative expenditures as well as hefty tax rebates would also have been possible. How the funds would actually have been used, had they been available, would have been a function of the political climate and power as well as of economic factors.

Preoccupation with what might have been changes nothing, but these exercises can shed light on future options. Therefore, Sheffrin also projected four different possibilities for the last quarter of the twentieth century, from 1976 to 2000. In each case unemployment was assumed to start at the actual 7.7-percent rate for 1976. The four options were:

1. A "European" range, recalling the past performances of these nations. In this scenario, unemployment is presumed to drop to 5 percent by 1980 and to 2 percent by 1984, where it remains.
2. A "conventional/modestly optimistic" route, with unemployment from 1980 on at 5.5 percent.
3. A "moderately pessimistic" case, with unemployment from 1978 to 2000 maintained at 6.5 percent.
4. A "pessimistic" projection, in which unemployment for the entire period averages 9.9 percent.[8]

On the basis of these assumptions, here are some of the findings. If the economy runs along the conventional/modestly optimistic route of 5.5-percent unemployment during most of the period instead of 2 percent, the cumulative loss of GNP is $6 trillion, and the cumulative loss in federal revenues is $1.3 trillion.

The moderately pessimistic course of 6.5-percent unemployment throughout most of the period yields a total loss of $7 trillion in GNP and $1.5 trillion in federal revenues, compared with the European range.

Compared with the European range, the most pessimistic course, with unemployment averaging 9.9 percent over these years, leads to a cumulative loss of GNP of $15 trillion and a total federal tax-revenue loss of $3.2 trillion.

These are staggering sums, but one need not project either an extreme depressionlike level of 9.9-percent unemployment or a European range of 2 percent to understand the problem. Even the 1 percentage point difference between the conventional/modestly optimistic 5.5-percent unemployment rate and the moderately pessimistic case of 6.5 percent leads to approximately $1 trillion less in total production during a quarter of a century and about $200 billion less in federal tax revenues.

Sheffrin's designation of 6.5-percent unemployment from 1978 to 2000 as a moderately pessimistic projection may actually be optimistic barring a drastic change in policy. Since 1977, when he did the study, unemployment dropped to the 6-percent range in 1978 and 1979. The seventh post-World War II recession, however, once more pushed unemployment up to an average of 7.1 percent for 1980. The 1981 average was 7.6 percent; and by mid-1982, in the wake of another mini-depression, it was nearly 10 percent.

Mounting Deficits

Both Jimmy Carter and Ronald Reagan gave high priority to balancing the federal budget upon entering the White House, and the federal deficit has become a topic of considerable interest. Much of the public, however, is unaware of the close interrelationship between the federal budget and unemployment. The relationship is direct. When unemployment rises, federal revenues fall. With declining income, unemployed persons pay less in taxes. Similarly, companies that experience falling profits because of the slowdown also pay less in taxes. The fact that employed workers usually receive smaller wage hikes during bad times further exacerbates the decline in revenues.

Rising unemployment also leads to more government expenditures— mostly on unemployment compensation and food stamps and to a lesser extent on welfare, Medicaid, and other social programs. In February 1980 the Congressional Budget Office (CBO) estimated that every 1-percentage-point rise in the jobless rate results in a $25-$29 billion increase in the federal deficit. From $5 to $7 billion of this amount was attributed to rising expenditures and from $20 to $22 billion to revenue shortfalls.[9]

The CBO based its estimates on a rise in unemployment from 7 to 8 percent. Above 8 percent these figures would have been even higher, since previous studies by the Congressional Research Service (CRS) show that the impact of unemployment on the deficit also depends on the initial level of the jobless rate. When that is higher, a 1-percentage-point increase in unemployment tends to generate higher deficits.[10]

On the other hand, the Reagan administration's budget cuts and more restrictive criteria for social programs including extended jobless benefits might reduce that figure somewhat. To the extent that states pick up the extra tab, it merely shifts more of the economic burden to lower levels of government, with narrower tax bases. Even if states or other local governments do not make up any of the difference, the cost does not disappear. Then it is paid for by the jobless through reduced income and living standards that result from the cuts in jobless benefits. Since the lion's share of the increase in the federal deficit comes about through reduced tax receipts due to falling income, however, even drastic budget cuts cannot eliminate the bulk of recession-induced deficits. That is why attempting to fight inflation by creating unemployment through budget cutting tends to increase rather than to decrease budget deficits.

Strain on Social Security

Not only does unemployment cause higher federal deficits in general, but the blow falls especially hard on the Social Security Trust Funds. Jobless workers do not pay Social Security taxes, nor do employers pay these taxes for the unemployed. Further, more has to be paid out to those who are forced into premature retirement. Starting with the recession of the mid-1970s, unemployment has contributed to short-term Social Security funding problems. One result was President Carter's proposal in 1977 that the federal government make a contribution from general revenues whenever unemployment exceeds 6 percent. Although this proposal was not approved by the Congress, the problem did not go away. High unemployment in the early 1980s continued to contribute to Social Security funding problems. In the future, as the proportion of older people in the population rises relative to the working-age population, this factor will become even more important. With a higher proportion of the working-age population employed rather than unemployed, it is easier for any nation to finance adequate Social Security benefits. This is true regardless of how these benefits are financed since, as has been shown, higher unemployment means less, and lower unemployment means more, output of goods and services.

Impact on State and Local Governments

The impact of unemployment on state- and local-government treasuries is not included in any of the studies cited. Yet recessions as well as the structural unemployment that persists between recessions add to their financial woes, especially those that are most affected by unemployment. In April 1981, Samuel M. Ehrenhalt, regional commissioner of the U.S. Bureau of Labor Statistics, described the impact of unemployment on New York City:

> The 1969-70 national recession plunged the city into an economic crisis which saw eight consecutive years of job loss totaling more than 600,000. An outgrowth of this debacle was the financial crisis of the mid-1970's and some fundamental changes in the city's economy. The past three years of job recovery, significant as they are, represent only a fraction of the jobs lost earlier in the 1970's.[11]

In 1975 the Senate Budget Committee estimated that state and local governments were losing about $20 billion in revenues annually as a result of the recession.[12] This figure does not measure the loss due to all unemployment, but only that amount attributable to the steep rise of joblessness in 1975. Regardless of the state of the national economy, however, unemployment continues to play havoc with areas hard hit by eroding job bases. Shifting more of the financing of social programs can only worsen their financial plight and lead to higher local taxes, cuts in services, and layoffs of public workers in areas already experiencing the most severe problems—thus adding still more to unemployment.

Economic Loss to the Unemployed

In the final analysis, the unemployed always bear much of the economic burden of unemployment. This is true despite the expansion of government benefits since the advent of the Great Depression of the 1930s. At best, unemployment insurance (UI) only partially and temporarily replaces income that is lost through being out of work. Furthermore, not all of the jobless collect benefits. Many, especially the young and women entering or reentering the labor force, do not have enough recent work experience or earnings to quality. Others are ineligible because they have exhausted their benefits or for other reasons.

In recent years only about half of the unemployed actually have collected benefits at any time.[13] That proportion was even lower in mid-1982, as growing numbers of the jobless exhausted their benefits. In June 1982, for example, the number of official unemployed was 10.4 million, but only 4.3 million—or 42 percent—were collecting UI benefits. These averaged $119 weekly, only 46 percent of before-tax average weekly earnings of nonagricultural production or nonsupervisory workers in the private sector—and only 36 percent of those in manufacturing.[14]

In the deep recession year of 1975, the *average* number of unemployed during the year was about 8 million, but an estimated 21 million persons were jobless *at one time or another* during the year. Yet according to a government survey, only 10.1 million of them—less than half—received any kind of income assistance.[15] In another survey of the unemployed in 1976, the U.S. Bureau of Labor Statistics (BLS) found that only 36 percent of its sample had income from UI the previous month.[16] Fewer—only 13 percent—had received food stamps, and 12 percent received public assistance. Five percent reported no income sources at all. The median family income for these workers was $450 a month, but 14 percent reported that their income from all sources was less than $200 a month. How did they meet their expenses? Seven out of ten had cut back on expenditures for food, clothing, and transportation; 27 percent had been forced to borrow money; and one in ten had moved to cheaper housing.

The financial burdens, of course, increase with the length of unemployment. Many of those who became unemployed as a consequence of the mini-depression of the mid-1970s began by cutting into savings; slicing normal expenses as much as possible; postponing nonessential spending; and eventually resorting to more drastic measures such as selling off insurance policies and other belongings, moving into less expensive housing, and even selling their automobiles—which often makes it more difficult to search for work.[17]

Although most workers do not exhaust their regular unemployment benefits when they are out of work, in the past that proportion increased during recessions from about one-quarter to two-fifths. In the future that proportion may be even higher. During the peak of the recession in 1975, 4.2 million jobless workers did exhaust their regular state UI benefits, which typically provide for a maximum of twenty-six weeks of coverage.[18] During periods of high unemployment the federal-state extended-benefits program adds up to thirteen weeks of coverage. In 1981, however, Congress tightened eligibility. Since then it has been much more difficult for states, even those hardest hit by unemployment, to qualify for the program. A special federal supplemental-benefits program enacted in 1975, which provided up to twenty-six weeks of additional coverage for workers unemployed during that recession, expired in fiscal 1977 and was not renewed. A temporary program of federal supplemental benefits enacted by Congress in the summer of 1982 and slated to expire in March 1982, only provides from six to ten additional weeks of benefits.

What happens to workers who do exhaust their UI benefits? A study of 2,000 unemployment-insurance exhaustees in four major urban areas in the mid-1970s recession provides some clues. There was extensive loss of job-related health insurance, a serious matter that affects many of the unemployed, even those who do not exhaust their benefits. About 25 percent received food stamps. (Restrictions enacted by Congress in 1981 will make that figure lower in the future.) Their average weekly family income was reduced from $271 to $178—from $14,092 to $9,256 annually. That figure, of course, includes the earnings of working spouses and children. Reemployment problems were severe. Only 24 percent were working four months after they had exhausted their benefits, 14 percent had dropped out of the labor force, and 61 percent were still unemployed.[19]

In addition to the loss of earnings and health benefits, other fringe benefits are lost. Seniority goes down the drain. Frequent unemployment can even affect retirement income—not only because private pension rights are often lost through unemployment, but also because the size of the Social Security benefit check reflects earned income, not jobless benefits. Thus Social Security payments in old age may be eroded by unemployment, even as drawing into savings at such times reduces any nest egg put aside for retirement. Long-term unemployment can also affect a disabled worker's eligibility for Social Security disability payments, which require relatively recent work experience in order to qualify.

Thus the monetary losses of unemployment, both to the nation and to the individual, are substantial.

The Human Costs

Despite the extent of these losses, perhaps the highest costs are the human ones. Unemployment means more than lost income, although that is not an insignificant consideration. Meaningful work plays an integral part in a person's development. In our society the work role is central in determining not only economic but also psychological and social well-being.

The 1930s

Numerous studies of the unemployed during the Great Depression on both sides of the Atlantic and in Australia have confirmed this obvious fact. A classic example is the extreme case of Marienthal, an Austrian village beset by almost total unemployment.[20] In demonstrating the severe economic deprivation of Marienthal's people, Paul Lazarsfeld, Marie Jahoda, and Hans Ziesel, then social scientists from the University of Vienna, only documented the obvious. The psychological effects the researchers observed in the months that they lived in close contact with the villagers were striking. Paramount among them were diminished activities and expectations, a disrupted sense of time, and growing apathy.

To a great extent, time is structured by work. For the unemployed of Marienthal, time lost its meaning. One day was the same as another. Days were no longer divided into hours. People no longer wore watches. Punctuality ceased.

John A. Garraty, a Columbia University historian who investigated responses to the problem of people out of work in the Western world since ancient times, has summarized the research findings of the 1930s in the various countries. These studies varied greatly in both scope and objectivity; individuals, not surprisingly, differed in the way they were affected by unemployment. Regardless of other differences, however, says Garraty, jobless workers initially searched feverishly for new employment. Then discouragment and sometimes disorganization set in. Finally, most sank into apathy, demoralization, humiliation, broken spirits, and hopeless despair. These were typical responses.[21] As writer Sherwood Anderson, who toured the United States during this era, observed, self-blame was typical.[22] Garraty has shown persuasively that blaming the unemployed for unemployment is one of the oldest traditions in the Western world. Internalizing this judgment, all too often the jobless blamed themselves for their predicament. What was clear, notes Garraty, was that very few people were able to survive long periods of enforced idleness without paying a psychological toll—even if their economic needs were met.

The Contemporary Era

Has all this changed since the 1930s? In the 1970s critics challenged the idea that unemployment causes large-scale human suffering. Not only were the unemployed made up of a higher proportion of youths and women, for whom unemployment was alleged to be of little consequence, but increased government benefits also were said to cushion the impact of job loss.

As already shown, such support is not complete in either coverage or wage replacement. It is certainly true, however, that many of today's unemployed do have more government support than did those of the 1930s. Although economic support is important, it cannot take the place of a job. An unemployment check can help pay the rent, put food on the table, and buy shoes for the children. But it cannot replace the feeling of dignity and self-worth for one who has been stripped of a role in society.

The Psychological Impact of Unemployment

There is considerable evidence that the psychological impact of unemployment persists into the present.

Crisscrossing the country in the aftermath of the mini-depression of the mid-1970s, writer Harry Maurer interviewed a wide variety of the jobless for his oral history of the unemployed—from farm workers and auto workers to engineers and editors, from droupouts to ex-college professors.

What astonished him more than anything else was the degree to which the unemployed blamed themselves—even those who were victims of mass layoffs. Among those Maurer interviewed, *worthless* was the word most used to describe their feelings.[23]

In 1975 City University of New York psychologist Hannah Levin found similar feelings among unemployed workers, all of whom had been steadily employed and came from stable communities in Brooklyn and Staten Island.[24] Far from providing a carefree period of leisure, joblessness proved to be psychologically devastating. Lack of hope for the future, boredom, the feeling of being in a rut and of time just dragging on were all pervasive. Some turned to drink to help pass away the hours. Depression was commonplace. Many men, too embarrassed to be seen near home, stayed off the neighborhood streets during the day. Aspirations dropped. Individuals felt a sense of powerlessness and loss of control, with adverse effects on their sexual relations. Some men were plagued by impotence, dreams of castration, or suicidal thoughts. Despite their own suffering and the depressed state of the national and local labor markets, over 90 percent of Levin's interviewees were victims of the dominant U.S. ideology: they blamed themselves for being unemployed.

Levin adds that roles played for eight hours a day become integrated into an individual's personality. Thus the loss of a job, when work is a central core of existence, can be quite threatening. It may lead to the loss of a sense of personal identity and to a growing feeling of meaninglessness.

The reactions of workers to loss of a job have also been likened to bereavement—loss of a loved one.[25] Ex-Chrysler workers who held a mock funeral in 1975 were expressing this feeling.[26] Even though they were receiving 95 percent of their take-home pay from Supplementary Unemployment Benefits (SUB) negotiated by the UAW, SUB could not adequately compensate for their painful loss or fears for the future.

Professionals in community-service organizations and mental-health centers often see at first hand the steep price of unemployment. Along with rising joblessness in 1975 and 1976, centers in New York's affluent Long Island suburbs reported a skyrocketing incidence of problems that had never before been common. These unemployed workers included middle managers whose jobs had been eliminated, as well as laid-off stockbrokers, teachers, and civil servants. All had assumed lifelong security, but some had received as little as twenty-four hours notice of termination. What followed was an upsurge of physical violence, white-collar crime, and sexual problems, as well as an increase in stress-aggravated illnesses such as asthma, hypertension, and colitis; these often went untreated because of the high cost of medical treatment and drugs. The children of the unemployed frequently withdrew, performed poorly in school, or became troublemakers. Some men had extramarital affairs in an attempt to prove their masculinity;

others abandoned their families, became paralyzed by inaction and apathy, or threatened suicide.[27]

From the Nashville, Tennessee, suicide-prevention center came this profile of the typical client: a man, never out of work before, with one or two children in college and mortgage payments to meet. A New England professional working with potential suicides observed that many people reached for an overdose after returning home from yet another unsuccessful job interview.[28] In Ohio, the director of Canton's Suicide Crisis Center reported in 1976 that two out of every three calls were related to unemployment. Similarly, the Akron Community Mental Health Center reported increasing its caseload because of high unemployment. In Youngstown, the executive director of the Mahoning Country Mental Health and Retardation Board told city-council members that wife and child abusers were often jobless persons who vented their anger on their loved ones.[29] Little wonder that the director of the Division of Mental Health Services of the National Institute of Mental Health was not surprised by an increase in emotional distress and utilization of mental-health facilities as the nation plunged into a recession, or by the finding that the unemployment rate of a given community mental-health center catchment area seemed to be correlated with its increased utilization.[30]

Estimating the Long-Term Costs of Unemployment

About that time, in February 1976, with unemployment still at 7.6 percent, Alan Greenspan, chairman of the Council of Economic Advisers, commenting on the state of the economy, noted that "we've healed a good deal of the damage" caused by the recession.[31] The suffering of many of the jobless was not included in that estimate, nor was any provision made for the economic or human toll that might have to be paid in future years.

Although the government has put great emphasis on assessing the impact of monetary and fiscal policy on income, prices, and employment, it has seldom analyzed the long-term human or social effects of economic-policy decisions.

An important exception is a major study done in 1976 by M. Harvey Brenner of Johns Hopkins University for the Joint Economic Committee of Congress.[32] This study was designed to provide guidance to policymakers seeking to evaluate the social and human impact of economic policy.

There is an extensive literature covering the short-term relationship between economic variables and one or two social indicators.[33] Indeed, Brenner himself had done many such studies. In one of them it was found that admissions to mental hospitals in New York State increased substantially during each recession since 1841.[34] Fluctuations in admissions to mental hospitals were more closely related to fluctuations in employment than to any other factor. The significance of the study for the Joint Economic Committee, however, is that it attempts to unearth long-term relationships between unemployment and other forms of economic distress and seven indexes of physical and social pathology for the whole country.

In the study, Brenner related changes in three economic indicators—unemployment, inflation, and per capita income—to seven indexes of pathology: suicide, admissions to state mental hospitals, admissions to state prisons, homicides, mortality from cirrhosis of the liver (mostly caused by alcoholism), mortality from cardiovascular-renal disease, and total mortality. Most of the analyses covered the period 1940-1973.

All seven of the indexes of pathology were statistically associated with changes in the three national economic variables. Moreover, the most consistent and statistically significant correlations were with changes in the unemployment rate. A similar pattern emerged from separate studies by age, race, sex, and geographic region, as well as for the three states that were studied individually—California, Massachusetts, and New York—covering general mortality, suicide, homicide, and cirrhosis of the liver; and for England, Wales, and Sweden, covering only general mortality.

Among other things, Brenner found that a sustained 1-percentage-point increase in the unemployment rate in the United States was associated five years later with: (1) a 1.9-percent increase in total mortality and mortality from cardiovascular-renal disease and from cirrhosis of the liver; (2) a 4.1-percent increase in suicides; (3) a 3.4-percent increase in state-mental-hospital admissions; (4) a 4-percent increase in state-prison admissions; and (5) a 5.7-percent increase in homicides.[35]

In a way, the changes in these indicators associated with fluctuations in unemployment are relatively small. That is, only a small proportion of *total* mortality, or state-mental-hospital admissions, or other pathologies is related to changes in unemployment. This is not surprising, considering the myriad of complex factors that influence the mental and physical states of individuals. Nevertheless, these seemingly small percentages are impressive when translated into human terms. They mean that a 1-percentage-point rise in the jobless rate is associated with:

36,887   total deaths, including
20,240   cardiovascular-renal deaths,
   920   suicides,
   648   homicides,
   495   deaths from cirrhosis of the liver,
 4,227   state mental hospital admissions,
 3,340   state prison admissions.[36]

These findings suggest that the full impact of even a sustained 1-percentage-point jump in unemployment may continue to take its toll on individuals and society many years after the initial rise. Thus loss of a job might precipitate or worsen hypertension, but death from coronary heart disease may occur only years later. Similarly, a long period of mental depression, anxiety, or agitation might precede a suicide or homicide attempt.

Can these findings be used to measure the impact of a recession? Utilizing Brenner's results, the staff of the Joint Economic Committee estimated the human toll of the 1.4-percentage-point rise in unemployment in the recession year of 1970, which was sustained over the next five years. Since a 1-percentage-point rise had been found by Brenner to be associated with a 1.9-percent rise in overall mortality, the committee estimated that the sustained 1.4-percentage-point increase in 1970 was associated with a 2.7-percent increase in total mortality (1.9 percent × 1.4 percent)—or 51,570 total deaths over the following five years, of which 26,440 were from cardiovascular-renal diseases. There were similarly higher figures for the other indexes.[37]

What does all this cost society? Excluding from these calculations factors such as broken lives, grief-stricken families, and fear of crime, the committee came up with a tab of "at least $21 billion."[38]

How did the committee arrive at this sum? Death, illness, and imprisonment reduce the nation's ability to produce goods and services. One measure of this loss is the foregone income of those who might otherwise be working. Estimates for this factor, added to medical, state-prison, and mental-hospital costs, yielded about $7 billion (in 1975 dollars); an additional estimate of $2.8 billion annually—$14 billion over the five years—brought the total to $21 billion.

These human and monetary costs may actually be understated. For instance, some deaths may occur over an even longer period. Moreover, these figures do not include estimates of the number of persons treated for illnesses that did not result in death or costs attributable to this extra morbidity. Also excluded are costs of federal prisons, police, and the criminal-justice system, as well as costs to the victims of crime. Numerous other items could be added to the list.

With large and sustained increases in unemployment since 1970, the additional impact on individuals and society in the second half of the 1970s and the beginning of the 1980s may reasonably be assumed to be many times greater than the Joint Economic Committee estimates.

Brenner's research techniques are essentially based on correlation and regression analysis. As in all such research, these procedures establish only a statistical relationship, not causation or direction of causation, which can be established only through sound theoretical considerations and empirical evidence from other research.[39] However, a substantial and growing body of empirical evidence backs up his findings. There are also explanations of the complex ways in which health may be affected by unemployment, in addition to the adverse impact of physical privation that might result from declining income.

The Role of Stress

Explanations that focus on psychological factors zero in on stress as an intervening link between unemployment and ill health. Medical researchers have gathered considerable evidence that implicates stress as a contributing factor in the precipitation or exacerbation of a host of physical as well as mental illnesses. Psychiatrist George Curtis, an expert on the psychophysiology of stress, acknowledges that it is already possible to demonstrate the complex physiological mechanism by which diabetes, heart disease, hypertension, arteriosclerosis, and resistance to infectious disease might be affected by stress. That, he notes, does not exhaust the list of potentially affected diseases. The relationship between stress and many other diseases is recognized, although the precise physiological mechanisms at work are as yet less well understood.[40]

What about the direction of causation, however? Which came first, the chicken or the egg? unemployment or illness? Using a macro approach—analyzing national figures—and using death rather than illness rates, Brenner reasons, makes this question easier to answer. At the individual level, one might reason that illness can lead to unemployment. But he points out, for example, that if the relationship between the national unemployment and suicide rates is considered, it simply cannot be argued that an individual's condition has any significant impact on the national unemployment rate.[41]

The impact of unemployment on health has, however, also been studied at both the individual and the plant levels. Research from plant closings has shown high uric-acid levels, increased cholesterol, and elevated blood-pressure and pulse rates among the suddenly unemployed.[42] Plant closings have been linked to increases in heart disease, hypertension, gout, hard drinking, self-destruction, and fatal accidents.[43] A study of New York State civil servants laid off in the budget cuts of the 1970s showed a marked increase in drinking—confirming a commonly observed fact.[44]

The relationship between unemployment and potentially complex pathological conditions is complex, however. There are many ways in which unemployment might be related to stress, and some of them also affect those who are not jobless—or not yet jobless.

Research by Stanislav V. Kasl and Sidney Cobb, stemming from a longitudinal study of the impact of a plant closing, demonstrates that different kinds of workers react differently to job loss. Equally significant is their finding of an anticipation effect that can start even before the job loss occurs. Elevations in physiological indicators or measures of psychological distress appeared even before the actual closing, after notices of the impending shutdown were given.[45] This suggests a way in which unemployment may affect even those workers who manage to hold onto their jobs. When layoffs are the order of the day, even employed workers may suffer from anticipation effects as they worry that their plant will shut down, their government agency will retrench, their school district will cut back on faculty, their library system will cut back on staff, or their job will simply be eliminated.

Once a mental or physical illness afflicts an unemployed worker, it may also act as a barrier to future employment, as Louis Ferman and John Gardner discovered in their research. Ferman and Gardner also suggest that some laid-off workers "skid" into jobs with less status, income, or fringe benefits and suffer detrimental psychological reactions as a consequence.[46] The study of laid-off New York State employees mentioned earlier revealed that 46 percent of all of those who later got jobs were earning less than their prelayoff salaries. Even among those who were subsequently reemployed by the state, 51 percent were receiving lower salaries.[47]

Impact on Families, Friends, and Communities

Unemployment affects families as well as individuals. Wives, husbands, children, parents, and others can also be involved. Once self-sufficient families often have to swallow their pride and apply for food stamps or welfare. In Detroit the welfare rolls went up by 64,000 in one year, as time and money ran out for tens of thousands of unemployed auto workers. Some of those who said they would rather die than put their families on welfare were forced to change their minds when their children were hungry. The strict qualifying rules were another shock, especially to those who were denied relief.[48] According to an official of Cleveland's food-stamp program, many cried as they applied for help.[49]

Marital strife, drinking, family strain, child abuse, and family breakup are all possible results that affect more than just the unemployed themselves. Even increases in infant mortality have been linked to rising unemployment, with the death rate for those under one day old showing the most striking increment within a year of the economic downturn. The exact causal mechanism is not known but is believed to be the result of marked deterioration in pregnant women's health following economic dislocation. This in turn is likely to stem from drastic changes in nutrition, high levels of stress and hypertension, increased use of alcohol or sedatives, or increased smoking.[50]

In areas of heavy unemployment, the quality of life for the employed and their families, as well as for the unemployed, often nosedives. Friends and families of the jobless are affected, especially if the unemployed are forced to leave the area. The whole social fabric of a hard-hit community can be seriously eroded. Simultaneously, financially hard-pressed communities may cut services.

In 1981 the Youngstown, Ohio, Little League season opened a month late, as did the city's playgrounds, baseball diamonds, and swimming pools. In Toledo, the Zoo Museum closed its doors. With an economy hard hit by unemployment, that city's 141 parks were serviced by only twenty-five people, with a sharp deterioration in cutting, trimming, and cleaning up.[51]

The long-term impact of these quality-of-life changes, which existed even before the deep federal budget cuts worsened the situation, is difficult to measure. One can speculate that by making it more difficult for people to relax, they increase stress or make it more difficult to relieve ordinary as well as extraordinary tension. These factors, however, are usually ignored.

Crime

It is not so simple to ignore a factor like crime. Thirty percent of the nation's families, according to the U.S. Bureau of Justice, were victimized by one or more crimes in 1980.[52] Not without reason, a pervasive fear of crime hangs over the land: 41 percent of Americans are highly fearful of becoming victims of violent crime, and another 29 percent are moderately fearful.[53]

The causes of crime are many and complex. It is simplistic to say that unemployment is *the* cause of crime. There is considerable evidence, however, of a close connection between high unemployment and rising crime rates—especially for crimes against property, but also for crimes of violence.

Of the many factors that have been studied in an attempt to predict the number of people going to prison, states Norman O. Carlson, director of the Federal Bureau of Prisons, unemployment is the only one that shows a positive correlation.[54] That is, the higher the unemployment rate, the higher the rate of commitment to prisons. Brenner's study showed that for every 1-percentage-point increase in unemployment, admissions to state prisons rose by about 4 percent. In 1975 the Federal Bureau of Prisons reported that since the early 1950s, increases in the national unemployment rate have been followed about fifteen months later by increased admissions to federal prisons.[55] Although crime is not synonymous with prison admissions, these studies are backed by others linking unemployment and/or labor-force participation rates with reported crime rates in cities, census tracts within cities, states, and the nation as a whole. It is not just the educated observations of those close to the action, like an Indiana state corrections official who notes that crime in that state seems to follow layoffs in the auto industry.[56] In one of these studies, Robert Mier, Thomas Vietorisz, and Jean-Ellen Giblin analyzed the homicide rate in fifty-one cities and found it to be significantly correlated with the official unemployment rate.[57] In another of his studies, Brenner estimated at a 1-percentage-point increase in unemployment in 1970 was related to 3.8 percent of all homicides, 5.7 percent of robberies, 2.8 percent of larcenies, and 8.7 percent of narcotics arrests that year.[58]

Not all crime is committed by the young or the poor—especially not white-collar crime. Nor is crime just an urban phenomenon. It has also been rising in the suburbs. The inner cities, however, where depression-level unemployment among minority youths has festered for decades, provide a fertile breeding ground. Crime flourishes in an environment where there are few jobs for youth; illegal activity becomes an alternative to work. The groups with the highest unemployment are the most prone to crime.

Justice Department data indicate that approximately 50 percent of property-crime arrests are of those in the 16- to 19-year-old age group.[59] Inner-city youths are between ten and twenty times more likley than other young people to be arrested for violent crime.[60] Some of these discrepancies might be attributable to a differential treatment of these youngsters by the police. Common knowledge and the magnitude of the gap, however, tell us that there are also real differences involved.

Not only does unemployment appear to be directly related to crime, but increased use of addictive drugs and alcohol induced by unemployment may also indirectly lead to more criminality. An alcohol or drug problem or a criminal record only compounds employment problems. Ex-offenders without jobs may soon be back in the crime business, but parolees with jobs are less likely to commit crimes.[61] The quality of the jobs is also crucial. The research of economist Ann Dryden Witte of Duke University suggests that higher-wage jobs and more stable jobs are associated with less crime among potential criminals.[62]

The circularity of the relationship between crime and unemployment is compounded even further in urban areas with high crime rates. High unemployment generates crime, which then helps to maintain high unemployment in these areas. A survey of 1,300 businesses in ten major cities confirms the fact that a high crime rate helps to push more jobs away from crime-ridden cities and often deters firms from expanding or relocating in these cities.[63]

Crime not only wastes lives and causes untold tragedies; it also robs the pocketbook as well as the quality of life. According to the Joint Economic Committee, the overall cost of crime to the nation was at least $125 billion, or $500 for each man, woman, and child.[64]

The potential financial benefit of preventing even a small part of criminality through employment is substantial. The cost of maintaining just *one* prisoner can be staggering. The prestigious public accounting firm of Coopers and Lybrand, for instance, conservatively estimated that in 1976, the out-of-pocket cost to New York City of maintaining one prisoner was $71.87 per day, or $26,000 per prisoner per year of imprisonment.[65] This figure includes personnel costs of the Department of Corrections and debt-service costs on capital construction projects, but not similar costs of the police department and the criminal-court system. It also includes supplies and other costs, such as medical services and hospitalization. Societal costs—only those commonly agreed on—were estimated at $39.55 per prisoner day, or more than $14,000 per prisoner year. Included in these costs were real-estate taxes foregone because city-owned property is exempt from these taxes, the cost of welfare payments to prisoners' families, and lost earnings—the contribution a prisoner could have made to national output had he or she not been incarcerated.

Together, these out-of-pocket and societal costs amounted to about $40,000 per prisoner year in New York in 1976 and would surely be even higher in the 1980s. Although the exact figures might vary somewhat from one place to another, they are substantial everywhere and represent a dead weight to society. To the extent that unemployment pushes youngsters into lives of crime, the cost to society is exceedingly high, over and above considerations like the fear of crime and the direct cost of crime to the victims.

Final Thoughts

This chapter has suggested some of the hidden costs of unemployment. No attempt has been made to present a complete catalog of costs or to present a precise quantitative estimate of the full bill. The important points are that over the years the price of unemployment includes income lost both to individuals and to the nation, and that the human costs of unemployment are also steep. Not only is there extensive human damage associated with joblessness; there are also hidden costs for hospital beds, police, prisons, welfare, disability and widow's pensions, and the like. These costs sometimes come due over a long period of time. Declining cities and regions as well as a decline in the quality of life are part of the picture.

Although the costs of unemployment are steep, they are not borne equitably. Much of the burden falls on the unemployed and on employed workers, whose own working standards and wages either fall or fail to rise as much as they would otherwise. In the unionized sector of the economy, unions have been considerably weakened. "Givebacks" are spreading.[66] In the automobile, meat-packing, newspaper, farm-implement, auto-supply, mining, smelting, railroad, airline, and other industries unions have agreed to significant concessions in wages and benefits, as have unions of teachers, public-transit employees, grocery workers, among others.

Lower- and middle-income people pay steeply for unemployment through an increasingly regressive tax system. Unemployment also intensifies racial and ethnic conflicts. It pits young against old, black against white, women against men, region against region in the fierce battle for scarce jobs.

In this environment, despite the heavy costs of unemployment, full employment seems to be a forgotten goal. If we temporarily leave the American scene, however, we see that full employment is not a forgotten goal everywhere. In Sweden, unemployment has long been maintained at rates far below those attained in the United States—averaging about 2 percent during the 1970s, compared with more than 6 percent in the United States. Such a record is no accident. It is the direct result of a conscious pursuit of full employment.

Why is full employment such an important goal? What techniques are used to achieve full employment? How do disadvantaged groups fare in the Swedish labor market? Is there anything that the United States can learn from the Swedish experience? We now turn to these questions.

Notes

1. U.S. Senate, Committee on the Budget, *First Concurrent Resolution on the Budget—Fiscal Year 1976, Report to Accompany S. Con. Res. 32*, 94th Cong., 1st Sess., 1975, p. 5.

2. Erik Lundberg, *Instability and Economic Growth* (New Haven: Yale University Press, 1968), p. 202.

3. Ibid., p. 350.

4. Ibid., p. 109.

5. This discussion draws heavily from Steven Sheffrin, *The Costs of Unemployment,* with an Introduction by Gar Alperovitz and Jeff Faux (Washington, D.C.: Exploratory Project for Economic Alternatives, 1977).

6. Ibid., pp. 9-13.

7. Ibid., p. xii.

8. Ibid., pp. 14-18 and tables IV-VI.

9. Cited in U.S. Library of Congress, Congressional Research Service, "Recessionary Labor Market Changes and Remedial Programs," by Dennis M. Roth et al. (Washington, D.C.: Congressional Research Service, 14 July 1980), p. 32.

10. Ibid.

11. Samuel M. Ehrenhalt, "Some Perspectives on the Outlook for the New York City Labor Market," Summary of remarks before the Fourteenth Annual Institute on the Challenges of the Changing Economy of New York City, New York, 14 April 1981, p. 5.

12. U.S. Senate, Committee on the Budget, *First Concurrent Resolution on the Budget, Fiscal Year 1976,* p. 7.

13. Congressional Research Service, "Recessionary Labor Market Changes," p. 14.

14. From and derived from *Monthly Labor Review* 105 (September 1982):66, Table 15; 67, table 16.

15. Congressional Research Service, "Recessionary Labor Market Changes," p. 24.

16. Carl Rosenfeld, "Job Search of the Unemployed," *Monthly Labor Review* 100 (February 1977):42-43.

17. National Advisory Council on Economic Opportunity, *Eleventh Report* (Washington, D.C.: U.S. Government Printing Office, 1979), p. 23.

18. Congressional Research Service, "Recessionary Labor Market Changes," p. 27.

19. Walter Corsen et al., *Experiences of Unemployment Insurance Recipients during the First Year after Exhausting Benefits* (Princeton, N.J.: Mathematica Policy Research, 1978), pp. 35-37.

20. Marie Jahoda, Paul Lazarsfeld, and Hans Ziesel, *Marienthal: the Sociography of an Unemployed Community* (Chicago: Aldine, 1971).

21. John A. Garraty, *Unemployment in History: Economic Thought and Public Policy* (New York: Harper and Row, 1978), p. 177.

22. Ibid., p. 181.

23. Harry Maurer, *Not Working: An Oral History of the Unemployed* (New York: Holt, Rinehart and Winston, 1979), p. 4.

24. Hannah Levin, "Unemployment—America's Major Mental Health Problem," Paper presented to the American Psychological Association Convention, Chicago, September 1975.

25. Walter Strange, "Job Loss: A Psychosocial Study of Worker Reaction to a Plant Closing in a Company Town in Southern Appalachia" (Ph.D. dissertation, Cornell University, 1977).

26. John E. Hession, "The Hidden Psychological Costs of Unemployment," *Intellect* 7 (April 1978): 390.

27. Barbara Shea, "The New Mental Problems of Hard Times," *Newsday* (Long Island, New York), 25 February 1976.

28. Nashville and New England cases cited in David Shaw, "Unemployment Hurts More Than Just the Pocketbook," *Today's Health,* March 1978, p. 25.

29. Ohio cases cited in Richard Kelly, *Industrial Exodus: Public Strategies for Control of Runaway Plants* (Washington, D.C.: Conference on Alternative State and Local Public Policies, 1977), pp. 8, 9.

30. Louis E. Kopolow and Frank M. Ochberg, "Spinoff from a Downward Swing," *Mental Health* 59 (Summer 1975):22.

31. Speech to the Investment Association of New York, quoted in *The New York Times,* 13 February 1976.

32. M. Harvey Brenner, *Estimating the Costs of National Economic Policy: Implications for Mental and Physical Health and Aggression,* Study prepared for the Joint Economic Committee, U.S. Congress, 94th Cong., 2d Sess., 1976.

33. For an extensive bibliography, see ibid. and Louis A. Ferman and Jeanne P. Gordus, eds., *Mental Health and the Economy* (Kalamazoo, Mich.: W.E. Upjohn Institute for Employment Research, 1979).

34. M. Harvey Brenner, *Mental Illness and the Economy* (Cambridge, Mass.: Harvard University Press, 1973).

35. Brenner, *Costs of National Economic Policy,* p. vi.

36. Ibid., p. 5.

37. Ibid., pp. vi, vii.

38. Ibid., p. ix.

39. For a discussion of these and other technical considerations, see ibid., pp. 46-64. For an extensive critique, see Ivar Berg and Michael Hughes, "Economic Circumstances and the Entangling Web of Pathologies: An Esquisse," in Ferman and Gordus, *Mental Health,* pp. 15-61. For a response to Berg and Hughes, see Brenner, "Health and the National Economy," in Ferman and Gordus, *Mental Health,* pp. 63-88.

40. George Curtis, "Psychophysiology of Stress," in Ferman and Gordus, *Mental Health,* pp. 235-254. An extensive bibliography provides references to the literature of stress.

41. Brenner, "Health and the National Economy," p. 75.

42. Arthur Shostak, "The Human Cost of Plant Closings," *AFL-CIO American Federationist,* August 1980.

43. Ibid.

44. Leonard Greenhalgh, *A Cost-Benefit Balance Sheet for Evaluating Layoffs as a Policy Strategy* (Ithaca, N.Y.: Cornell University, New York State School of Industrial and Labor Relations, CSEA-New York State Continuity of Employment Committee, 1978), p. 22.

45. Stanslav V. Kasl and Sidney Cobb, "Some Mental Health Consequences of Plant Closings and Job Loss," in Ferman and Gordus, *Mental Health,* pp. 255-300. See also Stanislav V. Kasl, Susan Gore, and Sidney Cobb, "The Experience of Losing a Job: Reported Changes in Health, Symptoms and Illness Behavior," *Psychosomatic Medicine* 37 (March-April 1975):106-122.

46. Louis A. Ferman and John Gardner, "Economic Deprivation, Social Mobility and Mental Health," in Ferman and Gordus, *Mental Health,* pp. 193-224.

47. Charles S. De Angelo, "Telephone Summary Report" (CSEA-New York State Continuity of Employment Committee, 1978), n.p., p. 4.

48. Iver Peterson, "Detroit Despairs of Regaining Jobs," *The New York Times,* 27 April 1981, p. A.18.

49. Steven V. Roberts, "An Ohio Family's Struggle to Survive Is Clouded by Plan to Cut Food Stamps," *The New York Times,* 8 March 1981, p. 24.

50. Brenner, *Costs of National Economic Policy,* p. 42, and National Advisory Council on Economic Opportunity, *Eleventh Report,* p. 28.

51. Iver Peterson, "Industry's Woes Hurting Midwest's Quality of Life," *The New York Times,* 31 May 1981, sect. 1, p. 22.

52. "Crime Said to Touch 30 Percent of Households," *The New York Times,* 8 April 1981, p. A.11. These figures are higher than those of the Federal Bureau of Investigation, which include only reported crime. The Bureau of Justice figures are for both reported and unreported crime and are based on a Census Bureau sample survey of 60,000 households.

53. James Lieber, "The American Prison: A Tinderbox," *The New York Times Magazine,* 8 March 1981, p. 28.

54. Harry Fleischman, "The Challenge of Crime," *The Crisis,* August-September 1977, p. 355.

55. U.S. Bureau of Prisons, "Correlation of Unemployment and Federal Prison Population" (Washington, D.C.: U.S. Bureau of Prisons, 1975).

56. James Lieber, "The American Prison," p. 60.

57. Robert Mier, Thomas Vietorisz, and Jean-Ellen Giblin, "Indicators of Labor Market Functioning and Urban Social Disorders," in *The Social Economy of Cities,* ed. Gary Gappert and Harold M. Rose (Beverly Hills, Calif.: Sage, 1975).

58. U.S. Congress, House Judiciary Committee, Subcommittee on Crime, *Hearings on Unemployment and Crime,* 95th Cong., 1st Sess., 1977, p. 25.

59. Barbara Becnel, "The Crime Unemployment Cycle," *AFL-CIO Federationist,* November 1978, p. 11.

60. Ibid., p. 9.

61. Ann Dryden Witte, testimony, U.S. Congress, Joint Economic Committee, *Hearing on the Social Costs of Unemployment,* 96th Cong., 1st Sess., 1979, pp. 31-32.

62. Ibid., p. 33.

63. Robert Reinhold, "Businesses' Moves Linked to Schools and Crime Rates," *The New York Times,* 14 January 1979, p. 24. (The survey was conducted by the Subcommittee on Fiscal and Intergovernmental Policy of the Joint Economic Committee of Congress.)

64. Fleischman, "Challenge of Crime," p. 355.

65. Coopers and Lybrand, "The Cost of Incarceration in New York City" (New York: National Council on Crime and Delinquency, 1978), p. 5.

66. William Serrin, "Unions Yielding 'Givebacks' to Employers at Rising Rate," *The New York Times,* 12 October 1981, p. 1.

Part II
Sweden

5 The Roots of Sweden's Full-Employment Policy

Sweden has a long history of concern about unemployment. From this concern, its full-employment policy has evolved.

Economic and Political Background

Before World War II

The Swedish Social Democratic party has traditionally emphasized full employment and social welfare rather than public ownership of industry. As far back as 1913 the party proposed a program that would now be called Keynesian. Hjalmar Branting, head of the Social Democratic party, and Gustav Möller proposed an economic policy to ensure full employment through expansion of the public sector and the use of fiscal policy.[1] The Swedish Parliament, barely one-quarter of whose members were Social Democrats, ignored the proposal; but it remained a central part of Social Democratic doctrine.

The 1920s were tough times for Swedish workers. Unemployment among union members—the only data available for those years—averaged 26.6 percent in 1921, dipped only slightly to 22.9 percent by 1923, and remained between 10 and 12 percent for the rest of the decade.[2] Intense industrial strife typified the decade as workers resisted managements' attempts to reduce earnings, increase hours, and worsen working conditions.[3] To make matters worse, emigration, which had provided a safety valve since the mid-nineteenth century, became more difficult. Changes in U.S. immigration policy cut the volume of emigration sharply, from more than 29,000 in 1923 to 3,000 at the end of the decade.[4] Not surprisingly, unemployment was the leading political issue of the 1920s.

Although the Social Democrats headed several short-lived coalition governments, they were too weak to implement full-employment policies.[5] Some Social Democrats also accepted the traditional economic wisdom of the age, which guided nonsocialist parties and employers: the cause of unemployment was that wages were too high; therefore, any support to the unemployed should not counteract the downward pressure on wages brought about by high unemployment, and any work projects for the unemployed should offer lower wages than the private sector.[6]

111

By 1932 unemployment was again as severe as it had been in the early 1920s. In Sweden, as in the United States, the depression was the main issue in the 1932 election. The Social Democrats proposed their solution: expand public expenditures and provide for employment at normal wages in order to increase purchasing power and hence demand. During a debate in Parliament that year, Social Democrat Ernst Wigforss used a concept similar to Keynes's multiplier. Four years before Keynes's publication of *The General Theory of Employment, Interest and Money*, Wigforss told the Swedish Parliament, ". . . if I want to start jobs for 100 persons, it is not necessary that I put all of the 100 to work."[7]

When the Social Democrats came to power in 1932 at the head of a minority government (supported by the Agrarian party, with whom they formed a formal coalition after the 1936 election), their first measure was to expand the economy and to stimulate employment through the use of public expenditures. The practical applications were designed by Wigforss, who had become finance minister.[8] During this period, Sweden broke with traditional economic ideas and adopted the use of the government budget as an instrument for economic stabilization. By 1937 Parliament officially abandoned the goal of balancing the budget annually in favor of balancing it over a longer period of time.

Sweden came out of the depression before most other countries, including the United States. Unemployment fell, and living standards rose. This recovery was partly attributable to the policies noted here, but other factors also should be mentioned: a low-interest-rate policy, stabilization of farm prices, modernization of industry, and depreciation of the kronor, to name a few.[9] Foreign trade, so important to Sweden's economy, picked up. This accelerated toward the end of the 1930s, when the arms race abroad—foreshadowing the coming of World War II—sharply increased the demand for Swedish iron ore. Thus, despite Sweden's neutrality, World War II had an impact on employment even before hostilities officially began. During the war it was no longer necessary to pursue an active full-employment policy through expansionary programs. Labor scarcities were prevalent, as in the United States. Training, recruitment, and relocation of labor were emphasized.

Post-World War II

During the war Sweden was governed by a broad coalition, with four participating parties. After the war only the Social Democrats remained in power, and they renewed their policy of conscious pursuit of full employment.[10] Unemployment continued to fall (see table 5-1).

By the end of the 1940s there was concern about the possible inflationary impact of full employment. What followed was a policy debate over the

Table 5-1
Unemployment in Sweden, 1935-1981
(Various Measures)

	Annual Rate of Unemployment		
Year	Trade Union Members[a]	Insured Unemployed[b]	Labor Force Sample Survey[c] Official Figures
1935	15.0	8.8	NA
1940	11.8	6.9	NA
1945	4.5	2.6	NA
1946	3.2	1.9	NA
1947	2.8	1.6	NA
1948	2.8	1.6	NA
1949	2.7	1.6	NA
1950	2.2	1.3	NA
1951	1.8	1.1	NA
1952	2.4	1.4	NA
1953	2.8	1.6	NA
1954	2.6	1.5	NA
1955	2.5	1.5	NA
1956	2.9	1.5	NA
1957	NA	1.9	NA
1958	NA	2.5	NA
1959	NA	2.0	NA
1960	NA	1.4	NA
1961	NA	1.2	NA
1962	NA	1.3	1.5
1963	NA	1.4	1.7
1964	NA	1.1	1.6
1965	NA	1.1	1.2
1966	NA	1.4	1.6
1967	NA	1.7	2.1
1968	NA	2.0	2.2
1969	NA	1.7	1.9
1970	NA	1.5	1.5
1971	NA	2.0	2.5
1972	NA	2.0	2.7
1973	NA	1.9	2.5
1974	NA	1.5	2.0
1975	NA	1.4	1.6
1976	NA	1.2	1.6
1977	NA	1.2	1.8
1978	NA	1.6	2.2
1979	NA	1.5	2.1
1980	NA	1.4	2.0
1981	NA	2.0	2.5

Source: Sweden, National Central Bureau of Statistics, *Arbetsmarknads-Statistisk Årsbok* (Yearbook of Labor Statistics, 1979-1980) (Stockholm: Liber Förlag, 1980), adapted from tables 2.13.2 and 2.13.3, pp. 138 and 139, and unpublished data.
Note: NA = not available.

[a]The rate of unemployment among trade-union members, available since 1911, is the oldest statistical series on unemployment in Sweden. It did not cover the whole labor force.

[b]From 1956 to mid-1974 these data measure the rate of unemployment among the insured unemployed who registered with the Employment Service, as a percentage of all members of unemployment-insurance societies. It is necessary to be registered at the Employment Service to get benefits. Figures for earlier years are estimates.

[c]Unemployment as a percentage of the total labor force. These are the official unemployment figures since 1962, as published by the National Central Bureau of Statistics, and are based on a labor-force sample survey. They are comparable to the official figures on unemployment in the United States, as well as to adjusted Swedish figures given in other tables.

full-employment-inflation issue. Although one prominent economist felt that the only solution to the presumed conflict was "to reduce aspirations with respect to employment,"[11] that policy option was rejected. Full employment remained the national goal. Inflation was to be held in check, but not at the expense of employment.

At the end of the 1950s the original Keynesian approach was replaced by the current one. This approach was initially developed by economists Rudolph Meidner, Gösta Rehn, and some others for Landsorganisationen i Sverige (LO), the Swedish Confederation of Trade Unions, which has been closely allied to the social Democratic party since LO's founding in 1898.[12]

The Rehn-Meidner model, which was endorsed by LO and then later became part of government policy, is post-Keynesian. That is, it starts with the assumption that it is neither desirable nor possible to eliminate all unemployment through traditional Keynesian economic policy. It rejects overreliance on general economic expansionary policy. This is considered neither sufficient nor desirable because it might cause inflationary bottlenecks in some parts of the economy without eliminating the most stubborn unemployment.[13] That is the theoretical framework for a less expansive general economic policy combined with expansionary selective measures that are designed to get at a wide variety of labor-market problems.

Using this approach, an *active* labor-market policy, with myriad government programs, plays an integral role in the pursuit of full employment. Moreover, by helping to eliminate labor shortages that may create production bottlenecks during boom periods, an active labor-market policy simultaneously plays a role in combating inflation. As Swedish economist Eskil Wadensjö explains it, an active labor-market policy consists of two parts. One part emphasizes the demand for labor by stressing job creation. The other part emphasizes the supply of labor by making it easy for workers to leave those areas and occupations with high unemployment to go to places and into occupations where there are jobs.[14] Starting with the recession at the end of the 1950s, the new, active labor-market policy became a permanent and leading part of the Swedish full-employment policy.

In sum, full-employment policy was originally developed by the Social Democrats in close collaboration with LO. During the forty-four years in which the Social Democrats remained at the helm, they developed a wide variety of policy tools. In the post-World War II years, joblessness seldom exceeded 2 percent. Expectations had risen, and there was little tolerance for unemployment.

In 1973 unemployment under the Social Democrats reached almost 3 percent, and that nearly cost them the election. In 1976 the Social Democrats did lose by a small margin to a center-right coalition. Full employment policy, however, was not an issue in dispute in that campaign; the opposition parties could not have won with an anti-full-employment stance. The main issue in the campaign was nuclear power, which had been supported by the Social Democrats.[15] The Center party, formerly the Agrarian party, gained support from its strong antinuclear position. In 1978 the center-right coalition split on the nuclear-power issue, and the Liberal party headed a minority government until the 1979 elections, when the center-right coalition won and retained the government. A shift within this coalition gave more seats in Parliament to the Conservatives. The coalition's margin in Parliament remained slim, however—a bare one-vote majority. The Social Democrats, though out of the government, remained the largest party. With 43.5 percent of the popular votes, they had more than double the 20.4 percent received by the second-largest party, the Conservatives. The latter, along with the Center and Liberal parties, made up the center-right coalition.[16] In spring 1981 that government resigned over a difference on tax issues and was replaced by a Liberal-Center minority government. After completion of this book, an unemployment rate of about 3.5 percent was a major issue in the September 1982 election, which returned the Social Democrats to the helm.

The ascent to power of nonsocialist coalitions did not alter the fact that full employment remained a central goal of the Swedish government. After 1976 new measures were developed to eliminate various types of unemployment and to meet new labor-market problems. Full employment has not yet become a partisan political issue in Sweden, where, unlike the case in the United States, support for full employment cuts across political party lines.

Sweden's Economy and Society

It would be useful now to consider briefly the social and economic context in which Sweden's full-employment policy operates and to make a few comparisons with the United States.

A small industrialized nation with a high standard of living, Sweden contains 8.3 million people in an area slightly larger than California. Sweden is Europe's fourth-largest nation, exceeded in area only by the USSR, France, and Spain. Stretching nearly 1,000 miles from north to south, Sweden lies partly in the Arctic Circle; in the southern third of the country, however, the climate is relatively moderate, especially considering its generally northerly location.

Poverty once drove Swedes to other countries. More than 1.2 million of them emigrated between 1860 and 1930. Growing affluence and rapid economic growth, however, typified the Swedish economy in the decades after World War II. Between 1950 and 1975 the annual per capita increase in real gross domestic product (GDP) averaged 3.1 percent, nearly 50 percent higher than the 2.1 percent recorded for the United States. Sweden thus emerged as an affluent nation whose 1975 per capita GDP ranked second in the world, just below that of Switzerland and above that of the United States, which followed in third place.[17] Sweden is still an affluent nation whose per capita GDP ranks above that of the United States, although its economic growth rate has been slow since the mid-1970s, generally below that of the United States.

Until recently, Sweden had an extremely homogeneous population. It still does, in comparison with the United States. There have been important changes, however. Immigration, much of it within the past two decades, has given the country something akin to a minority group. Five percent of the population is made up of immigrants. Ten percent is of foreign origin if foreign-born Swedish citizens and their children are counted.[18]

Welfare Capitalism

Sweden is well known for its comprehensive and generous social-welfare system. There is much more active government involvement in the economy than in the United States, but Sweden is not a socialist nation. The state has long owned the great iron mines in the extreme north. During World War II the government created a steel mill in Luleå, also in the far north, to help reduce the nation's dependence on imported steel and also to relieve local unemployment. Most business is privately owned however—proportionately more than in many western European countries. Private corporations still own about 90 percent of Sweden's manufacturing and mining.[19] Public enterprises and cooperatives share the rest. Ironically, government ownership increased when the nonsocialist parties were in power. For the most part it has taken the form of majority ownership of some shipbuilding, steel, and pulp and paper firms experiencing severe economic difficulties.

As in the United States, multinational corporations are an important and complicating part of the economic scene. A study of Swedish foreign investment shows that in 1974, 1,200 sales companies and 480 production companies had foreign subsidiaries.[20] The foreign-owned sector in Sweden is considerably smaller than that owned by Swedish companies abroad.

Labor and Management

One cannot understand Swedish labor-market policy without recognizing the different role played by organized labor in Sweden. Only a minority of U.S. workers belong to unions, whose membership has declined steadily from 23.0 percent of the total labor force in 1968 to 19.7 percent in 1978.[21] By contrast, most Swedish workers are organized, and unions are highly centralized. About 90 percent of blue-collar and 75 percent of white-collar workers are organized, as are many professional employees. Most blue-collar workers belong to LO, the dominant labor federation. With 2.1 million members, it is made up of twenty-five national unions. The leading white-collar federation, Tjänstemännens Centralorganisation (TCO), the Swedish Central Organization of Salaried Employees, has about 1 million members in its twenty-four affiliated national unions. Sveriges Akademikers Centralorganisation (SACO/SR), the Swedish Confederation of Professional Associations—representing professionals and other university graduates and government officers—has nearly 200,000 members such as physicians, dentists, academics, architects, psychologists, military officers, and higher salaried national civil servants in twenty-six different national unions.[22]

Swedish unions are more political than their U.S. counterparts, and they play a much more active role in all facets of society. As noted, LO is socialist in ideology (although TCO and SACO/SR are not and have no affiliations with political parties). LO has always been closely associated with the Social Democratic party. Full employment, however, is an important part of the agenda for all of organized labor, not only LO. In addition, LO is committed to a wage-solidarity policy. The aim of this policy is to reduce wage differentials in accordance with the principle of equal pay for equal work. The emphasis is on raising wages in low-wage industries and firms. A solidaristic wage policy was part of the original Rehn-Meidner proposal for Swedish economic policy.

Employers, too, are highly organized. Svenska Arbetsgivareföreningen (SAF), the Swedish Employers' Confederation, is the dominant private-sector employers' organization. It represents the majority of Swedish firms in manufacturing, building and construction, trade, transportation, and services. SAF was formed in 1902, stimulated by an LO-led general strike for universal suffrage, which was not actually attained until 1918. About 1.3 million Swedes work for 27,000 large and small companies affiliated with SAF through 37 employer associations. Most workers, however, are employed by the larger SAF members, over 40 percent of them in companies with more than 1,000 employees. It is the large firms that dominate SAF.[23]

In 1938, following years of intense labor-market conflict, SAF and LO entered into the historic Saltsjöbaden Agreement. Both parties agreed to self-regulate certain key issues, including the prevention of disruptive industrial conflicts that might otherwise lead to government control of industrial relations. This was part of a large compromise at the time that called for cooperation between capital and labor to achieve rapid economic growth. According to Swedish political sociologist Walter Korpi, this cooperation was the result of a widespread feeling in Sweden that the Social

Democrats were going to remain in political power for a long time. Thus political power had become separated from economic power. Within the foreseeable future, neither capital nor labor could hope to resolve their conflicts of interest through surrender of the other party. The compromise was designed to benefit both parties. Business would gain because it was to be given favorable conditions for growth and expansion. Labor would gain because unemployment was to be allowed to decrease and growth was to provide the economic basis for both improved living standards and more extensive social-welfare policies. The government, which had often intervened in favor of employers, was to remain neutral in labor-management relations, with the emphasis on self-regulation mentioned earlier.[24]

Consequently, there is considerably less government intervention into and regulation of collective bargaining in Sweden than in the United States. Collective bargaining is also highly centralized. Since 1956 SAF and LO have conducted an unbroken series of collective negotiations, which have resulted in joint recommendations to affiliates to make national agreements within the centrally set framework.[25] In U.S. terms, that would be like the heads of AFL-CIO and the National Association of Manufacturers sitting down at the bargaining table—an unheard-of scenario.

Extensive labor-management cooperation and relatively few strikes and lockouts have characterized Swedish industrial relations for decades. Between 1971 and 1975, for example, an average of 63 days a year were lost through labor disputes per 1,000 employees, compared with 347 in the United States.[26] The strikes and lockouts that kept about one-quarter of Sweden's workers from their jobs for ten days in May 1980 represented a sharp departure from the more usual labor relations.[27]

Labor Force and Employment Trends

Employment trends in Sweden are similar to those in the United States. There has been a dramatic shift out of agriculture and forestry, with less than 7 percent of total employment in 1975. About 26 percent work in manufacturing and mining, a proportion that has been declining in recent years. The most rapid growth has been in the service sector, which employs 58 percent of the labor force. Within that sector, public employment has grown most rapidly since 1960, much more so than in the United States.[28]

Viewed from a U.S. perspective, Swedish unemployment is exceedingly low. It averaged 1.8 percent in 1977, 2.1 percent in 1978, 2.1 percent in 1979, and 2.0 percent in 1980. Despite a fierce recession, it was only 2.5 percent in 1981 (see table 5-2). In the first half of 1982, during that recession—when unemployment in the United States was soaring past 9 percent—Sweden's hovered around 3 percent. Rates that low have not been attained

Table 5-2

Civilian Labor-Force Participation and Unemployment Rates, Sweden and the United States, 1972-1980, Adjusted to U.S. Concepts
(Percentage)

	Labor-Force Participation Rate[a]		Unemployment Rate[b]	
Year	United States	Sweden	United States	Sweden
1972	60.4	64.1	5.6	2.7
1973	60.8	64.1	4.9	2.5
1974	61.2	64.9	5.6	2.0
1975	61.2	65.9	8.5	1.6
1976	61.6	66.0	7.7	1.6
1977	62.3	65.9	7.0	1.8
1978	63.2	66.1	6.0	2.2
1979	63.7	66.8	5.8	2.1
1980	63.8	67.2	7.1	2.0

Source: Adapted from Joyanna Moy and Constance Sorrentino, "Unemployment, Labor Force Trends and Layoff Practices in Ten Countries," *Monthly Labor Review* 104 (December 1981), table 3, and U.S. Department of Labor, Bureau of Labor Statistics, *Statistical Supplement to International Comparisons of Unemployment: Bulletin 1979* (Washington, D.C.: Bureau of Labor Statistics, 1981).

Note: Statistics for the Swedish labor force, as originally published, related to the population aged 16 to 74, but these figures have been adjusted to include persons 75 and over. The noninstitutional population has also been excluded to conform to the U.S. concepts.

[a]Civilian labor force as a percentage of the civilian population 16 and older.

[b]Unemployed as a percentage of the civilian labor force 16 and over.

in the United States since World War II. It is significant that low unemployment has gone hand in hand with a high and growing labor-force participation rate, which now exceeds that of the United States (see table 5-2). In other words, Sweden's low unemployment is not a statistical artifact, masking, for example, a low labor-force participation rate for women. In fact, the main reason for the labor-force growth is that Swedish women, like their U.S. counterparts, have been flocking into the labor force in large numbers, although many work only part time. Their participation rate is even higher than that of U.S. women (see table 5-3). As in the United States, the sharpest rise has been among mothers of preschool children. Similarly, the labor-force participation rate of Swedish men, as well as that of U.S. men, has been declining slowly, partly as a result of lowered retirement age and other pension changes that mainly affected men.

Even when unemployment is as low as it has been in Sweden, its distribution is uneven. As in the United States, women and young people are more likely to be jobless than others are. The unemployment rate for women is somewhat higher than for men. Moreover, the real gap between the sexes is actually higher than unemployment figures imply. As in the United States, there is more hidden unemployment among women, who are

Table 5-3
Labor-Force Participation Rates, by Sex, 1970-1980, Sweden and the United States, Adjusted to U.S. Concepts
(Percentage)

| | Labor-Force Participation Rate | | | |
| | Men | | Women | |
Year	United States	Sweden	United States	Sweden
1970	79.7	78.5	43.3	50.0
1971	79.1	78.0	43.3	50.9
1972	79.0	77.3	43.9	51.5
1973	78.8	76.8	44.7	51.7
1974	78.7	76.9	45.6	53.3
1975	77.9	77.0	46.3	55.2
1976	77.5	76.5	47.3	55.8
1977	77.7	75.6	48.4	56.7
1978	77.7	75.1	50.0	57.5
1979	77.9	75.2	51.0	58.7
1980	77.4	75.0	51.6	59.7

Source: Adapted from Joyanna Moy and Constance Sorrentino, "Unemployment, Labor Force Trends and Layoff Practices in Ten Countries," *Monthly Labor Review* 104 (December 1981), table 2, and U.S. Department of Labor, Bureau of Labor Statistics, *Statistical Supplement to International Comparisons of Unemployment: Bulletin 1979* (Washington, D.C.: Bureau of Labor Statistics, 1981).

Note: Civilian labor force as a percentage of the civilian population 16 and over. For a description of the methodology used to adjust Swedish figures to U.S. concepts, see footnotes to table 5.2

often deterred from entering or remaining in the labor force in the face of adverse labor-market conditions. The highest unemployment rates in Sweden are experienced by young people. Teenage unemployment has ranged from 7 to 8 percent since the mid-1970s and has been a cause of grave national concern. The jobless rate among immigrants (those who do not hold Swedish citizenship) is about twice the national average, a ratio similar to that of blacks to whites in the United States. Older workers and the handicapped are groups that also face special labor-market problems.

In the United States, unemployment in recent years has been especially severe in large urban areas. Some regions, like the northeast and the industrial midwest, have suffered extensively from growing unemployment. Although unemployment in Sweden has not been concentrated in large cities, it does have a strong regional dimension. The north, with about one-seventh of the population, typically has about 40 percent of Sweden's unemployment.[29] (The special problems faced by these groups and regions are discussed in more detail in later chapters.)

More Difficult Times

Compared with the 1960s, the 1970s was a decade of more unemployment in Sweden, as in the United States. From 1960 to 1969 joblessness averaged 1.7 percent in Sweden, compared with 4.8 percent in the United States. From 1970 to 1979, however, these figures (adjusted to U.S. methods of measurement) rose to 2.1 percent and 6.2 percent (see table 5-4).

Although full-employment policy in Sweden was maintained in the 1970s, it had to be implemented in a much harsher economic climate than in the previous decade. Two international recessions and rising energy costs during the 1970s adversely affected both nations' economies, although the potential of these factors to add to employment problems is actually greater in Sweden. Sweden is highly dependent on exports, much more so than the United States. About 25 percent of GDP is exported, compared with 7 percent for the United States.[30] Some sectors are even more dependent on exports. The engineering industry, with its metal manufacturing, machinery, electrical products, and transport equipment, accounts for half of all exports;

Table 5-4
Unemployment in Sweden and the United States, 1960-1979, Adjusted to U.S. Concepts
(Percentage)

Year	Unemployment Rate[a]		Year	Unemployment Rate[a]	
	United States	*Sweden*		*United States*	*Sweden*
1960	5.5	NA	1970	4.9	1.5
1961	6.7	1.4	1971	5.9	2.5
1962	5.5	1.5	1972	5.6	2.7
1963	5.7	1.7	1973	4.9	2.5
1964	5.2	1.5	1974	5.6	2.0
1965	4.5	1.2	1975	8.5	1.6
1966	3.8	1.6	1976	7.7	1.6
1967	3.8	2.1	1977	7.0	1.8
1968	3.6	2.2	1978	6.0	2.2
1969	3.5	1.9	1979	5.8	2.1
Average,			Average,		
1960-1969	4.8	1.7	1970-1979	6.2	2.1

Source: U.S. Department of Labor, Bureau of Labor Statistics, *International Comparisons of Unemployment* (Washington, D.C.: U.S. Government Printing Office, 1978), table 3, p. 19, for 1960-1976. Data for 1977-1979 for the United States are from *Monthly Labor Review* 103 (May 1980): 67, table 1; for Sweden, from Central Bureau of Statistics, Labor Force Surveys, 1977, 1978, and 1979, mimeo.

Note: Adjustments made by U.S. Bureau of Labor Statistics for 1960-1976.

[a]Unemployed as a percentage of the civilian labor force 16 and over.

some large engineering companies export as much as 70-80 percent of their production.[31] Per capita imports are also among the highest in the world.[32]

The length and depth of the 1974-1975 international recession cut sharply into foreign demand for Swedish exports. With one of the world's highest wage levels, Sweden now faces increasing competition in foreign markets. To make matters worse, in some traditionally important export industries such as steel and shipbuilding, long-term structural problems have surfaced. Finally, with no domestic oil or coal, Sweden is potentially more vulnerable to rising energy costs, since three-quarters of its energy supply is imported.[33]

The Swedish response to the more difficult challenge of unemployment in the 1970s was quite different from that of the United States, where there was an upward escalation in the amount of unemployment considered tolerable. Although passage of the Humphrey-Hawkins Full Employment and Balanced Growth Act of 1978, with its interim goal of reducing unemployment to 4 percent by 1983, seemed to represent a new policy direction, that goal was soon postponed by President Carter. By mid-1980 unemployment was once again soaring upward and as it neared 8 percent there was hardly a political outcry. That rate seemed as tolerable as 4 percent once had.

In Sweden during the same years, the worsening economic situation led to more strenuous efforts to combat joblessness. Why were efforts accelerated rather than goals pared down? A closer look at the Swedish philosophy of full employment and its relationship to other aspects of Swedish life provides some clues.

The Swedish Philosophy of Full Employment

As one Swedish official has observed, "Swedes are not particularly religious, but one thing we do hold almost sacred is everybody's right to work."[34]

Full employment is not a peripheral issue. It has been regarded by Swedes as an important means of increasing the output of goods and services by using otherwise idle resources. But full employment is not viewed solely in economic terms. Equally significant is its linkage to other important aspects of Swedish society. Full employment is the linchpin of Sweden's comprehensive social-welfare policy, is essential to LO's wage policy, and is considered the practical means of breathing life into a widely shared egalitarian philosophy.

Sweden's generous and comprehensive social-welfare system is rooted in the notion of jobs for all. First, high unemployment would mean less output and greater dependency. Expenditures on income transfers would be a greater economic burden.[35] Equally important, income transfers alone are not considered a solution for persons who want to work, whether they are normal or physically, psychologically, or socially handicapped. The concept of *normalization* is fundamental to the Swedish social-welfare system.[36] The goal is to enable everyone to live as normal a life as possible and "to reduce the risk of isolation, loneliness, and alienation."[37] Work is considered the key to a normal life. In short, a job is considered a basic right.

Job development that stems from full-employment policy has been used to meet other highly regarded social-welfare goals such as expanding and upgrading services for the ill, disabled, elderly, children, and parents.

Full employment is an essential part of LO's wage-solidarity policy, which aims at reducing wage inequalities and raising the earnings of low-wage workers. The goal is equal pay for equal work, regardless of the profitability of the firm. Unions of more highly paid workers accept smaller wage hikes for themselves and use their strength to help low-wage earners get larger wage gains. This policy necessitates the centralized agreements negotiated between LO and SAF that are then recommended to affiliated unions. The least profitable firms, which cannot pay these wages, however, may be squeezed out or undergo rationalization to increase their productivity. LO recognizes that this wage policy requires full employment and an active labor-market policy if workers who become unemployed are to find jobs in other, more profitable firms and sectors. This was part of the Rehn-Meidner proposal adopted by LO in 1951.[38]

Finally, with a strong egalitarian ethos, there is heavy reliance on employment policy to bring about more equality among regions and income groups, as well as for women, the handicapped, immigrants, and other less favored groups.

Inflation

Swedish policy, as already noted, has not been guided by a feeling that concern about unemployment must be dampened because of fear of inflation. This is not to say that inflation has not been a concern. Like those of other Western indusrial nations, Sweden's economy has not been inflation free. However, although unemployment is lower, Swedish inflation has also generally been somewhat lower than that of European members of the Organization for Economic Cooperation and Development (OECD) though higher than that of the United States. For example, according to the OECD, from 1971 to 1978 the annual increase in consumer prices averaged 8.9 percent in Sweden, 9.9 percent in OECD European nations, and 6.7 percent in the United States. In 1979 inflation was lower in Sweden than in either OECD European countries or the United States. In 1980 inflation was lower in Sweden than in OECD European countries but higher than in the United

States. In the six-month period ending in April 1982, inflation was higher in Sweden than in either OECD European countries or the United States.[39]

Unlike that of the United States, Swedish policy has not been based on any belief in an inevitable trade-off between unemployment and inflation. There has been concern over both unemployment and inflation, and efforts have been made to deal with them simultaneously. Sweden long ago rejected the policy option of simply heating up the economy as the way to achieve full employment. Meidner and Rehn pointed out that such an approach could worsen inflation without getting at the most stubborn unemployment. Thus a major aim of labor-market policy has been to develop jobs in those sectors of the economy and among those groups where they are needed. At the same time, policies are also aimed at preventing inflationary bottlenecks due to specific labor shortages when the economy is expanding, through, for instance, labor-market training and retraining.

With full employment such an overriding goal of Swedish society, one might now ask: How is full employment attained? What are the main techniques?

Notes

1. Bernard K. Johnpoll, "Sweden's Socialists: Hoist with Their Own Success," *The Nation*, 4 December 1972, p. 553.

2. Solomon Barkin, "Swedish Active Manpower Policy: Its Evolution and Chronological Development" (Amherst, Mass.: University of Massachusetts Labor Relations and Research Center, 1977), p. 4, mimeo. Figures for union members are the only ones available for those years.

3. Ibid., p. 5.

4. Ibid., p. 5.

5. Walter Korpi, *The Working Class in Welfare Capitalism: Work, Unions and Politics in Sweden* (London and Boston: Routledge and Kegan Paul, 1978), p. 80.

6. Ibid., p. 80.

7. Ibid., p. 81.

8. See Korpi, *Working Class*, p. 81; Johnpoll, "Sweden's Socialists," p. 553; and Barkin, "Swedish Active Manpower Policy," pp. 9-11.

9. I am indebted to Eskil Wadensjö for pointing out the intense debate that has been taking place among Swedish economists about the relative roles of fiscal stimulus of the economy and other factors in this recovery. See also Barkin, "Swedish Active Manpower Policy," pp. 10-12.

10. Assar Lindbeck, "Theories and Problems in Swedish Economic Policy in the Post-War Period," *Surveys of National Economic Policy Issues and Policy Research, American Economic review*, 58 (June 1968): supplement, p. 2, esp. pp. 18-27. See also Berndt Öhman, *LO and Labour*

Market Policy since the Second World War (Stockholm: Bokförlaget Prisma, 1974), esp. chap. 2, and Eskil Wadensjö, "Job Creation and Job Maintenance in the Private Sector: A New Course in Labor Market Policy," paper prepared for a conference in Padeborn, Germany, February 1979, photocopy. For an overview of the Swedish economy from 1945 to the mid-1960s, see Erik Lundberg, *Instability and Economic Growth* (New Haven, Conn.: Yale University Press, 1968), chap. 5.

11. Lindbeck, "Theories and Problems," p. 19.

12. Korpi, *Working Class*, p. 3.

13. This strategy is discussed in Lindbeck, "Theories and Problems," esp. pp. 10-32; Öhman, *LO*, esp. chap. 2; and Wadensjö, "Job Creation."

14. Wadensjö, "Job Creation," pp. 4-5.

15. Nils Elvander, "In Search of New Relationships: Parties, Unions and Salaried Employees' Associations in Sweden," *Industrial and Labor Relations Review* 28 (October 1974):72-73. See also Robert Skole, "Sweden's Nuclear Election," *The Nation*, 9 October 1976, pp. 334-337.

16. Sweden, Ministry of Economic Affairs and Ministry of the Budget, *The Swedish Budget 1980/81*, Summary (Stockholm: Liber Förlag, 1980), p. 164.

17. Skandinaviska Enskilda Banken, *Some Data about Sweden, 1977-1978* (Stockholm: Skandinaviska Enskilda, 1977). Data on emigration are from p. 3, data on GDP from table 5.5, p. 16.

18. "Immigrants in Sweden," *Fact Sheets on Sweden* (Stockholm: Swedish Institute, 1978), p. 1. Immigration is discussed in greater detail in chapter 8.

19. "General Facts on Sweden," *Fact Sheets on Sweden* (Stockholm: Swedish Institute, 1979), p. 2.

20. Skandinaviska Enskilda Banken, *Some Data about Sweden, 1977-1978*, p. 51.

21. U.S., Department of Labor, Bureau of Labor Statistics, *Directory of National Unions and Employee Associations, 1979*, Bulletin 2079 (Washington, D.C.: U.S. Government Printing Office, 1980), table 6, p. 59. If employee associations are included, the figures are 25.2 percent for 1968 and 22.3 percent for 1978.

22. Data for LO and TCO are from Skandinaviska Enskilda Banken, *Some Data about Sweden 1979-1980*, p. 80. Data for SACO/SR are from SACO/SR, *SACO/SR, the Professional Organization for University Graduates and Others with Higher Education* (Stockholm: SACO/SR, n.d.), p. 4.

23. Swedish Employers' Confederation, *SAF and the Swedish Labour Market* (Stockholm: Swedish Employers' Confederation, 1976), pp. 9-10, 13.

24. Swedish Employers' Confederation, *SAF and the Swedish Labour Market*, p. 11; "Labor Relations in Sweden," *Fact Sheets on Sweden* (Stockholm: Swedish Institute, 1977), p. 3; and Korpi, *Working Class*, pp. 80-86.

25. "Labor Relations in Sweden," *Fact Sheets on Sweden*, p. 3.

26. Skandinaviska Enskilda Banken, *Some Data about Sweden, 1977-1978*, table 4-6, p. 13.

27. John Vinocur, "Labor Strife Brings Sweden's System to a Turning Point," *The New York Times*, 5 May 1980, p. 2.

28. Skandinaviska Enskilda Banken, *Some Data about Sweden, 1977-1978*, table 4-7, p. 13.

29. "Swedish Labor Market Policy," *Fact Sheets on Sweden* (Stockholm: Swedish Institute, 1980).

30. Skandinaviska Enskilda Banken, *Some Data about Sweden, 1977-1978*, table 27-3, p. 73.

31. Swedish Association of Metalworking Industries and Swedish Engineering Employers' Association, *The Swedish Engineering Industry* (Stockholm: Swedish Association of Metalworking Industries and Swedish Engineering Employers' Association, 1976), p. 22.

32. Skandinaviska Enskilda Banken, *Some Data about Sweden, 1979-1980*, p. 21.

33. Ibid., p. 73.

34. Berit Rollén, "Equality Between Men and Women in the Labor Market: The Swedish National Labor Market Board," in *Equal Employment Policy for Women: Strategies for Implementation in the United States, Canada and Western Europe*, ed. Ronnie Steinberg Ratner (Philadelphia: Temple University Press, 1980), p. 179.

35. Gösta Rehn, "The Fight against Inflation," 29 October 1975, p. 12, mimeo.

36. Leif Holgersson and Stig Lundström, *The Evolution of Swedish Social Welfare* (Stockholm: Swedish Institute, 1975), p. 12.

37. Ibid., p. 12.

38. Öhman, *LO*, chaps. 2, 3.

39. *OECD Economic Outlook* 31 (July 1982):51, table 19. For an interesting analysis of the mechanism of Swedish inflation, see Hans Brems, "Swedish Fine Tuning," *Challenge*, March-April 1976, pp. 39-41.

6 Labor-Market Policies for Full Employment: An Overview

For several decades an active labor-market policy has been the guiding star in Sweden's unending quest for full employment. Yet there is no single technique that can be described as *the* most important. Instead, a staggering array of selective policies is targeted to overcome the myriad unemployment problems that afflict specific groups, regions, and industries. The approach lends itself to flexibility. As the problems shift—with the large-scale entry of women into the work force or the rise of youth unemployment—new tools are developed while old ones are retained or refashioned.

Some tools, such as the investment-reserve fund and inventory subsidies (discussed later) are not used in the United States. Others, like direct job creation, have also been used in the United States but on a smaller scale or mainly during times of crisis. In Sweden, on the other hand, they are used extensively even when unemployment is at or less than 2 percent, well below what most U.S. policymakers and economists regard as full employment.

The National Labor Market Board

Although the broad guidelines of labor-market policy are set by the government and Parliament, the main body for shaping and implementing these policies is the National Labor Market Board (Arbetsmarknadsstyrelsen, or AMS). AMS is a Swedish institution with no exact counterpart in the United States. Funded by Parliament via the annual budget, the AMS governing body, which meets every two weeks, is tripartite, with labor, business, and government representation. Three of its fifteen members come from LO, two from TCO, and one from SACO/SR. SAF has three members; agriculture and female labor have one apiece. There are also two AMS staff representatives and a deputy director. The director-general, who heads the board, is appointed by the government for six years. Although unions have a plurality of votes and are the source of most new ideas, nearly all decisions are unanimous.[1]

The presence of labor and management on the AMS board has been a key factor in securing their cooperation on a continuing basis at every level. It also enables AMS to secure vital information and expertise that would not otherwise be available. Unions assign high priority to their involvement with AMS. Their representatives are bound in a general way to LO, TCO, and SACO/SR convention decisions. The Metalworkers, as well as other national unions affiliated with the labor federations, also devote a great deal of convention time to questions of employment policy and programs.[2] Even though they work full time on employment policy, union and SAF representatives stay with, are paid for, and are accountable to their parent organizations. This gives them much-needed channels back to national and local branches.

AMS also functions through regional offices and supervises the twenty-four County Labor Market Boards and the Employment Service, with its 220 local offices, all with local tripartite representation similar to that of AMS. Labor and management are also the backbone of the working groups that are constantly involved in investigations and development work. Their presence enables AMS to get a realistic picture of actual labor-market and workplace conditions, and to anticipate possible stumbling blocks to the implementation of proposed policies. When AMS finally embarks on a policy, the unions and SAF also inform their members and help to secure their much-needed cooperation—an important ingredient for success.

Since AMS reaches down to the local level, it plays a vital role in tailoring policies to the needs of different areas. The County Labor Market Boards are in day-to-day contact with local unions and firms. They keep AMS continuously abreast of labor market conditions. On the basis of the state of the labor market, AMS then allocates funds to the County Labor Market Boards, along with guidelines about the main groups to be served.

Labor-Market Techniques

The best way to understand this rich assortment of labor-market tools, mostly administered by AMS, is to take a closer look at some of them. Most policies focus on the creation or maintenance of employment and advance planning; job information, placement, guidance, and training; geographic mobility; advance warning; regional job development; or unemployment benefits. Others are aimed at groups such as the handicapped, women, the young, the elderly, and immigrants. Many policies, of course, fit into several categories. Some of these policies will be examined in this chapter, and those aimed at special groups form the core of chapters 7 and 8.

Job Creation and Advance Planning:
Established Methods

At the heart of Swedish full-employment policy are various measures to create and maintain employment. The availability of jobs is crucial to the success of policies such as job training. Job-creation policies range from those that influence private-sector investment to direct job creation and advance planning. They are well-established methods.

Investment-Reserve Funds. The ups and downs of the business cycle bring in their wake large changes in employment.[3] Starting in 1938, Sweden developed its unique system of investment-reserve funds, which are used to help smooth these fluctuations. The aim is to influence the timing of capital expenditures, usually the most volatile sector of a capitalist economy. Firms are induced to curb potentially inflationary investment during boom periods and to speed up investment during recessions to help stimulate additional employment. Companies can set aside up to 50 percent of pretax profits with substantial tax advantages; 50 percent of these must be deposited in a blocked, no-interest account with the Bank of Sweden. During an economic downturn—and this was done extensively in the 1970s—the government can authorize release of these funds for tax-free use in approved projects, and AMS handles the applications. Reserves that are used without permission within five years of deposit are taxable. After five years, 30 percent can be used tax free without authorization. Since the mid-1960s the reserves have also been used to stimulate investment in depressed areas regardless of the stage of the business cycle.

Relief Work. Direct job creation by government is another long-established instrument of Swedish labor-market policy that still plays a major role in efforts to combat unemployment.[4] Relief work (*beredskapsarbete*; literally "preparedness work") is designed to provide transitional, short-term employment for the jobless, usually for no more than six months. From the Works Progress Administration (WPA) of the Great Depression to the Comprehensive Employment Training Act (CETA), special job creation has also been used in the United States at various times.

Relief jobs are similar to public service employment in the United States, except that in Sweden these jobs always pay regular wages and fringe benefits, or else wages are determined through special collective-bargaining contracts, whereas in the United States they often have paid low wages. In Sweden there are no special job programs for the poor or for relief recipients. In line with Swedish social philosophy, special programs for the poor or for the relief recipients are regarded with disdain as stigmatized programs. Programs that have the potential to zero in on a specific problem are preferred. Thus if a person is jobless, it is thought that he or she may require assistance regardless of income or skill level. In the United States eligibility has often hinged on factors such as low income, disadvantaged status, or receipt of public assistance.

U.S. critics have often charged that jobs programs are "make work" or that their expansion in a recession is not very useful because implementation takes too long. Sweden takes great pains to avoid these potential pitfalls.

Most relief jobs are specially created on national- or local-government projects, with a few on private projects. Advance planning is the key word. The main idea is to have a reserve of projects that can be started without delay if unemployment rises. To ensure their social usefulness, the emphasis is on projects that would normally be undertaken within the next few years. Projects are drawn from annual plans of national and local government authorities. Each County Labor Market Board compiles an annual plan of suitable projects. As an incentive for advance planning, municipalities and counties receive grants covering 75 percent of the cost of producing the plans and blueprints in advance, so that projects can be started swiftly.[5] The ability to terminate a project quickly is also a consideration in selecting projects because the aim is to return the unemployed—who must be registered as job seekers with the Employment Service—to regular employment.

The information that the County Labor Market Boards collect is then consolidated and used by AMS in planning for the country as a whole in the next fiscal year. This is necessary since projects are fully or partially financed by AMS from funds received from Parliament for this purpose every fiscal year. It is also possible to receive additional funds from Parliament during the year if the employment situation should suddenly deteriorate.

AMS then allocates money to different regions via the County Labor Market Boards, which, in the light of local needs, select the projects and decide when to stop and to start them. Central-government projects are fully financed. Local-government and private-sector sponsors formerly received grants covering 33 percent of wages, but since 1978 they have received 75 percent.[6]

Relief work is also used to counter seasonal and structural unemployment. Projects are often timed to prevent seasonal unemployment. This is especially important in northern Sweden, with its long, cold winters. There are also about forty industrial workshops that provide relief jobs for factory workers. (Since 1980, these have been part of Samhällstöretag, the organization of sheltered workshops, discussed in chapter 8.) Most of these workshops were originally private plants that closed. They were later taken over by the government to provide jobs for laid-off handicapped or older workers, or women who are tied down to a particular location that has few job prospects for them. Many of them would otherwise remain unemployed. Unlike other relief jobs, industrial relief is often permanent. Special relief projects for the handicapped also exist.

Once, relief work almost certainly meant road and other construction work, forestry, and nature conservation. This changed, however, spurred by the increasing number of women and young people who joined the ranks of the jobless and by the appearance of unemployed university graduates. Partly as a result of the rapid expansion of university enrollments in the 1960s, not all graduates could be absorbed in the labor market in jobs traditionally available to them. SACO, the union of professionals that was a predecessor of SACO/SR, pressed from its seat on AMS for the development of new forms of relief work for university graduates, many of whom had become junior members of SACO while still students. As a result, the development of new community-health programs, social services and services for children were speeded up. Also, many existing preschool programs were qualitatively improved by the services these young graduates provided in relief jobs. Afterward, many remained as regular workers.[7]

The variety of relief jobs has therefore been greatly expanded and their composition shifted to serve white-collar and service employees as well as blue-collar workers, women as well as men, and the young as well as the mature jobless. This shift can be seen by noting the rise in the proportion of relief jobs in public services; health services; and the care of the sick, the aged, and children from 13 percent of the total in fiscal 1972-1973 to 74 percent in fiscal 1979-1980.[8]

Relief jobs are found in public agencies, institutions, municipalities, county councils, and private industry. CETA also developed a diversity of jobs and sponsors. A major difference, however, is the scale on which Sweden uses public service jobs to fight unemployment. For example, in 1978, when the jobless rate soared to 2.2 percent—a cause for alarm in Sweden—the number of unemployed averaged 95,000 and the number of relief jobs averaged 43,000—45 jobs for each 100 unemployed persons, exclusive of specially subsidized jobs for the handicapped (table 6-1). The equivalent that year (as a proportion of the jobless) in the United States, when unemployment was 6 percent and 6 million were officially jobless, would have been about 2.7 million public service employment jobs. The actual number of CETA public service job slots in 1978 was at a historic peak of 725,000 and subsequently fell sharply despite rising unemployment. At the beginning of 1981, with unemployment at 7.3 percent for February (representing 7.8 million persons), the Reagan administration announced proposals to phase out these jobs completely by fiscal 1982; and budget cuts approved by Congress eliminated them in October 1981.

It is important to note that not all specially created jobs in Sweden come under relief-work programs. Numerous special programs exist for handicapped workers; these are discussed in chapter 8.

Other Means of Influencing the Timing of Employment. The theory behind relief work and investment reserves is to alter the timing of projects that would ordinarily be undertaken at a later date. Other methods, however, are also used to influence the timing of employment.

Table 6-1
Unemployment, Government Job Creation, and Labor-Market Training in Sweden, 1965-1979

Year	Unemployed Total Number (1)	Percentage of Labor Force (2)	Employed in Government-Created Jobs (Average per Month) (3)	In Labor-Market Training Courses (Average per Month) (4)	Total in Government-Created Jobs and Training[a] (5)	Ratio: Jobs and Training to Unemployed, (5)/(1) (6)
1965	44,000	1.2	9,800	15,900	25,700	58.4
1966	59,100	1.6	9,200	18,800	28,000	47.4
1967	79,500	2.1	13,700	23,500	37,200	46.8
1968	84,900	2.2	20,300	29,600	49,900	58.8
1969	72,700	1.9	15,600	31,600	47,200	64.9
1970	59,100	1.5	14,600	33,900	48,500	82.1
1971	100,600	2.5	19,000	39,400	58,400	58.1
1972	107,300	2.7	32,400	43,100	75,500	70.4
1973	98,000	2.5	33,300	46,000	79,000	79.8
1974	80,300	2.0	23,400	40,700	64,100	77.4
1975	67,300	1.6	16,600	35,700	52,300	77.8
1976	66,300	1.6	26,300	38,000	64,300	97.0[b]
1977	76,000	1.8	28,200	42,000	70,200	92.4[b]
1978	95,000	2.2	43,000	47,000	90,000	94.7[b]
1979[c]	93,000	2.2	50,000	50,000	100,000	107.5

Source: From and derived from Sweden, Ministry of Economic Affairs and Ministry of the Budget, *The Swedish Budget 1980/81: A Summary*, Stockholm, 1980, p. 90.

[a]These are called *relief work* by the Swedes, but they are more comparable to public service employment; they are not tied to any public-assistance programs, nor is there any income eligibility. Unemployment is the criterion.

[b]These figures exclude in-plant training for workers threatened with layoffs. For all years, they exclude all persons in various forms of subsidized employment for the handicapped, although handicapped persons who are in government-created jobs and labor-market training courses (columns 3 and 4) are, of course, included. In 1978 an average of about 45,000 persons were in special programs for the handicapped. In 1977 and 1978 about 100,000 workers a year received some in-plant training.

[c]First three-quarters.

When the labor market weakens, the central government can and does advance its own construction or renovation—buildings, airports, railways, and universities, for example. It can also influence local government and private industry. Stepping up public works has been a fairly common countercyclical measure in the United States, but it is interesting to note several unique ways that Sweden has used this measure to reinforce other public policies to meet social needs.

Economic slumps have been used at various times to increase central-government grants to municipalities for day nurseries and after-school centers and to speed the clean up of the environment—a strong national goal in Sweden. During the 1971-1973 recession, the central government temporarily increased the grants to municipalities for the construction of sewage-treatment plants from 25 to 75 percent of investment costs. Private-industry grants for investments to prevent water and air pollution and for noise abatement were temporarily raised from 25 to 50 percent.[9] The impact was two-pronged: first, employment was boosted considerably, especially in the construction and engineering industries. Second, environmental protection was improved. Sweden now has probably the most extensive and efficient wastewater-purification system in Europe. The new sewage-treatment plants built by the municipalities have transformed many once-polluted lakes into clean, clear water where people can swim safely and enjoyably.[10]

With its harsh winter, Sweden also makes a major effort to reduce seasonal unemployment. As a U.S. Department of Labor study put it, "One would also expect very large seasonal unemployment swings related to the winter in Sweden, but this has been mitigated as a result of massive government programs to stimulate winter employment."[11] In fact, the study also found that despite its more severe winter, seasonal swings in construction are less pronounced in Sweden than in the United States.

Much of Sweden's success in reducing seasonal unemployment stems from its strong emphasis on spreading out construction work—in addition to relief jobs—throughout the year. Over 90 percent of all housing is built with state loans, and this in itself is an important potential for stabilization.[12]

More specifically, since 1954 government authorities have been required to plan contract construction work so that it is balanced throughout the year. For projects lasting less than one year, contractors are required to ensure that peak employment comes during the slack winter season. At the local level, County Labor Market Boards, which also control the issuance of starting permits for construction, keep a close eye on their seasonal impact and might require, for example, that a construction starting date be rescheduled from May until November. This is often feasible because technological advances have been developed that now permit construction even in severe winters.[13]

A shift to more cold-weather construction in the United States would do more than reduce seasonal unemployment. According to the U.S. Labor Department, it would lead to substantial savings and efficiencies through reduced unemployment payments, more efficient use of capital and equipment, and reduced inflationary pressures, which would more than offset the estimated cost increase of 1-2 percent.[14]

In Sweden stepped-up government orders are not limited to construction. Machinery and equipment orders, for example, have sometimes been stepped up; advance orders have also occasionally been targeted to specific industries experiencing difficulties, such as engineering and textiles, in order to gain time for consultation or to arrange for other work for employees threatened with layoffs.

Maintaining Employment: New in the 1970s

In contrast to methods that create new employment, during the recessions of the 1970s, Sweden developed several ways to prevent layoffs or speed up hiring that directly subsidized firms. These include the stockpiling subsidy, the in-plant training grant, and the new-recruitment grant.

Stockpiling Subsidy. The stockpiling subsidy, used temporarily in both the recessions of the 1970s, was designed to prevent layoffs by enabling firms to maintain production despite falling demand.[15] Most of the decline was the result of the slack in exports caused by international recessions. In brief, the policy encouraged the accumulation of manufactured and semimanufactured goods that could not be sold immediately.

Subsidies as high as 20 percent of the value of the increase in the firm's inventory were granted—provided employment did not decline during the period of support. The firm also had to be located in an area affected by unemployment or by the risk of unemployment. The subsidy provided an important cushion against the impact of the international recessions on domestic employment and production. It was also hoped that when foreign recovery came, Sweden would be ready to fill export orders quickly, whereas firms in other countries would need time to gear up to meet the rising demand. This strategy worked approximately as planned during the first —relatively short—recession. The second recession of the 1970s, from which recovery was expected in 1976, lasted longer and was deeper than had been anticipated. This led to large-scale inventory accumulation. Although stockpiles were eventually reduced, in some cases the excess had to be sold at much lower prices.[16]

In-Plant Training Subsidy. The in-plant training subsidy was another new approach developed in the 1970s to prevent layoffs. Instead of continuing the same level of production, it aims to use slack periods for worker education. Companies hit by an economic crisis that withdrew a planned layoff and provided training instead of resorting to layoffs or firings were eligible for training grants of 25 kronor per student hour.[a] This was reduced to 20 kronor per student hour in 1979. Educational programs of up to 960 hours have to be jointly developed by management and unions. Part of the education has to be general and unrelated to the work tasks. The need for these grants is assessed by AMS on the basis of data jointly submitted by companies and unions.

In-plant training grants started in a minor way in 1974 under the Social Democrats. In February 1977 the new center-right coalition raised the subsidy from 8 kronor to 25 kronor an hour, and the program expanded greatly. During 1977 and 1978, at one time or another, a total of about 200,000 employees—a little more than 5 percent of the labor force—spent some time in in-plant worker education covering a wide range of subjects.[17] Programs ran the gamut from purely vocational training for upgrading or for different work, to courses in employee participation in decision making, occupational health and safety, and the issue of women's equality.

Some problems did arise. Instructions were not always followed; in a few cases firms were paid for more hours than were actually justified; and in some cases production continued unchanged despite the subsidy, which simply turned the subsidy into a direct payment to the company. However, these abuses were infrequent and, on the whole, the program proved to be very popular. Companies gained through increasing the quality of their labor force. Workers preferred avoiding the trauma of unemployment and the ability to use time that would otherwise be idle to enhance their skills and for general education. There was also a saving in unemployment benefits that would have been paid.

In-plant training has become a permanent though little-used tool against unemployment. Rules have been tightened, and employers must pay for each participant's first forty hours of training. Also, the hourly subsidy has not been increased from 20 kronor, which means that its real value has eroded. Thus in-plant training has become relatively more expensive for firms to use as a method of preventing layoffs.[18]

New-Recruitment Grants. While the stockpiling and in-plant training subsidies were both designed to maintain employment, the recruitment grant, introduced temporarily in mid-1978, aimed to speed up new hiring.[19]

Companies that increased the size of their work force through new recruitment were eligible for grants of varying size, depending on the date of hiring. For employees newly hired in the third quarter of 1978, the subsidy

[a]One Swedish *krona* was worth approximately $0.22 in 1977 and 1978, $0.23 in 1979 and also in 1980. After a devaluation in September 1981, it was worth approximately $0.18.

was 12,000 kronor; in the fourth quarter it was 8,000 kronor, and in the first quarter of 1979 it was 4,000 kronor. To keep firms from simply hiring and firing, each new employee had to represent a net increase in employment from the date of hiring until mid-1979, when the subsidy became payable. The Employment Service also had to be notified in advance of the firm's intent to recruit so that it could try to place a jobless person in work. Finally, in a provision targeted to help inexperienced young people, thirty hours of work training, jointly agreed on by management and union, also had to be given.

The program was publicized widely on television, and one positive benefit was that the Employment Service reached a new group of smaller employers. In all, some 3,700 firms, small and large, recruited 16,100 persons through the program. According to a subsequent evaluation by AMS, however, a majority of them would have been recruited even without the grant.[20]

Job Placement, Information, Guidance, and Job Training

Sweden's full-employment policy has developed in an environment characterized by major occupational, sectoral, and regional shifts in the demand for and supply of labor. In fact, the Rehn-Meidner model stressed labor mobility.[21] Full employment was to be accompanied by a movement from less to more productive jobs. In this dynamic labor market, the public Employment Service was assigned a major role.

The Employment Service, administered by AMS, has district and local offices throughout Sweden, as well as mobile units that serve sparsely populated areas. Among its clients are the middle-aged man who has become unemployed because of a plant closing, the housewife who wants to work, the youngster who cannot find a job, and the disabled worker with no idea of how to earn a living. Depending on the needs of the individual, the Employment Service can help with job placement, information, guidance, and rehabilitation.

Job Placement. A Swede who is jobless or wants to change jobs has a strong incentive to visit the Employment Service office. As in the United States, recipients of unemployment benefits must be registered job seekers. In contrast to the United States, however, with a few minor exceptions, private employment agencies are not permitted, so the Employment Service is an important source of job information as well as the initial source for all other services that might ultimately lead to job placement.

Nevertheless, with too few and too limited a variety of job listings, the Employment Service was unable to serve all job seekers adequately. It was more likely to be notified about blue- than white-collar jobs and was notified about only 60 percent of regular job openings (excluding relief jobs).[22] The situation bore a slight resemblance to the even greater limitation of the public labor exchange in the United States, where the Job Service (formerly also called the Employment Service) gets only a fraction of job openings and overwhelmingly handles low-wage jobs. The average placement wage in fiscal 1980 was only $3.99 an hour, not much above that year's $3.10 an hour federal minimum wage.[23]

To facilitate placement and to reduce frictional unemployment, it was considered essential for the Swedish Employment Service to have better information and a wider coverage of job openings. In 1976 pilot studies were initiated for the compulsory notification of job openings with the Employment Service in several counties. The findings were positive: a 40-percent increase in listings, favorable employer reaction, and an increase in the number and variety of job seekers using the service.

As a result, the mandatory listing of most jobs lasting more than ten days was extended by legislation to the whole country. There are some exceptions, such as managerial jobs and jobs that the employer intends to fill with an existing employee or with a member of the employer's family, as well as jobs for political or religious organizations that presuppose certain convictions. Mandatory job listing does not mean mandatory hiring. The employer still does the hiring and is not obligated to employ persons referred by the Employment Service. Other forms of recruiting still exist, such as newspaper ads, personal contacts, employer recruiting, and so forth. The Employment Service, however, must be notified first of any vacancies.

LO supported this measure; but SAF opposed it, motivated by a generalized opposition to a weakening of what it perceived to be an employer's prerogative. Possibly a fear of mandatory hiring was also involved, since many employers thought of Employment Service referrals as less desirable—as persons who could not get jobs themselves. Since the Employment Service, like its U.S. counterpart, services a disproportionate number of those with a weak labor-market position, a company that did not list certain jobs—or any jobs—could automatically curb the number of applications from women, the handicapped, immigrants, and youths, and thus could engage in a subtle form of discrimination.

Mandatory job listing is helping to change the negative image of the Employment Service, has expanded the range of job openings, has attracted more job seekers in all occupations, has improved the Employment Service's ability to serve more groups, and has enhanced the Labor Market Board's job-planning function. It benefits both employers and job seekers through reducing job-search and recruiting time and costs.

How do the job listings actually work? Consider the job seeker who comes to the Employment Service. He or she first sees a placement officer.

As in the United States, in some offices openings can be checked on a computer terminal. There are also printed lists of job openings, which resemble the want-ad section of a U.S. newspaper. Job descriptions are given, as are the name and phone number of the employer and, often, those of the local trade-union representative, who can be contacted for further information. The job lists are computer based. All reported vacancies are added to the county lists, which are printed three times a week. They are supplemented twice weekly by lists covering several counties. Local job lists, as well as those from the rest of the country, are available to all job seekers. Other nationwide lists, issued less frequently, include specialized ones for teachers, for physicians, and for job openings with the national government.

While it was once considered adequate to rely on a self-service system, now it is felt that everyone who comes to an Employment Service office should at least be offered some personal assistance. If a particular kind of job is not available, the placement officer might discuss other possibilities. Free telephones are available at the cheerfully decorated centers for job seekers who want to contact, employers on their own. Others can get help in making contacts, something that proved necessary for foreigners not fluent in Swedish and for young people, who often were too shy to phone employers by themselves.

Information. On a day-to-day basis, the Employment Service tries to match job seekers and job vacancies. But just as the Job Service in the United States has a broad range of responsibilities that goes well beyond job placement, so does the Employment Service in Sweden.

Information about training possibilities, vocational guidance, unemployment benefits, and subsidies available to workers moving to another part of Sweden comes from the Employment Service. It also serves the special needs of immigrants, the handicapped, students, and vocational counselors from compulsory school to university. For example, groups of students are often given information and brochures about job placement, relief work, labor-market training centers, guidance, and unemployment benefits. Many informational brochures are available in a variety of languages, and in some larger cities there are interpreters. Advertisements, slides, and television films inform other audiences about available services and fields of employment.

Brochures also provide information about programs available to firms. As in the United States, employment officers also visit firms to discuss recruitment and the employment of groups with special problems. When a firm requires large-scale recruitment, the Employment Service can provide special assistance.

Guidance. Finding a job may be a relatively simple task—check the job list, pick up the phone, report for an interview, and start to work—but not always. Therefore, the Employment Service also provides individualized job planning and guidance for persons with employment problems or for new entrants or reentrants into the labor market. With few ideas about their qualifications, their potentials, or the workings of the job market, the handicapped, youths, housewives, and older workers find this especially useful. Job planning may involve vocational training, a change of occupation, assistance to persons starting their own businesses, or special employment or rehabilitation programs for the handicapped. Employment Service specialists can provide aptitude and other psychological tests, work-capacity assessments, and medical consultations.

Although U.S. Job Service personnel are also involved in similar activities, their ability to help the jobless has more often been frustrated by the lack of listings or by the inability to meet the needs of many of the unemployed because of program restrictions. This situation has been worsened by the Reagan administration's drastic cuts in some programs and by the complete elimination of others. Moreover, services have been severely affected by budget cuts that have led to the closing of hundreds of local employment offices and large staff layoffs.

The Employment Service in Sweden has been given a large task. It is clear that whatever the problem its focus is on employment. As a Swedish official put it: "We hold that an unemployed person who visits an Employment Service office should always have some kind of assistance. Otherwise we run the risk that the Employment Service Office will be regarded as an unemployment center."[24]

Job Training. Sometimes the Employment Service recommends job training. Sweden's extensive and permanent but flexible system of labor-market training, called AMU (*arbetmarknadsutbildning*), is a long-established and integral part of its full-employment policy.[25] Although it expanded greatly during the recession of the 1970s, it is important to realize that AMU is not simply a crisis measure. Ongoing labor-market training is considered essential if a dynamic economy characterized by structural changes is to attain full employment. The Rehn-Meidner model recognized its pivotal role. As the supply and demand for certain skills shifts, as obsolete technology is replaced, as some sectors of the economy expand while others contract, as new firms are formed while others go out of business, training and retraining of labor are considered absolute necessities. There are several important reasons for this: to prevent unemployment of displaced workers; to ensure an ample supply of workers with the required skills for the available jobs; and to gain more equality for regions and groups with more severe labor-market problems, so that they can catch up with the rest of the country.

Labor-market training aims to make it easier for people to find work. The main emphasis is vocational—to provide skills needed for gainful employment.

Who is eligible? An interesting philosophy is evident here. In general a person must either be unemployed or be considered hard to place or in danger of becoming unemployed. The latter category might include a worker whose recent back trouble signals the need to shift from a job involving heavy lifting to less strenuous work. Unlike the United States, where training programs have often been linked to relief (for example, the Work Incentive Program—WIN—for applicants or recipients of AFDC), or limited to the economically disadvantaged (for example, Title II of CETA and almost all of CETA after 1978), Sweden does not link training to public assistance, nor is eligibility income tested. As with relief jobs, there are no separate programs for the poor, although the special training needs of various groups and individuals are given careful consideration. The housewife with little or no experience who wants to work, even if her husband has an income, and the handicapped are included as much as the jobless worker in need of retraining because of a plant closing, or the university graduate in a field with too few jobs.

There is also a limited amount of training for which employed workers may be considered. This so-called bottleneck training for shortage occupations is geared toward preventing or eliminating labor shortages, most of which occur during periods of economic expansion. Like many labor-market tools, it is anti-inflationary in intent. By allowing for a smoother economic expansion than would otherwise be possible, bottleneck training prevents sectoral shortages that could lead to escalating costs.

Labor-market training is designed for adults. It is not meant to conflict with the existing educational system. Thus, as a rule, trainees have to be 20 years old or over. Exceptions are usually made for handicapped, for foreign refugees, and for parents with children to support. With the rise in youth unemployment, some programs were developed for youngsters under 20 years old.

How does someone find out about labor-market training? An unemployed person may have heard about it from family members, co-workers, or friends, or in other informal ways, since the program is an integral part of Swedish society. Formal information and placement come from the Employment Service, which decides whether trainees—all of whom must be registered as job seekers—meet the qualifications. Afterwards, it helps them find employment.

Training is free, and a grant covers the cost of course materials. Trainees also receive a taxable stipend, indexed to the inflation rate, that varies with entitlement to unemployment benefits. In 1981 this ranged from 155 to 210 kronor a day for five days a week for those aged 20 and over.[26] (In 1980 the average industrial worker earned about 300 kronor a day.[27]) Persons who are eligible for regular unemployment benefits or have exhausted them get up to 11/12 of their most recent income from work, within the set minimum and maximum. Others automatically receive the minimum.

Young people under 20 who are not entitled to regular unemployment benefits receive a smaller stipend, 75 kronor a day in 1981, unless they have children to support. Trainees who do not live near the training center may also receive additional subsistence and a travel allowance. Different rules apply to in-plant trainees. As already noted, as employees they receive regular pay and benefits, while the firms receive the training subsidy.

Most courses are arranged by the National Board of Education at the request of AMS, which determines their scope, scale, vocational emphasis, and location. The National Board of Education is responsible for their administration and educational, technical, and financial management. Costs are defrayed from a special AMS-administered fund.

AMS bases its request for courses on a national plan that uses information gathered by the County Labor Market Boards. Every year a plan is developed with input from a joint advisory delegation made up of representatives of AMS, the National Board of Education, LO, SAF, TCO, and SACO/SR.

The plan is not rigid. Changes can be made during the year to meet unforeseen needs. The active participation of labor and management at the local level is an integral part of the process, since each county has tripartite course and special-training committees, the latter for various trades and occupations.

This sort of training is usually given at the more than fifty Labor Market Training Centers located throughout Sweden. Individual courses are also given in many other places. Most courses are vocational, but some are purely preparatory because many trainees know little about the labor market or their own potential. A popular course of this sort that lasts about four weeks is entitled "Working Life and Education"; this has also been adapted for various groups with special problems. (Since 1980 this has been given at the Labor Market Institutes discussed in chapter 8.) It combines intensive vocational guidance with short periods of practical experience in different kinds of jobs at different workplaces or at the center. The aim is to give trainees a better idea of the kind of work they might like. For example, a trainee might choose to work in an optician's office, to draw maps in a municipal office, and to spend time in a dental laboratory before selecting a specific vocational course.

Compensatory general education is often necessary before vocational training can begin, especially for those with little formal education. Many middle-aged and older trainees have had no more than six to eight years of formal schooling. They get a special eight-week nonvocational course that covers subjects such as Swedish, civics, English, mathematics, physics, and chemistry. Additional academic preparation is often required before entering training for certain occupations. For example, technical subjects might be prerequisites for studying electronics and other related trades, whereas more English and Swedish are often given in preparation for studying office occupations. Special courses lasting up to about sixteen weeks have been developed for these situations.

Vocational courses mostly range in length from two to seventy-two weeks. One-year courses are common, especially in mechanical trades and office occupations. A few courses take two years or longer. Approved curricula have been developed for about four hundred different occupations, and at any given time about three hundred of them are in use in various parts of Sweden.

Flexibility is the keynote at the centers. In order to permit the unemployed to start job training without unnecessary delay, courses are structured, when feasible, to admit students at frequent intervals. This is possible because classes are small—usually having no more than fifteen to twenty students—and there is heavy use of specially developed self-instructional and self-testing materials to supplement traditional teaching methods. Independent study, with tests and teaching highly individualized, is typical of labor-market training. This is useful not only because of the flexible admission policy but because of the wide difference in the backgrounds, experience, and aptitudes of students, who can work at their own pace. In any labor-market training center, traditional instruction goes on in some classes; but in most classes students work by themselves under the guidance of a specially trained teacher who gives help as required. Training time is forty hours a week, the same as working hours in Sweden.

Since the students' backgrounds vary, the range of skill levels taught must be broad enough to encompass those with considerable education as well as those with little. In the Labor Market Training Center in Östersund, in northern Sweden, for example, there are classes in traditional skills such as typing, automotive mechanics, and cooking. Since the late 1960s there has also been a university-level environmental course that concentrates on noise-, water-, and air-pollution control and is useful to unemployed engineers and others with the appropriate background.[28] In southern Sweden, at the Furulund Labor Market Training Center—not far from the historic university city of Lund—there is a two-year professional-level course in optometry to which a few carefully selected students are admitted, among them university graduates with different backgrounds.[29]

Labor Market Centers also have courses for immigrants in the Swedish language. Formerly they had a specially adapted ten-week course in working life and education, which has also been transferred to the Labor Market Institutes. The physically, socially, and mentally handicaped—about one-third of the trainees—can often take ordinary courses; but special preparatory courses are also given, as necessary, depending on the handicap.[30]

If it seems more appropriate, training can also be taken in the regular educational system. Consider a newly divorced, middle-aged woman entering the job market with only seven years of education.[31] She might first be placed in a working-life and education course at a Labor Market Institute and then in a preparatory course designed to refresh her memory of what she once learned in school; but the local Employment Service might feel that if she is to find permanent work, she will have to finish compulsory schooling (grades 7-9). Thus it could approve training grants for attendance at an adult municipal school, where she could complete her schooling in about one and a half years. Afterwards, still receiving the grants, she might be placed in an upper-secondary-school vocational course for about the same amount of time. With such a long-range training plan, a job-placement officer would be in close contact with her during the entire period to make sure her schooling was going well; and the grant would be made one stage at a time.

In addition to the in-plant training subsidy introduced in the 1970s to prevent layoffs, there are other kinds of in-plant training that are permanent instruments of labor-market policy. These include training of the handicapped, who are hard to place, and training for regional-development purposes.

In recent years labor-market training has undergone certain significant changes in addition to the extensive use of in-plant training to prevent layoffs. Until 1980 some special courses were developed for teenagers. The proportion of women has also jumped sharply, from a bare 15 percent of all trainees in 1960 to 53 percent in 1970.[32] During the rest of the 1970s, in most years, they continued to make up half or slightly more of all trainees.[33] Finally, in addition to the extensive use of in-plant training to prevent layoffs, there has been a secular increase in the number of people enrolled in labor-market training courses; and more extensive use has been made of labor-market training as a major countercyclical tool. Table 6-1 shows both tendencies. In both 1966 and 1976, for example, the jobless rate was 1.6 percent, and the average number of unemployed was quite similar; but the average number of persons in labor-market training, excluding in-plant training, had about doubled by 1976. The countercyclical quality can be appreciated by observing the large expansion in training programs during recession years, especially 1971-1973 and 1978. In this respect Sweden differs considerably from the United States. As labor economists Vernon Briggs, Allan King, and Ray Marshall (secretary of labor during the Carter administration in the United States) note, "there has been a tendency to reduce training commitments during recessions, believing that it is superfluous to train people when there exists an abundant number of unemployed people."[34] Many European nations rejected that view during the 1970s; and, according to a study by the National Commission on Manpower Policy, Sweden was the most committed to the expansion of training during periods of recession.[35] It is considered desirable to use time that would otherwise mean unemployment to build the skills of the labor force and to prevent the human damage caused by unemployment.

In the early 1980s the number of people in relief jobs and labor-market training, as well as in firm-oriented measures, was decreased rather than increased in a weakening economy. The rising unemployment that resulted contributed to the victory of the Social Democrats in 1982.

The results of labor-market training are usually regarded as positive. Most people who begin training complete it. About 75 percent of these graduates are employed within three to six months, 80 percent of them at work for which they have been trained. There is some cyclical variation. In the recession of the late 1970s, about 70 percent were working within six months.[36]

Table 6-1 shows the average number of people in government-created relief jobs, as well as in labor-market training. It gives some indication of the magnitude of Sweden's commitment to fight unemployment, even in years in which unemployment was hovering around 2 percent, a figure not seen in the United States since World War II.

Even with unemployment that low, joblessness in Sweden was a bigger problem in the 1970s than a decade earlier. In 1968 and 1978 unemployment was 2.2 percent. In 1968, however, 59 persons were in relief jobs and labor-market training combined for every 100 who were unemployed. In 1978, on the other hand, the ratio was 95 persons in these special programs for every 100 of the jobless. That is, nearly as many were in labor-market training and relief jobs as were out of work. These figures actually understate the number of persons helped by *all* forms of training, job creation, and job maintenance. They do not include in-plant trainees; beneficiaries of other job-maintenance programs, such as workers in plants that received stockpiling subsidies; or handicapped persons in special programs for the disabled. (For example, in 1978 the number of persons in special programs for the disabled averaged about 45,000, whereas in 1977 and 1978 a total of about 100,000 workers a year also received some in-plant training.)

Geographic Mobility

Despite all these efforts, some jobless workers may not be able to secure employment unless they relocate. The Rehn-Meidner model assumed that geographic as well as occupational mobility would be necessary to achieve full employment. This was also an anticipated effect of the solidaristic wage policy. Workers from areas with high unemployment would migrate to jobs in regions with labor shortages. These workers, Meidner and Rehn reasoned, should be assisted in their job-seeking efforts and should not have to bear the costs of relocation, especially since their mobility would contribute to the nations's faster economic growth and more efficient use of resources.[37] Consequently, since the late 1950s a variety of mobility grants have been an integral part of the AMS arsenal of weapons against unemployment.

Grants and Allowances. Swedes who are unemployed or in danger of being unemployed—perhaps because of an impending plant closing—can get a great deal of assistance to ease the financial burdens and personal adjustments that stem from moving to another area.[38] To qualify, a worker must be unable to get a job within a reasonable distance from home and must be registered with the Employment Service.

These grants and allowances take various forms. A jobless worker may receive travel and subsistence allowances that cover the cost of checking out opportunities elsewhere. Their wives' and husbands' costs are also covered because it has been found that workers with spouses who are dissatisfied with the new communities are more likely to quit their new jobs.

What if a worker does decide to relocate? In that case AMS pays the family's moving and travel expenses and, if necessary, an allowance for the expense of temporarily maintaining two households for up to six months or, under special circumstances, for nine months. When a family moves, there are usually additional household expenses. The old rug may be the wrong size, or the drapes may not fit the new windows. Therefore, an additional starting grant is provided for curtain money. This grant was 3,000 kronor for single workers and 6,000 kronor for married workers in 1981.[39] As in the United States, a jobless worker who lives in a declining area may find it difficult to sell a home. Although it is a small program, AMS can even buy the home of a worker who agrees to take a job in another part of Sweden. This program not only helps those who would otherwise be unable to sell their homes. It also prevents an unemployed worker from being forced to sell at a financial loss. Afterwards, AMS sells these homes—often for vacation use, since they are mostly in rural areas.

In addition to these resettlement grants, workers who continue to live at home but accept employment outside their home districts can get daily travel allowances.

Issues. Clearly, an unemployed worker benefits from these generous and extensively used relocation allowances, which in the 1970s were granted to about 20,000 Swedish workers annually.[40] In the United States that would be the equivalent of about 500,000 workers; but an unemployed U.S. worker who wants to seek a job elsewhere typically gets little assistance. (A minuscle number has received relocation allowances under the Trade Adjustment Assistance program.) Yet despite their widespread use in Sweden, there is less than complete satisfaction with mobility grants.

One criticism concerns their adequacy. A study by an Expert Group for Labor Market Research, released in 1978 by the Swedish Ministry of Labor, found that, even considering the grants, removals to other regions have often meant sacrifices or only small gains to the individual, but considerable gains to society as a whole.[41] Since the beginning of 1982, mobility grants have been tax-free, which greatly enhances their real value.

Migration obviously entails social as well as economic adjustments. In fact, fully 35 percent of one group of migrants studied had returned to their original district within five years. To improve this situation, the Expert Group recommended that more public resources should be allocated to helping migrants adjust to their new living and working conditions. For some people, however, reverse migration might be the best solution. Thus the Expert Group also recommended that mobility grants should be given to migrants who wish to pull up stakes and return to their home areas. This solution, they reasoned, would be fairer to those who regretted their initial decision to move and would make others more willing to try geographic mobility as a possible solution to their employment problems.

Another, perhaps more basic, criticism questions migation as a solution to the problem of unemployment. Uprooting workers and separating families and friends, after all, is only one possible solution. Bringing jobs to economically depressed areas is another.

Regional Development

In the 1960s popular opposition to the policy of migration mounted in the north from Swedes who did not want to pull up stakes. AMS was decried as a travel agency whose initials were said to stand for *All Must Southwards*—in Swedish, *Alla Måste Söderut*. Regional development became a hot topic. The Center party, which had originally championed regional development, gained enormous support when it made regional-development policy a leading political issue. Then, under political pressure, the Social Democrats also espoused regional development as an approach to unemployment.[42] As a result, since the mid-1960s the government has put considerable emphasis on developing jobs in areas with the most severe unemployment—and in equalizing interregional economic, social, and cultural gaps.

The Strategy. Regional assistance was not an entirely new approach, since relief work had traditionally been used more extensively in northern Sweden than elsewhere.[43] Other policies were subsequently added, however; and their main thrust was to stimulate private job development in depressed areas. The use of investment reserves in these areas is encouraged, and an array of support measures are offered to new and expanding companies—loans and grants for investment in plant and equipment, subsidies for in-plant training of new workers, and employment subsidies. Transportation subsidies help to reduce the high cost of shipping goods out of the north.

Regional-development planning has gone through a number of stages, starting with the division of the country into two parts: a development area eligible for special support, and the rest of the country. The development area had about two-thirds of the land—from the far north to the upper-middle part of Sweden—but only about 15 percent of the population. It was then divided into an inner and an outer aid area. The former, with more pervasive problems, received relatively more assistance. Later, border areas and a few depressed localities in the south—the so-called gray zone—also became eligible for assistance. Finally, in 1979 Parliament divided these areas into six regions for purposes of development support, considering factors such as population trends, the labor-force participation rate, and the employment situation. The grants are now diversified, with relatively more aid going to Area Six, the far north, and the least going to Area One (similar to the former grey zone), which might still be eligible for some support. For example, in Area Six a firm might be able to get grants covering up to 70 percent of building costs. In Area One, however, an eligible firm can get only a maximum of 10 percent.

Assistance can be given to both new and existing companies in industrial and related activities, as well as to tourist and service enterprises. In order to qualify for support, the investment must be potentially profitable and must not harm existing enterprises. Initially the emphasis was on investment in plant and equipment, but gradually more attention came to be paid to the actual lasting employment impact of the project.

Thus employment subsidies are an important part of the strategy. They are targeted to *increases* in employment rather than to total employment. Hence they are only granted for *increasing* the number of persons on the payroll and for maintaining that increase. Area Six gets the largest employment subsidies—130,000 kronor over a seven-year period for every man-year the firm increases and maintains employment. As a safeguard, the subsidy is payable annually rather than all at once. Firms in Areas Four and Five may be eligible for smaller grants, but those in other areas are not eligible for employment subsidies of this sort.

Because employment opportunities for women have been especially poor in the north, regional support is given only to firms that provide employment for at least 40 percent persons of each sex. (This is discussed in greater detail in chapter 7.)

Another part of the regional strategy is to slow down the growth of Sweden's three largest cities (Stockholm, Göteborg, and Malmö) and to build up smaller communities that will be able to provide work, services, and a good environment for their inhabitants. This should help curb migration; or, if someone must move from a sparsely inhabited rural area or small town, the move will not necessarily involve a great distance, a change in region or county, or a drastic change in life-style.

The country has been divided up into a structural plan for developing all of Sweden. In addition to the three largest cities, there are 23 designated primary centers (one in each county), as well as 70 secondary and 278 tertiary centers.

The goal is to stimulate development in primary centers rather than in the largest cities. Industry is to be built in clusters for greater economic viability and in order to provide each center's inhabitants with a greater variety of jobs. There has also been an attempt to decentralize government employment, which is quite concentrated. Some central-government authorities have already been relocated out of Stockholm.

Secondary and tertiary centers are much smaller communities, which will not be able to provide as complete an array of employment opportunities and services as the primary centers. They will be developed more extensively than at present, however. The aim is to make them more attractive places in which to live and work. Tax-equalization grants help local governments with inadequate tax bases provide adequate community services.

How Successful Is the Policy? How extensive and how successful has Sweden's development policy been? There is no doubt that AMS expenditures on regional-development assistance have risen sharply. Between 1963 and 1966 these expenditures rose from zero percent of the AMS budget to more than 10 percent, and from fiscal 1969-1970 to fiscal 1977-1978 they averaged 11 percent.[44] Between mid-1965 and the end of 1978, 1,876 firms received a total of 5.8 billion kronor in regional-development support, nearly 80 percent as loans and the rest in the form of grants and subsidies. The government reported that 51,000 jobs had been created as a result of this policy, a number equal to a little more than 1 percent of the labor force.[45] In the United States that would be equivalent to more than 1 million jobs.

When jobs come to the north, there is no erosion of working standards, since workers are unionized throughout Sweden and the north is not a low-wage area. This contrasts with the United States, where firms often go South mainly to avoid unions and to pay lower wages. Since development subsidies are financed by the central government, localities do not have to compete with each other by offering low taxes as an incentive to firms. This common practice on the part of states and localities in the United States often causes them to have revenues that are too low to finance adequate services.

In the 1970s migration often took the form of movement into the primary centers rather than from north to south. Gösta Rehn points out that between 1965 and 1979 development policy helped manufacturing employment in the north to grow by about 75 percent while it declined in the rest of the country.[46] Nevertheless, as an LO report concluded, the main impact has not been to eliminate the differences but to prevent them from worsening.[47]

The persistence of regional differences can be seen by comparing the unemployment rate in the northern two-thirds of Sweden with the average in the three metropolitan counties that contain the three largest cities. In 1970 it was 91 percent higher in the forestry counties in the north than in the metropolitan counties. In 1978 it was still 89 percent higher. Because of the recession, unemployment rates had risen in both areas, from 2.3 percent to 2.7 percent in the north and from 1.3 to 1.5 percent in the metropolitan counties. Although the labor-force participation rate had risen in the north, it still lagged behind the cities.[48]

There are a number of reasons for this situation. Job expansion through development policy has had to offset the loss of employment in other important sectors. Forestry, for example, has been rationalized. Thus although productivity has risen, forestry now employs fewer workers. Long-term problems beset other industries that are concentrated in the north. As in the United States, the steel industry has suffered from structural problems. Nor have the recessions in the last half of the 1970s helped. They made it more difficult to create new jobs anywhere, let alone in the north. Increasingly, moreover, Swedish-based multinationals simply invest outside of Sweden.

Therefore, despite generous subsidies, firms often prefer not to locate in the north. Among the various reasons they offer are marketing problems caused by being so far from central Europe; high transportation costs, even with subsidies; a desire to remain close to decision-making centers and important people in the larger cities; and difficulties in recruiting scientists and engineers.[49]

In line with this last reason, SACO/SR does not support efforts to decentralize central-government employment.[50] Although in the long run greater reliance on local recruiting may be possible, in the short run decentralization often entails some transfer of professionals to other locations. Professionals in SACO/SR used to be quite mobile as they moved up in their careers. They are now less inclined toward mobility than in the past, partly because the emergence of the two-earner family has complicated matters. A geographical move often means that a spouse must also look for another job. For some, such as physicians and teachers, this is not a great problem, since they can get employment anywhere in Sweden. For others, opportunities may be limited in smaller communities. More home ownership may also make some reluctant to move.

Private firms have much of the power to affect regional development through their investment-location decisions. The inducements are offered, but companies are free to accept or reject them. Since 1976 the government has at least voluntarily gotten large companies to *consider* regional development policy as early as possible in the planning of their investment projects. A company may, nevertheless, decide not to go north.

In 1979 the government renewed its own earlier commitment to regional policy when Parliament approved a new, 7.4-billion-kronor, five-year program for regional development, later adjusted to 8.2 billion kronor.[51] Many in the north and elsewhere feel it still is not enough to eliminate that region's employment problems. Thus for the foreseeable future, moving workers to jobs and jobs to workers both remain integral parts of Sweden's full-employment policy.

Advance Warning

Part of Sweden's ability to maintain low unemployment lies in its system of advance warning. An employer cannot simply announce on a Friday afternoon that a plant is closing permanently and will not reopen next week, nor can a permanent retrenchment or temporary layoff be carried out in such a fashion. A Swedish worker who is threatened with a job loss receives a great deal of protection, with the emphasis on preventing unemployment *before* it happens. The 1970s was a period of sweeping labor legislation, and many of that decade's laws spell out these protections. Noncompliance is rare.

The Security of Employment Act, in effect since 1974, requires reasonable cause for dismissal and mandates that advance warning be given to the employee and to the union.[52] In the case of a planned layoff due to lack of work or for other economic reasons, the union must be notified at least one month in advance. A worker must always be given at least one month's notice and, in turn, is required to give an employer one month's notice before leaving a job. Actually, most workers are entitled to more than a month's notice. If they have been employed by a company for at least six consecutive months or for a total of twelve months in the previous two years, different rules apply. Then the length of the notice varies with age, rising from one month for those under 25 years old up to six months for those 45 years old and over, with seniority determining the order of the layoff. A worker who questions the validity of his or her dismissal can go to one of Sweden's Labor Courts for a prompt hearing if the dispute cannot be resolved by other means.

Under the Codetermination Act, which went into effect in 1977, personnel cuts cannot be implemented until negotiations with the union take place.[53] All decisions related to the cuts are subject to negotiation, including the number of jobs to be eliminated. In the United States in a similar situation, even if there is a union, it may not be able to judge an employer's claims.[54] A Swedish union, however, is legally entitled to financial and other information that may be needed for a proper evaluation of the company's situation. Is the layoff justified? If the union thinks it is not and cannot convince the employer, an appeal can be made to the Labor Court, which is empowered to modify or postpone a layoff.

The County Labor Market Board plays a pivotal role in the advance warning system. The Promotion of Employment Act, in effect since 1974, requires that the County Labor Market Board be notified of any impending dismissals or layoffs involving five or more workers. In the case of dismissals the notification period varies from two months if not more than twenty-five employees are involved to six months if more than twenty-five workers are affected. Temporary layoffs require one month's notice.[55]

Including the County Labor Market Board in the early-warning system gives it time to try to minimize the extent of unemployment and the hardships associated with it. As soon as notice is given, the Employment Service is triggered into action. When there is a large cutback or a plant closing, additional Employment Service staff may be deployed from other areas to the affected locality.

The County Labor Market Board or the Employment Service then quickly brings together its own personnel and all interested parties, including the union, management, affected workers, and municipal-government officials. The purpose of this meeting is to explain the myriad forms of assistance that are available. This often leads to the formation of a joint consultation group that works as a team to tailor the different labor-market programs to the specific needs of the workers.[56]

The exact details vary from one situation to another, but it is not unusual for the Employment Service to move right into a workplace when a large personnel cut or plant closure is involved. The Employment Service may even install a computer terminal right on the premises with the most up-to-date information on job vacancies throughout Sweden. Particular attention is paid to the needs of the most vulnerable workers—those who would have the toughest time finding other jobs. The handicapped and the elderly are in this category and receive special protection under the promotion of Employment Act. Unless a firm shuts down, they are usually retained.

The early-warning system gives the Employment Service valuable time to arrange for retraining while the workers who have received notice are still on the job, to help them with a thorough job search, and to alert potential employers to their availability. Everyone who works for the company, not just those slated to be terminated, is eligible for help in finding a job. This is important because some of them may find other work, and the resulting attrition may greatly reduce the need for dismissals.

Advance warning also provides time to see if the dismissals or threatened plant closing can be averted. This is crucial when a firm dominates the local labor market, which is not uncommon in Sweden. In these cases, after the statutory notice period is over, a firm may be given a temporary grant covering 75 percent of the wage costs to enable it to continue its operations a while longer. The aim is to give the Employment Service more time in which to help employees find new jobs or to arrange for them to get needed retraining. Under such circumstances *all* workers in the company are entitled to retraining or resettlement grants, not just the affected workers. The hope is that over this extended period of time, additional attrition may help to cushion the blow.

In July 1981 a new measure was introduced—an adjustment grant to firms that reduce their personnel by more than three hundred persons. Its purpose is to enable these firms to keep their employees longer than necessary under the Security of Employment Act and, at the same time, to encourage and help the workers find other work. The subsidy amounts to 75 percent of total wage costs for a maximum of six months. It is paid even for workers who leave before this period has expired, but in such cases the employee is entitled to half the previous wages. The aim is to give both employers and employees an incentive to speed up the adjustment process.[57]

If an enterprise is bankrupt and faced with imminent closure, limited support may also be granted, normally for up to six months but sometimes for as long as a year. This gives the workers more time to solve their employment problems. Sometimes the enterprise is able to work out its own problems and to carry on afterwards. A worker never is left unprotected during the required period of notice, even if a firm goes bankrupt. If that should happen, there is often some money available. Even if there is not, the government will continue wage payments for the statutory period from a special insurance fund into which employers pay. It works on the principle of guaranteed savings accounts in the United States, for which member banks pay insurance premiums.

Placing government orders with a firm facing cuts or closing is another way of buying time for the Employment Service to carry out its job-placement activities. Stockpiling subsidies and other techniques such as in-plant training, discussed earlier in this chapter, have been used during certain recessionary periods.

When a period of advance warning involves a plant closing, attempts are often made to prevent the closure. The community, as well as AMS and the union, may also get involved, since the loss of industry can be a severe blow to a local economy. In the final analysis, however, the decision to close down an operation remains a firm's prerogative. Under the Codetermination Act the union does not have the right to veto a firm's decision in such a matter. This holds true even if the facility is operating at a profit but the firm considers the rate to be inadequate. Many workers are reportedly dissatisfied with this aspect of the law, especially since most of the time the closing eventually takes place.[58]

The advance-warning period is also often used by local officials as a time to try to attract other employers into their community to make up for the anticipated loss of jobs. There is, of course, no guarantee that new business can be attracted to the area. It goes without saying that this task is more difficult during a recession.

Various tools are available, such as the release of investment-reserve funds or development subsidies, depending on the region. Workers may be retrained in advance for the skills a new employer requires, if one is found; and they can be ready to work by the time the new facility opens.

Information is invaluable in locating potential employers. Since 1976 Sweden's largest companies—those with 500 or more employees—including some subsidiaries of U.S. multinational companies, have voluntarily provided the government with detailed prospective information about their five-year investment and employment plans, as well as with semiannual updates. Informal discussions are held between government and management to try to mesh these private investment plans into the employment needs of specific areas.[59]

Even with all these efforts, some workers end up out of work. For them, there is Sweden's system of unemployment benefits.

Unemployment Benefits

Unemployment benefits appear at the end of this chapter because Swedish labor-market policies for full employment are geared toward employment rather than unemployment. Although jobless benefits are generous by U.S. standards, they make up only a small proportion of the expenditures of AMS, averaging about 9 percent in the 1970s.[60]

These benefits play an important role in maintaining income and living standards for the jobless, however. Compared with the United States, in some ways they reflect a different social philosophy concerning the unemployed.

There are two systems.[61] The older and more basic one is government subsidized but run by government-approved unemployment-insurance societies. These societies have close links to the unions, which originally created the system. Membership is compulsory for the union members and must be open to other employees, for whom it is voluntary. Since most Swedish workers belong to unions, coverage is extensive. In the late 1970s about 70 percent of the income of these societies came from the government. Member fees and employer payroll taxes financed the rest—the latter being the method of financing used in the United States.

To qualify, an unemployed worker must have belonged to a benefit society for twelve months, have worked for at least five of the previous twelve months, and be registered for work with the Employment Service. Payments, which are taxable, can go as high as 91.7 percent of former income up to a maximum that, like the labor-market training stipend, was 210 kronor per day in 1981.[62] The average payment was 200 kronor per day, or about two-thirds of the average daily income of an industrial worker.[63] Because of Sweden's high marginal rates, that figure represents a substantially higher proportion of after-tax income. Unlike the U.S. system, duration varies with age: up to age 55, benefits are payable for sixty weeks; but, in recognition of their special difficulties, those between 56 and 64 years old can collect for ninety weeks if they cannot find work; benefits cease at age 65, the normal pensionable age.

In 1974 Sweden established a complementary system, *labor-market cash assistance,* to make coverage complete. The government contributes half of the cost, and the rest comes from an employer payroll tax. It covers those who do not belong to benefit societies, as well as those 60 years old and over whose regular benefits have run out.

A unique feature, which contrasts with the U.S. system and with those of most countries, is coverage of new entrants and reentrants into the labor market. Eligibility requires that one must have worked for five of the previous twelve months. Those who have finished secondary school or the equivalent may also qualify, if they have been actively seeking work through the Employment Service for at least three months.[64] Targeted to help housewives and young people who enter the labor market but cannot find work, the underlying philosophy is that if you want to work but cannot find a job after a reasonable period of time, you should be entitled to some compensation for the loss of potential income—even if you have never worked before. The emphasis of the Employment Service, however, is still to find work or training for the recipient, since unemployment payments are not considered a real solution to the problem.

Cash assistance pays less than the basic benefits—75 kronor per day in 1981, payable for only thirty weeks.[65] Persons over 55 can receive them for sixty weeks; and those who are over 60 can receive them until their sixty-fifth birthday. This is also possible for some structurally unemployed persons who are over 55 years old.

Under both the basic unemployment and the cash-assistance programs, the jobless continue to receive health benefits, since national health insurance applies to the whole population. Also, both kinds of unemployment benefits are credited toward the national pension plan. This contrasts with the United States, where the unemployed usually lose their health benefits, and unemployment benefits are not credited toward Social Security, which can result in lower retirement benefits.

The existence of two unemployment-benefits systems is somewhat of an anomaly; and a government commission of inquiry has been established to see whether a single national system can be created. In the interim the separate systems coexist, and the hope is to minimize the number of people who must rely on them.

Continuing Challenge

Sweden's commitment to full employment is deep rooted and unending, and the pivotal role assigned to AMS stems from that commitment. The significance and status given to labor-market policies is confirmed by the funding that Parliament gives to AMS.

During the 1970s, when unemployment generally was more severe than in the 1960s, AMS was allocated a relatively larger share of government expenditures. In the last half of the 1960s, for example, AMS expenditures averaged only 5 percent of the national-government budget, compared with about 7 percent in the 1970s.[66] In fiscal 1977-1978, when unemployment was above 2 percent—considered a recession for Sweden—AMS got 9 percent of the national budget—almost as much as the 10.1 percent that went to the defense budget that year.[67] During that period Sweden was ruled by a center-right coalition. Between 1965 and 1978 AMS expenditures rose from 1 to 3 percent of GNP.[68] Thus, by comparison, in 1978 Sweden was expending almost as much of its resources on the battle for full employment as on defense expenditures, which amounted to 3.4 percent of GNP.[69]

From a U.S. perspective, continuity of funding has also been a factor that has enabled AMS to produce positive results. The uncertainty and intense political controversy over funding in the United States has always made it difficult, if not impossible, for any government agency to undertake the kind of planning that AMS does. Since most labor-market policies are administered by AMS, the overlapping and fragmentation so characteristic of U.S. policies have also been averted.

Not every policy has been equally successful, of course. Some policies are acknowledged to be stopgap measures. But it is considered preferable to have more people temporarily in training and relief jobs during a recession than openly unemployed. Nor have all unemployment problems been solved. Taken together, however, these policies have helped Sweden maintain unemployment rates that seldom exceed 2 percent. Much of the social cost and the human damage caused by unemployment has been minimized. People who are working rather than idle are producing output. And people who are learning rather than unemployed are increasing the nation's human capital as well as enhancing their own abilities.

Even when unemployment is in the 2-percent range, however, not every group fares equally well. The questions one might ask now are: Who are the groups with the employment problems? What approaches are taken to their problems?

Notes

1. Information about AMS and its policies is found in its annual reports. See, for instance, Sweden, National Labor Market Board, *Swedish Employment Policy 1979/80*, Annual Report Reprint (Solona: National Labor Market Board, 1980). Much of what follows is drawn from interviews with Bertil Rehnberg, director-general of AMS, members of the AMS staff, and representatives of other organizations—such as SAF, LO, and the Swedish Engineering Employers' Association—whose names are listed in footnotes or in the acknowledgments at the beginning of the book.

2. United Automobile, Aerospace and Agricultural Implement Workers of America (UAW), United Steelworkers of America (USW), and International Association of Machinists and Aerospace Workers (IAM), *Economic Dislocation: Plant Closings, Plant Relocations and Plant Conversions, Policies and Programs in Three Countries; Recommendations for the United States,* Joint Report of Labor Union Study Tour Participants, May 1979.

3. More details about investment funds are given in "The Swedish System of Investment Funds," *Fact Sheets on Sweden* (Stockholm: Swedish Institute, 1980), from which this section is drawn.

4. For a general description of relief work, see Sweden National Labor Market Board, *Relief Work as an Instrument of Labour Market Policy*, Labor Market Seminars (Solna: National Labor Market Board, May 1978).

5. "Swedish Labor Market Policy," *Fact Sheets on Sweden* (Stockholm: Swedish Institute, 1979), p. 3.

6. Fredrik Winter, Research Section, National Labor Market Board, personal correspondence, Solna, Sweden, 18 January 1982.

7. Sten Markusson, Swedish Confederation of Professional Associations (SACO/SR), personal interview, Stockholm, 3 September 1979.

8. Sweden, National Labor Market Board, *Jämställdhet på arbetsmarknaden: Statistik (Equality in the Labour Market: Statistics)* (Solna: National Labor Market Board, 1981). Derived from table 12, pp. 15-16.

9. Ingemund Bengtsson (then Swedish minister of labor), Testimony, U.S. Senate, Committee on Labor and Public Welfare, Subcommittee on Labor and Public Welfare, *Hearing, Labor Market Policy in Sweden,* 93rd Cong, 2d Sess., November 1974, pp. 5-7.

10. Ibid., p. 7.

11. U.S. Department of Labor, Bureau of Labor Statistics, *International Comparisons of Unemployment, Bulletin 1979* (Washington, D.C.: U.S. Government Printing Office, 1978), p. 54.

12. Ibid., p. 55.

13. The Swedish Construction Industry," *Fact Sheets on Sweden* (Stockholm: Swedish Institute, 1981), p. 2.

14. U.S. Department of Labor, Employment and Training Administration, *Employment and Training Report of the President,* Transmitted to the Congress 1979 (Washington, D.C.: U.S. Government Printing Office, 1979), pp. 210-211.

15. This section draws heavily from a personal interview with Alan Read, Research Section, National Labor Market Board, Solna, Sweden, 31 August 1979.

16. Sweden, Ministry of Economic Affairs and Ministry of the Budget, *The Swedish Budget 1979/80: A Summary* (Stockholm: Liber Förlag, 1979), pp. 14-15.

17. Bo. A. Ericsson, "The Employment Situation in Sweden: Some Main Issues Looking Ahead to the 1980s," *Election Year '79,* no. 2 (New York: Swedish Information Service, June 1979), p. 3.

18. Fredrik Winter, Research Section, National Labor Market Board, personal correspondence, Solna, Sweden, 8 December 1981.

19. This section draws heavily on a personal interview with Sten Borg, Research Section, National Labor Market Board, Solna, 31 August 1979.

20. Fredrik Winter, personal correspondence, 8 December 1981.

21. The Rehn-Meidner model is covered by Berndt Öhman, *LO and Labour Market Policy Since the Second World War* (Stockholm: Bokforlaget Prisma, 1974), and Eskil Wadensjö, "Job Creation and Job Maintenance in the Private Sector: A New Course in Labor Market Policy," Paper prepared for a conference in Padeborn, Germany, February 1979, photocopy.

22. Information about mandatory job listing draws heavily on Sweden, National Labor Market Board, *Compulsory Notification of Vacancies,* Labor Market Seminars (Solna: National Labor Market Board, May 1978), and Leif Tallskag, Research Section, National Labor Market Board, personal interview, Solna, 31 August 1979.

23. U.S. Department of Labor, Employment and Training Administration, *Employment and Training Report of the President,* transmitted to the Congress, 1981 (Washington, D.C.: U.S. Government Printing Office, 1981), p. 47.

24. Ingemund Bengtsson, *Hearing, Labor Market Policy in Sweden,* p. 4.

25. For a description of labor-market training, see Sweden, National Board of Education, *Labour Market Training* (Stockholm: LiberLärmedel, 1975), and Swedens, National Labor Market Board, *Labour Market Training in Sweden* (Solna: National Labor Market Board, May 1978), from which this section draws heavily. In August and September 1979, the author also visited Labor Market Training Centers in Östersund and in Furulund and interviewed their directors.

26. "Labor Market Policy in Sweden," *Fact Sheets on Sweden* (Stockholm: Swedish Institute, 1981), p. 3.

27. Ibid.

28. The description of the Labor Market Training Center in Östersund is based on the author's visit and interview with the director, 21 August 1979.

29. Based on the author's visit to the Labor Market Training Center, Furulund, Sweden, 7 September 1979, and on an interview with Gilbert Andersson, director.

30. National Board of Education, *Labour Market Training,* p. 5.

31. This example is based on a case study described by Eva-Len Ahlqvist, "Helping the Job-seeker: On Local Employment Offices," in *Labor Market Reforms in Sweden: Facts and Employee Views,* ed. Allan Larsson (Stockholm: Swedish Institute, 1979), pp. 44-47. This book also describes interesting on-the-scene examples of other aspects of labor-market policy such as relief work, labor market training, codetermination, and employment security.

32. National Labor Market Board, *Labor Market Training in Sweden,* p. 13; idem, *Jämställdhet på arbetsmarknaden: Statistik,* table 10, p. 13.

33. Ibid.

34. F. Ray Marshall, Allan G. King, and Vernon M. Briggs, Jr., *Labor Economics: Wages, Employment and Trade Unionism* (Homewood, Ill.: Richard D. Irwin, 1980), p. 583.

35. National Commission for Manpower Policy, *Reexamining European Manpower Policies,* Special Report no. 10 (Washington, D.C., 1976), cited in Marshall, King, and Briggs, *Labor Economics,* p. 553.

36. Jan Johannesson, *On the Outcome of Swedish Labour Market Policy from the 1960s up to 1981* (Berlin: International Institute of Management, 1982), p. 35.

37. Öhman, *LO,* chaps. 3, 4.

38. A general description of this is in *Information for Immigrants: The Public Employment Service in Sweden* (Solna: National Labor Market Board, 1978), pp. 8-9.

39. Letter to the author from Fredrik Winter, 8 December 1981.

40. "Swedish Labor Market Policy," *Fact Sheets on Sweden* (Stockholm: Swedish Institute, 1981), p. 2.

41. Sweden, Ministry of Labor, Expert Group for Labor Market Research (EFA), *Labour Market Policy in Transition:* Summary of *Arbetsmarknadspolitik i förändring,* SOU 1979:60 (Stockholm: Liber Förlag, 1978). Analysis of migration and recommendations are on pp. 39-45.

42. Wadensjö, "Job Creation," pp. 5-6.

43. Information on regional policies and planning draw heavily on a personal interview with Alan Read, National Labor Market Board, Solna, 31 August 1979.

44. EFA, *Labour Market Policy in Transition,* derived from data in table 1, pp. 8-9.

45. Sweden, Ministry of Economic Affairs and Ministry of the Budget, *The Swedish Budget 1980/81* (Stockholm: Liber Förlag, 1980), p. 116. That may be a high estimate. A more recent government study has estimated a smaller impact. Eskil Wadensjö, Swedish Institute for Social Research, Stockholm, personal correspondence, 21 December 1981.

46. Gösta Rehn (Sweden) and K. Helveg Petersen (Denmark), *Education and Youth Employment in Sweden and Denmark,* A study prepared for the Carnegie Council on Policy Studies in Higher Education, 1980, p. 88.

47. Swedish Trade Union Confederation—LO, *Report on Labour Market Policy* (Stockholm: Swedish Trade Union Confederation, 1975), p. 34.

48. Taken from and derived from Sweden, Central Bureau of Statistics, Labor Force Survey, unpublished data.

49. Gunnar Lindström, Swedish Employers' Confederation, personal interview, Stockholm, 29 August 1979.

50. Sten Markusson, Swedish Confederation of Professional Associations (SACO/SR), personal interview, Stockholm, 3 September 1979.

51. Ministry of the Budget and Ministry of Economic Affairs, *Swedish Budget 1980/81,* p. 116.

52. Sweden, Ministry of Labor, *Swedish Laws on Security of Employment: Status of Shop Steward, Litigation in Labour Disputes* (Stockholm: Ministry of Labor, 1977), pp. 1-2, 6-20.

53. See Sweden, Ministry of Labor, *Towards Democracy at the Workplace: New Legislation on the Joint Regulation of Working Life* (Stockholm: Ministry of Labor, 1977), and Swedish Trade Union Confederation, *Co-Determination in Sweden: An Up to Date Analysis of Developments and the Reforms Implemented in the 1970s* (Stockholm: Swedish Trade Union Confederation, 1979). The latter publication gives the background and discusses security of employment, representation on boards of directors, and other aspects of industrial democracy, as well as the law on codetermination.

54. For an interesting description of the process from the perspective of U.S. trade unionists, see UAW, USW, and IAM, *Economic Dislocation,* pp. 11-20, from which this section draws heavily.

55. Ministry of Labor, *Swedish Laws on Security of Employment,* pp. 21-24.

56. Description draws from UAW, USW, and IAM, *Economic Dislocation,* pp. 13-14, and Sweden, National Labor Market Board, *Measures of Labour Market Policy for a Local Employment Crisis,* Labor Market Seminars (Solna: National Labor Market Board, 1978).

57. Fredrik Winter, personal correspondence, 8 December 1981.

58. UAW, USW, and IAM, *Economic Dislocation,* p. 13.

59. Ibid., pp. 14-15.

60. Bo Jangenäs, "Employment and Labor Market Policy in Sweden During the Recession of the Late 1970s," *Current Sweden,* no. 266, February 1981 (Stockholm, Swedish Institute), calculated from table 4, p. 7.

61. For a brief description, see Lennart Forseback, *Industrial Relations and Employment in Sweden* (Stockholm: Swedish Institute, 1980), pp. 97-98.

62. Ibid., p. 97.

63. "Labor Market Policy in Sweden," *Fact Sheets on Sweden,* 1981, p. 4.

64. Sweden, National Central Bureau of Statistics, *General Description of Labour Market Policies* (Stockholm: National Central Bureau of Statistics, 1979), p. 9. This gives a complete description of eligibility. See also Sweden, National Labor Market Board, *Working in Sweden: Information for Immigrant Job Applicants in Sweden* (Solna: National Labor Market Board, 1979).

65. "Labor Market Policy in Sweden," *Fact Sheets,* 1981, p. 4.

66. Calculated from data in EFA, *Labour Market Policies in Transition,* table 1, pp. 8-9, and in Jangenäs, "Employment," figure 4, p. 7.

67. Jagenäs, "Employment," figure 4, p. 7; "The Swedish Defense," *Fact Sheets on Sweden* (Stockholm: Swedish Institute, 1971), p. 2.

68. EFA, *Labour Market Policy in Transition,* table 1, p. 9.

69. U.S. Arms Control and Disarmament Agency, *World Military Expenditures and Arms Transfers, 1970-1979* (Washington, D.C., 1982), p. 78.

7

The Disadvantaged in a Full-Employment Labor Market: Women and the Quest for Equality

The Swedish government bill of 1966, which forms the basis of labor-market guidelines, states that the aim is to "achieve and maintain full, productive and freely chosen employment."[1] That goal was reinforced and strengthened by another bill, passed by Parliament in 1976, which stresses the need to remove barriers that keep people unemployed or outside the labor market. Now the concept is *work for everyone*, and there is a recognition that this means more than simply providing jobs for those who actively seek them. As a Swedish publication expressed it, the ambition is also "to change the conditions of persons whose unemployment is of a more latent nature."[2]

The goal has not yet been translated into reality for all young people, women, immigrants, older workers, and the disabled. By U.S. standards the proportion that is unemployed in most of these groups is very small—but not by Swedish standards. Providing members of these groups with jobs and removing barriers that keep them jobless or outside the labor market are major challenges of Swedish society.

Background

As in the United States and many other industrial nations, Swedish women have been entering the labor market in record numbers. Between 1965 and 1979 women made up the entire increase in the Swedish labor force.[3] While the number of men in the labor force remained unchanged, the number of women grew by more than half a million—39 percent. The labor-force participation rate for men fell from 80.0 percent to 78.5 percent, but for women it climbed from 40.5 percent to 63.5 percent. At the beginning of this period women constituted 37 percent of the labor force; but by 1979, 45 percent of the labor force was made up of women, although many of them work only part time.

The main shift occurred among married women, and it was especially pronounced among mothers of young children. In 1965 only 36.8 percent of women with children under 7 years old (the compulsory school-starting age) were in the labor force, but by 1979 that proportion had escalated to 70.6 percent.

Like immigrants, women were welcomed into the labor force during the 1960s, with its tight labor markets. Once the trend had started, even recessions did not drive them out again. An important change in 1971 also made it more advantageous for wives to work—by taxing each individual's earned income separately.

Although Swedish women have higher unemployment rates than men, (table 7-1), that figure does not tell the whole story. Lower labor-force participation rates mask part of women's unemployment. The latent or hidden unemployed (discouraged workers) are overwhelmingly women, as are part-time workers. Latent unemployment among women, however, has declined in recent years.[4]

It is interesting to contrast the attitudes toward the unemployment of women in Sweden and the United States during the 1970s, a decade in which the labor force of both nations became increasingly feminized. In the United States the structural hypothesis came into vogue. Many policy-makers and economists considered contemporary high levels of unemployment less significant than in earlier periods because women had become a larger share of the labor force and their unemployment was considered less important than that of men. Women were viewed as not quite legitimate members of the labor force.

In Sweden, on the other hand, the response was to try to provide employment for these women, despite a softening of the job market. The underlying philosophy is expressed by the labor-market guidelines in the Swedish bill of 1966. This bill stresses the fact that the aim of full employment cannot be achieved once and for all: "Full employment can only be ensured through measures which are constantly adjusted to current requirements. Aspirations with regard to the provision of meaningful employment have risen and our efforts must be stepped up accordingly."[5]

Table 7-1
Unemployment Rates in Sweden, by Age and Sex, 1979-1981
(Percentage Unemployed)

	Both Sexes			*Male*			*Female*		
Age	*1979*	*1980*	*1981*	*1979*	*1980*	*1981*	*1979*	*1980*	*1981*
16-74	2.1	2.0	2.5	1.9	1.7	2.4	2.3	2.3	2.6
16-19	7.4	7.6	9.4	7.0	6.5	8.2	7.9	8.8	10.5
20-24	3.7	3.7	4.7	3.6	3.5	4.8	3.8	3.9	4.6
25-34	1.9	1.8	2.3	1.8	1.5	2.2	2.1	2.2	2.5
35-44	1.2	1.1	1.4	0.9	0.9	1.3	1.5	1.4	2.5
45-54	1.0	1.0	1.3	0.9	0.9	1.4	1.1	1.1	1.3
55-64	2.0	1.6	2.0	1.8	1.6	2.2	2.2	1.6	1.8
65-74	0.0	0.0	0.0	0.0	0.0	0.0	0.0	0.0	0.0

Source: Sweden, Central Bureau of Statistics, Labor Sample Survey.
Note: The *unemployment rate* is the percentage of the labor force that is unemployed.

Thus the basis of policy is the *present* aspirations of women for work—not nostalgia for the past, when women were content to stay at home. Women's right to work is to be recognized as equal to men's right to work. The policy also is geared toward those who are outside the labor market: the hidden unemployed.

The Goal of Equality between Men and Women

The official attitude of the government goes beyond a grudging recognition that women have a right to enter the labor market. It sees the goal as equality between men and women in work, home, and society. This concept was first spelled out in a 1968 report to the United Nations:

> . . . every individual, irrespective of sex, shall have the same practical op-portunities, not only for education and employment, but also in principle the same responsibility for his or her maintenance as well as a shared responsibility for the upbringing of children and the upkeep of the home.[6]

In 1972 an advisory council to the prime minister on equality between men and women was appointed, which acknowledged that measures were needed to support women in the labor market and to combat the segmenta-tion of the labor market by sex. This council was superseded in 1976 by a Parliamentary-appointed Equality Committee assigned to concentrate on long-range issues of equality and to recommend legislation.[7]

Sex Segregation in Labor Markets

The large-scale entrance of women into the labor market has not been suffi-cient to bring about equality. Sex segregation is strongly embedded in the Swedish labor market, as it is in the U.S. labor market. Three-quarters of all Swedish women were concentrated into twenty-five occupations in 1970 and into thirty occupations in 1975.[8] Women's occupations are similar to those in the United States: secretarial and clerical work, nursing, teaching, retail sales, and so on. By contrast, almost all workers in some occupations are men: electrician, engineer, machinist, carpenter, welder, and lumber-jack, to name just a few. More than half of employed women work in the public sector, compared with only one-quarter of the men. In manufactur-ing, men make up three-quarters of the work force. Just under one-fifth of women work in that sector, although it is important for immigrant women, nearly half of whom are employed in it. Since they are unlikely to work in white-collar occupations, immigrant women usually are found in different occupations than other women. Some typical occupations of immigrant women are cleaning woman and so-called male jobs such as shop mechanic and machine fitter.

Although women in general are occupationally segregated, some progress was made in the 1970s in increasing their entry into male-dominated professional and blue-collar occupations. To cite a few examples, between 1970 and 1975 the proportion of female physicians rose from 18 to 23 percent, opticians from 11 to 16 percent, precision mechanics from 8 to 13 percent, and machine fitters and repairers from 2 to 8 percent. On the other side of the coin, the proportion of male preschool teachers rose from 1 to 4 percent.[9]

Although substantial differences still persist—and despite pervasive sex segregation—considerable progress has been made in narrowing the gap between women's and men's wages. This contrasts with the United States, where under similar circumstances the earnings gap has not eroded. Unlike U.S. women, most Swedish women belong to unions and have gained from dramatic changes in union policies.

Until 1960 lower wages for women were actually written into union contracts in the private sector, although they had been abolished in the public sector considerably earlier.[10] Equal pay for equal work is now written into collective-bargaining contracts, which cover most of the labor force. In 1960 female blue-collar workers in manufacturing earned 69 percent as much an hour as men, but by 1970 that average had risen to 80 percent. By 1977 it was 87 percent.[11] Much of this improvement stems from LO's wage-solidarity policy, which emphasizes raising low wages. Women benefit because they are still concentrated in lower-wage industries and occupations, even within manufacturing. Female white-collar employees working full time in that sector made gains, but greater inequality remains. Between 1970 and 1977 the wage gap narrowed from 59 to 70 percent of male wages. This reflects women's concentration on the lower rungs of white-collar occupations. Among white-collar workers in SAF's collective-bargaining domain (which extends beyond manufacturing) women in comparable positions now earn 95 percent as much as men. With occupational segregation, however, many are not in comparable positions. Female civil servants also made gains. Between 1970 and 1976 the salaries of those affiliated with the Swedish Federation of Civil Servants rose from 66 to 80 percent of average male pay. Despite these gains, studies show that women are generally concentrated in lower positions throughout the Swedish economy and have fewer opportunities for promotion, and that women's jobs are simply given lower status and lower pay than men's occupations. Moreover, the annual earnings gap between *all* working women and men—including those women who work reduced hours—would look substantially larger than most of the figures cited. One reason is that so many women work part time—46 percent in 1980.

Policies of AMS

AMS has been actively involved in carrying out the government's equality policy by helping to provide jobs and job training for unemployed women and through outreach and regional policy, for the latent unemployed, who do not appear in the jobless statistics. Although another important objective of AMS is to work to eliminate sexual stereotyping and to make all jobs open to both men and women, it has been more successful in providing jobs and training than in breaking down sexual stereotyping.

In 1970 women held only 3 percent of all relief jobs, compared with 41 percent by 1979. At that time these female relief workers were mostly under 25. Their unemployment was most severe: 83 percent of women compared with 57 percent of men in relief work were in that age group. The rising proportion of women in relief jobs represents a conscious effort to expand opportunities for them, since the County Labor Market Boards are instructed by AMS to strive to ensure that the needs of unemployed women are considered in planning relief work. This has meant going beyond the traditional forestry and road work into a wider range of jobs, including white-collar work, social services, and especially nursing and allied occupations. The idea, says an AMS official,

> is not to extend traditional sex roles in relief work. On the contrary, we strive to use relief work so that girls and women have an opportunity to try untraditional occupations, while boys and men have an opportunity of doing traditional female work, e.g., at a nursery school or a hospital.[12]

This direction was also related to the government's desire to expand services for the elderly, the sick and disabled, and children; most such jobs have been women's work. Thus, although women are better represented, and there have been efforts—and some success—in getting men and women to try nontraditional jobs, most relief workers are still in the traditional roles.

A similar situation exists in labor-market training. Women are now well represented, even more so than in relief work. In 1979-1980, 52 percent of persons starting such training were women, compared with only 15 percent in 1959-1960.[13] Nearly half of all women starting training courses in 1979-1980 were trained for office or health-care work, however, compared with only 8 percent of the men.[14] When selections are made for training courses, priority is given to the underrepresented sex if there are applicants from both sexes. Although some progress has been made in training men in health and medical-service occupations and women in men's occupations, most trainees of both sexes still select and are trained for traditional jobs. As Berit Rollén of AMS observed, "unfortunately, we cannot yet claim that labor market training has become the instrument we would like it to be for equality."[15]

Pragmatic as well as ideological factors govern the interest AMS has in opening nontraditional jobs to women. Simply to achieve the goal of providing jobs for Swedish women—especially if the hidden unemployed are considered—necessitates widening women's employment options. Wider options are needed because the aim of Swedish labor-market policy also includes bringing jobs to those who do not appear to be unemployed according to the official statistics on unemployment. This problem is particularly severe in the north, where employment opportunities for women are most lacking, and also in the many smaller towns that dot the Swedish landscape in all regions. In such places, women's unemployment is higher; and, equally significant, their lower labor-force participation suggests another dimension of the problem. For example, 77 percent of 16- to 64-year-old women in Stockholm County were in the labor force in 1977, compared with only 65 percent of those in small towns (called municipal centers) in nonmetropolitan counties. Similar differences existed among all age groups.[16] There has been an impressive narrowing of the male-female differential in labor-force participation rates in the north and elsewhere, however,

In addition to relief work and labor-market training, AMS uses other techniques to deal with open and hidden unemployment and occupational segregation. For example, small groups of about ten women reentering the labor force after years at home are sometimes brought together in *guidance groups*.[17] For several days they are offered labor-market information and advice by a placement officer, and they gain moral support and confidence from each other. They also are encouraged to sample different kinds of jobs—including nontraditional ones—for a week at a time, as arranged for by the Employment Service, before deciding on a job or training choice. Another approach, the *Kristianstad model*, combining guidance and practice, stresses outreach and information to recruit and train women for traditionally male jobs in a local area. It was introduced in one county in the early 1970s and is now used all over the country.[18]

This works best when firms, unions, and local authorities are willing to cooperate. But without an actual local labor shortage this cooperation has been lacking. *Equality grants* have also been available since 1974 to subsidize employers who train women for men's jobs or men for women's jobs. Originally set at 8-14 kronor an hour, these subsidies did not prove enough of an inducement to stimulate the use of equality grants. In 1979 the subsidy was raised to 20 kronor an hour, and Parliament removed a restriction that there must also be a local difficulty in recruiting labor for the occupation contemplated for training. Then the number of firms using these grants rose substantially.[19]

Another technique has been especially designed for women in depressed regions like the north. Since 1974, to obtain a regional-development grant or loan, a firm has had to reserve at least 40 percent of its new jobs for each sex. In the program's first two years, women were 35 percent of all new recruits—not 40 percent because some exemptions are possible. In the first four years the proportion of women employed by firms receiving development aid rose from 17 to 22 percent.[20] AMS regards these quotas as one of its most effective instruments.[21] When firms apply for the aid, if suitably trained women are not available, arrangements are made to train them. Women in these areas, AMS feels, have been given a "better chance of asserting their right to employment in the face of prejudice and tradition."[22]

Antidiscrimination Legislation

During the 1970s many other attempts to promote equality in the labor market got under way in both private and public sectors. The most far-reaching measure is the Act on Equality between Men and Women in Working Life, which became effective on 1 July 1980.[23] The new law, which applies to all public- and private-sector employers, bans sex discrimination in hiring, promotion, and training, and calls for positive measures to promote equality. Part of the law calls for positive discrimination—that is, affirmative action—if there is an uneven distribution of men and women at the workplace.

Negative reactions from SAF, LO, and TCO prior to the law's enactment led to the stipulation that this affirmative-action section can be replaced by labor-management agreements on equality, which had already been concluded by private-sector employers and unions in 1977.[24] Where these are lacking, an equal-opportunity ombudsman and an Equal Opportunity Commission have been established to ensure compliance. In their criticisms, both SAF and the unions stressed the traditional voluntary approach as preferable, pointing to their already negotiated equality contracts. SAF's opposition is not surprising, considering that the law seeks to break deeply rooted patterns of discrimination perpetrated by management. As for the criticisms made by these unions, it should be noted that sweeping labor legislation in the 1970s had already made vast inroads into the voluntary approach and that much of this had been at the behest of LO. LO and TCO also felt that they should have been invited to participate in drafting the law but were not, although some of their objections (and those of SAF) led to the changes noted here. Not only are few women to be found at the top echelons of Swedish business, but they are also practically nonexistent in the union hierarchy, although 38 percent of LO's membership and 47 percent of TCO's are women.[25] As a study by the National Committee on Equality between Men and Women notes about union women at the lower levels, "their muscle-flexing has yet to make itself felt in the higher echelons."[26]

It is still too early to know the act's impact. Few in Sweden, however, believe that workplace equality can be accomplished without substantial changes in other areas of life. The educational system—which turns out men and women who have chosen different courses and which in turn reflects existing norms—has been subject to numerous changes.[27] These include considering child-care experience as a positive factor (worth extra points) for adults who apply for admission to colleges and universities; requiring both boys and girls to study home economics, child care, and shop; and trying to woo men into preschool-teacher training—with some success. Between 1965 and 1977 the proportion of men in this field did increase from less than 1 percent to 8 percent.[28] Even so, educational decisions are still strongly correlated with gender.

Family Policy and Employment Policy

Perhaps the biggest issue that has been raised is family policy.[29] This contrasts sharply with the United States, where, although married women and mothers have flocked into the labor market, public policy toward the family has scarcely acknowledged the fact. In Sweden, myriad policies have been introduced or are being considered that affect both parents and children. The reasons for these policies vary, and they raise or respond to a host of issues: What happens or should happen to children when both their parents work? Shall society pretend they are not there or hope they will fend for themselves? Should there be any adjustments in the workplace to these new developments? Should child care be the responsibility of the mother? If so, is that compatible with the goal of equality between the sexes in the labor market, in the home, and in society? Or should both parents share the responsibility of homemaking and raising children? Can women's role change if men's does not? This hardly exhausts the issues that have been raised. The next question is: What specific policies are involved?

Children's allowances, housing subsidies for families with children, prenatal care, health care, an extensive school lunch system all help families with children. Starting in the mid-1970s, however, new policies were more explicitly designed to take cognizance of the new labor-market trends and to attempt to encourage fathers as well as mothers to share the responsibility—and the pleasures—of raising children.

In 1974 Sweden switched from maternity benefits, common in most industrial nations, to parenthood benefits. Gradually extended, these now entitle parents to twelve months of leave from work in connection with the birth or adoption of a child. Like sickness benefits, they are paid from the national health-insurance fund, and the first nine months usually amount to 90 percent of lost earnings. The parents decide how to allocate the first six months: they can share it, or one parent can use it all, but both cannot use it at the same time. Another three months are given as forty-five days to each parent. This is an attempt to encourage fathers to use parenthood leave, but there is a loophole because the time can be transferred from one parent to the other. These days can be used at anytime before the child reaches the age of 8 and can be taken all at once or bit by bit—as quarter, half, or whole days. In the newest addition to parenthood leave, parents of children born after the beginning of 1979 get an additional three months, which pay a flat 37 kronor a day to one parent. Parents are also entitled to a leave of absence from work without compensation until the child is eighteen months old.[30]

Also introduced in 1974, and paying about 90 percent of lost earnings, are benefits that enable either parent to take time off from work to care for a sick child under 10 years of age. These were initially payable for ten days a year but were gradually raised. In 1980 they became payable for a maximum of sixty days a year for each child.[31] A physician's note is required after seven days. Although few parents require such a long leave, it was felt that those whose children had lengthier illnesses should also be covered. Already existing nursing allowances, given for children so seriously handicapped that one parent must stay home with them, were expanded. These child-care leaves have wide support. Although the Social Democrats initiated them, nonsocialist governments expanded these benefits.

Who actually takes these leaves? Mostly, though not entirely, mothers do. A small but growing proportion of fathers, primarily white-collar and professional workers, take parenthood leave—up from a mere 2.4 percent in 1974 to about 12 percent by 1977. They report overwhelmingly favorable experiences, and it is hoped that more men—especially blue-collar workers—will use this leave in the future. Although in most cases the mothers still take off time to care for sick children, a larger proportion of fathers do use this leave. In one-third of the families that used these benefits, the father stayed home at least one day.[32]

A big issue in family policy is the expansion of publicly supported child-care facilities, which by U.S. standards are very plentiful. These grew rapidly in the 1970s, and in 1976 Parliament approved a plan for a major expansion of such facilities.[33] Despite considerable progress, however, public facilities for preschool-age children are available for no more than one-third of all such children and one-half of those with working parents.[34] Shortages still keep many mothers from entering the labor force.

Swedish day-care centers are of very high quality. A group of U.S. trade-union women visiting these centers were especially impressed by the high ratio of adults to children, the low-key family style, and the fact that they look more like homes than schools or institutions.[35]

Any slowdown in public-sector growth, such as that started by the nonsocialist coalition toward the end of its term in office, could curb the expansion of child-care facilities and help keep mothers out of the labor market. Since that sector also has provided the lion's share of jobs for women (albeit at traditional woman's work) it would also cut out part of the demand for women in the labor market. Expansion of public child-care, however, still is a very high priority in Sweden.

Even with excellent, though not universally available, child-care facilities, there is concern that working parents and their children need more time to spend with each other. Since 1979 all parents with children under 8 years old have had the right to a six-hour day instead of the normal eight hours, with a proportionate reduction in earnings. This reform, introduced by the nonsocialist bloc, has been criticized by the Social Democrats, who feel that it favors higher-income families who can afford to take time off from work, and discriminates against lower-income and single-parent families, who need the income. Instead they favored expanding parenthood leave on the principle of compensating for loss of income and speeding up the expansion of day-care facilities.[36] But the current way that many women actually "solve" their conflict between family and work outside the home is through part-time employment. Social Democrats, unions, and most women's groups tend to regard this expansion of part-time work for women negatively, since it provides only limited employment opportunities and, they contend, may impede the development of equality between the sexes by reinforcing women's homemaker role and giving men a good excuse for not sharing more responsibilities.[37] In fact, however, most Swedish women are not yet equal in the home, even when they work full time. In a majority of families in which both partners are fully employed, women usually still do most of the household tasks.[38] Yet there has been some progress. According to a study by Marianne Pettersson of the Center for Working Life, the proportion of men who share household duties in families where the wife works either full or part time has risen in recent years.[39]

Conservatives have proposed paying a small allowance to compensate a parent who stays home with a young child because of preference or lack of space in a child-care center or it could be used to pay for child care. This, too, is regarded negatively by the Social Democrats, who think it will also reinforce the women-in-the-home syndrome. Most other parties feel some combination of expanded day care and a version of the Conservative proposal might be a reasonable approach.

Shorter hours for everyone have also been considered a solution to the dilemma. The Social Democrats as well as most other political parties and unions support a six-hour day in their long-term programs, although hardly anyone foresees this happening in the near future. In contrast to many European labor movements and the International Labor Organization, Swedish unions *do not* support a universal shorter work week as a means of reducing unemployment. It is seen as a goal on its own merits. The six-hour day has largely been considered a family, a women's, and a leisure issue. The claim is that it will give children and parents more time to spend with each other; that the sexes will be able to share household tasks, rather than women working part time and men full time; and that everyone, especially women, will have more time to work with popular movements, especially unions. The four-day week, with little or no reduction in the work day, seems to be preferred by men but is viewed from a perspective of equality as reinforcing traditional roles. Women, they say, will still work part time and men full time. Men will use the day off to go fishing, and guess who will do the dishes! Besides, say critics, child care cannot be concentrated in one extra day a week, nor can political or union activities.

Political Factors

Swedish women are far better represented in political than in economic life, and intense interest in family policy and day care partly stems from this fact. In 1979 about 26 percent of Parliament members were women, compared with about 3 percent of the U.S. Congress.[40] Although Parliament heavily subsidizes day care, municipalities pay about one-third of the cost and parents' fees about 11 percent. But a recent study shows that in municipalities where women were well represented in local politics, the expansion of child-care facilities has proceeded more rapidly.[41] "The local authorities say they are hamstrung by the wretched state of their finances," observes sociologist Rita Liljeström, "but it is hard to avoid the suspicion that the expansion is also being braked by a traditional view of the family."[42]

Publicly, all political leaders support the idea of the equality of the sexes, and it is written into the programs of all the political parties and unions. "Nobody," says Berit Rollén of AMS, "would dare state what a Republican county chairman said in Houston [National Conference on International Women's Year], to the effect that participants were a gaggle of outcasts, misfits and rejects." Nevertheless, she adds, sometimes we "wish they would openly say what they think instead (for often they think differently)."[43] The official sanction of equality, she admits, does make it easier to talk to people who have not yet accepted the concept.

Conclusion

Extension of the commitment to full employment to women has not yet brought about sex equality in the labor market, but striving toward that goal has raised a host of issues and led to profound reforms that also affect policies toward families and children. In these efforts the ideology is equality and sharing of roles for the benefit of both sexes and the children, rather than simply women's liberation. Women need to work outside the home.

Fathers need to participate more in child care, not just because the mother works but also because children need parenting, not just mothering—because child care helps humanize the lives of men.

Much has been written about attempts to eliminate the assembly line in Sweden because that method of production seems incompatible with the welfare of human beings. But Margereta Beckérus former secretary of the Swedish Committee on Equality between Men and Women, calls for a reorganization of work because "the world of work seems to be poorly designed for human beings—especially those who happen to have children."[44] The call for this reorganization of work as well as the call for equality may be some of the most important by-products of Sweden's commitment to full employment for women.

Notes

1. "Swedish Labor Market Policy," *Fact Sheets on Sweden* (Stockholm: Swedish Institute, 1979), p. 1.

2. Ibid., p. 1; see also "Swedish Labor Market Policy," *Fact Sheets on Sweden* (Stockholm: Swedish Institute, 1981), for a discussion of the concept of work for everyone.

3. Unless otherwise specified, all data on the labor force and the labor market in this chapter are taken or derived from Sweden, National Central Bureau of Statistics, *Arbetsmarknadsstatistisk Årsbok, 1979-1980 (Yearbook of Labor Statistics, 1979-1980)* (Stockholm: Liber Förlag, 1980), or from unpublished data from Swedish Central Bureau of Statistics, Labor Force Surveys, various years.

4. Christina Jonung and Bodil Thordarsson, *Women Returning to Work, Sweden,* Reprint no. 34, (Lund, Sweden: Department of Economics, Lund University, 1980), p. 123.

5. "Swedish Labor Market Policy," *Fact Sheets on Sweden* (Stockholm: Swedish Institute, 1980), p. 1.

6. Sweden, National Labor Market Board, *Equality in the Labor Market: Programme—Adopted by the Labor Market Board,* Solna, 1977, p. 3.

7. Birgitta Wistrand, *Swedish Women on the Move* (Stockholm: Swedish Institute, 1981), pp. 13-15.

8. All data in this paragraph are from National Committee on Equality between Men and Women, *Step by Step: National Plan of Action for Equality,* SOU 1979-56 (Stockholm: Liber Förlag, 1979), pp. 48-49.

9. Ibid., pp. 50-51.

10. Alice H. Cook, "Collective Bargaining as a Strategy for Achieveing Equal Opportunity and Equal Pay: Sweden and West Germany," in

Equal Employment Policy for Women ed. Ronnie Steinberg Ratner (Philadelphia: Temple University Press, 1980), p. 57.

11. Figure for 1960 from Nancy S. Barrett, "Have Swedish Women Achieved Equality?" *Challenge,* November-December 1973, table 2, p. 17; all other data on wages in this paragraph are from National Committee on Equality, *Step by Step,* p. 51.

12. Berit Rollén, "Equality between Men and Women in the Labor Market: The Swedish National Labor Market Board," in *Equal Employment Policy,* ed. Ratner, p. 189.

13. Sweden, National Labor Market Board, *Swedish Employment Policy, Annual Report 1979/80* (Solna: National Labor Market Board, 1980), p. 16, and Sweden, The National Board of Education, *Labor Market Training: A Presentation,* 2nd rev. ed. (Stockholm: Liber Lärmodel, 1975), p. 15.

14. National Labor Market Board, *Swedish Employment Policy, Annual Report 1979/1980,* p. 16.

15. Rollén, "Equality," p. 190.

16. National Committee on Equality, *Step by Step,* table 3, p. 45.

17. National Labor Market Board, *Equality in the Labor Market: Programme,* p. 13.

18. Ibid., p. 13.

19. Ibid., p. 14, and National Committee on Equality, *Step by Step,* p. 63.

20. National Committee on Equality, *Step by Step,* p. 63.

21. Rollén, "Equality," p. 194.

22. Ibid., p. 194.

23. Act on Equality between Men and Women at Work, effective 1 July 1980.

24. National Committee on Equality, *Step by Step,* pp. 65-66, and Wistrand, *Swedish Women,* pp. 15-16.

25. National Committee on Equality, *Step by Step,* table 18, p. 132. Data are for 1976.

26. Ibid., p. 132.

27. For a discussion of the education of men and women, see "Education and Training," in *Step by Step,* pp. 23-41.

28. Ibid., p. 23.

29. See, for example, Lillemor Melsted, "Swedish Family Policy, *Election Year '79,* no. 4 (New York, Swedish Information Service, July 1979); Rita Liljeström, "Integration of Family Policy and Labor Market Policy in Sweden," in *Equal Employment Policy,* ed. Ratner, pp. 388-403; Siv Gustavsson, "Women and Work in Sweden," *Working Life in Sweden,* no. 15 (New York: Swedish Information Service, December 1979); Jonung and Thordarsson, *Women Returning to Work: Sweden;* National Committee on

Equality, *Step by Step,* esp. pp. 71-91; Swedish Trade Union Confederation, *The Trade Union Movement and the Family Policy* (Stockholm: Swedish Trade Union Confederation, 1977); and "TCO's View of Family Policy and Equal Opportunities," Stockholm, Central Organization of Salaried Employees, 15 May 1978.

30. "Social Insurance in Sweden," *Fact Sheets on Sweden* (Stockholm: Swedish Institute, 1981), p. 1; National Committee on Equality, *Step by Step,* pp. 85-86; and Wistrand, *Swedish Women,* pp. 32-33.

31. Ibid.

32. National Committee on Equality, *Step by Step,* pp. 74-75.

33. For a complete explanation of child-care programs see, "Child Care Programs in Sweden," *Facts Sheets on Sweden* (Stockholm: Swedish Institute, 1980), and National Committee on Equality, *Step by Step,* pp. 81-82, 86-87, 89. For a comprehensive comparison of Swedish and U.S. attitudes toward working mothers, see Carolyn Teich Adams and Kathryn Teich Winston, *Mothers at Work: Public Policies in the United States, Sweden, and China* (New York: Longmans, 1980).

34. Fredrik Winter, Research Section, AMS, personal correspondence, Stockholm, 12 December 1981.

35. Ruth Jordan, *A Commitment to Children: The Report of the Coalition of Labor Union Women Child Care Seminar,* Committee of Labor Union Women, 1977, pp. 3-5.

36. For a detailed account of the different political parties on family policy, see Melsted, "Swedish Family Policy,"

37. Ibid., p. 7; "TCO's View of Family Policy and Equal Opportunities"; National Committee on Equality, *Step by Step,* p. 68. A more positive interpretation of part-time work is given by Marianne Pettersson, "Part-Time Work—a Threat to Equality?" (Stockholm, Arbetslivcentrum, mimeo.; Christina Jonung, "Sexual Equality in the Labor Market," *Monthly Labor Review* 101(October 1978):34.

38. National Committee on Equality, *Step by Step,* pp. 47-48.

39. Marianne Pettersson, *Deltidsarbetet i Sverige. (Part-time Work in Sweden)* (Stockholm: Arbetslivscentrum/Akademilitteratur, 1981), p. 160.

40. Maud Edwards, "The Swedish Woman in Political Life," *Political Life in Sweden* (New York: Swedish Information Service), p. 1, and U.S. Bureau of the Census, *Statistical Abstract of the United States: 1980* (Washington, D.C.: U.S. Government Printing Office, 1980), derived from table 843, p. 51. Nineteen were in the House of Representatives and one was in the Senate.)

41. Margareta Beckérus, secretary of the Swedish Committee on Equality between Men and Women, Speech, Dublin, 15 May 1979, Stockholm, Jamstalldhetskommittén, p. 16, mimeo.

42. Liljeström, "Integration of Family Policy and Labor Market Policy," p. 399.

43. Berit Rollén, "Gently towards Equality, *Working Life in Sweden,* no. 5 (New York: Swedish Information Service, May 1978), p. 3.

44. Beckérus, Speech, Dublin, May 15, 1979.

8

The Disadvantaged in a Full-Employment Labor Market: Immigrants, Youth, Older Workers, and the Disabled

Immigrants in a Homogeneous Society

Immigrants are relative newcomers on the Swedish scene. Unlike the United States, which has always been a land of immigrants, Sweden was traditionally an extremely homogeneous nation. As recently as 1930 only about 16,000 foreigners lived within its borders. But this has changed dramatically.

By the end of the 1970s about 1 million of Sweden's 8.3 million people were either immigrants themselves or had at least one parent who was a post-World War II immigrant. Of that number about 430,000 were foreign nationals.[1]

In the wake of World War II, northern and central European refugees from nazism settled in Sweden. Later, political refugees came from Hungary in 1956, from Poland and Czechoslovakia in 1968, and from many other countries. There were also nonpolitical motives for coming. During Sweden's boom period, with its labor shortages, immigrants were specifically sought for jobs that were hard to fill with Swedes as long as opportunities for other employment were plentiful. The biggest wave of these foreign workers entered in the 1960s, the first decade in which large numbers of southern Europeans came to Sweden. During the 1960s workers came from many countries, especially Yugoslavia, Greece, Turkey, and Finland, to help maintain the rapid growth of the Swedish economy.[2]

Since the early 1970s, with the end of the boom economy, immigration of workers from non-Nordic nations has practically ceased. An agreement signed in 1954 by the Nordic nations enables Scandinavians to seek work freely in any of these countries. Beginning in 1967, however, others coming to Sweden for that purpose have been required to obtain a work permit before entering Sweden. Non-Scandinavian immigrants do still come to Sweden, but mostly as refugees, as relatives of immigrants already living in Sweden, or as adopted children of Swedish parents. A few also come illegally.

Unlike some European countries, Sweden rejected the "guest-worker" system. Foreign workers, who cannot be sent back to their country of origin if they become unemployed, were encouraged to bring their families. Equality, such an important part of the Swedish ethos, became one of the foundations of immigration policy as laid down by Parliament. Foreigners were to have the same living conditions, social benefits, and right to work as

177

the rest of the population. Although eligible to become citizens after five years of residence, they were to be treated equally even if not citizens. Sweden even broke with the old tradition that voting rights should be based on citizenship. Since 1976, immigrants who have lived in Sweden for three years but are not citizens have been able to vote and run for office in municipal and regional, though not national, elections.[3]

Finns, with a different culture and with a native language linguistically remote from Swedish, are the largest group of foreign nationals in Sweden, followed by Yugoslavs. There are about one hundred foreign-language newspapers and magazines, and a polygot of languages is now part of the Swedish landscape. One can get an idea of what this means by looking at Norrköping, a city with a population of 121,000. The 7,000 foreign citizens who live there speak sixty different languages.[4] Except for the Finns, some of whom also live in the north, most immigrants live in the cities of central and southern Sweden. They do not live in slums; there are none in Sweden. They enjoy the same modern housing standards as others, although with their larger families they are somewhat more overcrowded. In many cities, however, immigrants are concentrated in certain neighborhoods—ones that often contain more than their share of Swedes with the most severe social problems. In Tensta and Rinkeby in Stockholm, about 40 percent are foreigners. And this is replicated elsewhere.[5]

Immigrants in the Labor Market

Immigrants come to Sweden to work, and work they do. Foreign nationals make up about 5 percent of the labor force, and the figure would be about 10 percent if all the foreign born and their children were included, regardless of citizenship status. An integral part of the Swedish work force, immigrants are highly concentrated in certain industries and occupations. In 1979 about 43 percent of foreign nationals, compared with 25 percent of Swedish citizens, worked in manufacturing.[6] Large numbers also work in the private services, especially restaurants and commercial cleaning. In one commercial cleaning firm in Stockholm, 98 percent of the cleaners are foreign, most of them Greek.[7] Others are clustered in Sweden's vast health-care network, most often in low-level hospital jobs but also as physicians. Immigrants are a diverse group, not a monolith. Some with professional backgrounds came as political refugees or to fill shortages in fields such as medicine. For the most part, however, their occupational structure is quite different from that of the rest of the population—overrepresented in blue-collar and underrepresented in white-collar occupations. Since foreigners were only recruited for occupations in which there was an excess demand, some white-collar workers from poor countries moved to affluent Sweden to become industrial workers.[8]

In their work, immigrants are much more likely to be exposed to very high noise levels and to very dirty conditions. They are also overrepresented in occupations with higher rates of industrial injuries.[9]

Despite their different occupational structure, a 1977 survey of the Central Bureau of Statistics reveals that immigrants have a somewhat higher average income than Swedes. This is partly because they work more hours; they are less likely than others to work only part time and more likely to hold an extra job in addition to their regular one. Also, proportionately more immigrants than other workers work inconvenient hours, which pay shift differentials.[10]

The majority of foreign workers in Sweden belong to trade unions, and their wages are determined by the same collective-bargaining contracts as those of their Swedish colleagues. Because of the solidarity wage principle of LO, wage differentials in Sweden are narrower than in the United States. Thus, even if they were not working longer hours than others but were overly concentrated on the lower rungs of the Swedish job ladder, the spread between the wages of immigrants and those of others would be less pronounced than for similarly situated workers in the United States.

The disadvantaged position of immigrants in the labor market shows up markedly in the unemployment statistics (table 8-1). The incidence of unemployment among foreign nationals is about twice that of Swedes. Their heavy concentration in manufacturing has made them more vulnerable to cyclical and structural problems in that sector, and their small

Table 8-1
Unemployment Rates of Immigrants in Sweden, by Age and Sex, 1980 and 1981
(Percentage Unemployed)

Age	Both Sexes		Male		Female	
	1980	*1981*	*1980*	*1981*	*1980*	*1981*
16-74	4.0	4.8	3.9	4.5	4.2	5.1
16-19	9.9	12.5	9.5	13.3	10.3	11.8
20-24	6.3	8.4	6.5	7.4	6.1	9.3
25-34	4.1	4.9	4.2	5.1	4.1	4.8
35-44	2.8	3.1	2.7	2.9	3.1	3.3
45-54	1.9	2.5	2.1	2.7	1.7	2.2
55-64	1.2	0.9	1.5	1.3	0.7	0.3
65-74	0.0	0.0	0.0	0.0	0.0	0.0

Source: Sweden, Central Bureau of Statistics, Labor Force Sample Survey.

Note: The *unemployment rate* is the percentage of the labor force that is unemployed. *Immigrants* are foreign nationals.

representation in white-collar and professional fields, which have greater stability, has given them less immunity to unemployment than Swedes.

Language difficulties compound immigrants' labor-market problems and add to the general problems of adjustment that are common to immigrants anywhere. Short-run policies have been developed that aim to help those already in the labor market, whereas long-run policies are aimed at their children.

Since 1973 the law has required employers to grant their immigrant employees 240 hours of time off from work with full pay in order to receive instruction in Swedish, if they have not already mastered the language.

One problem with this program has been its failure to reach very deeply into the immigrant work force. Many who are eligible have not been enrolled. Since the cost of an employee's released time is paid for by his or her firm, the program has been unpopular with business. Noncompliance—in itself, fairly uncommon in Sweden—is widespread. In some ways the law may even have added to the problems of immigrants by making it harder for them to get jobs. One econometric study posing that question found mixed evidence to support that view, but it did not go beyond the first six months after the law went into effect.[11] In 1975 an LO report on labor-market policy noted that many employers were disinclined to hire non-Swedish-speaking immigrants after the law's passage. LO was also forced to demand of AMS that employers stop the discriminatory practice of stating that only Swedish-speaking persons should apply when listing job openings with the employment service.[12]

Suggestions to strengthen and finance this program to prevent these consequences—for example, a payroll tax—have been mentioned, but so far no change has been made. One proposal that may be enacted by Parliament was made by a government committee at the end of 1981, with support from committee members of the four main parties. Paid time off for instruction in Swedish for foreigners would be increased to 600 hours. That would enable them to get a better grasp of the language. But their wages would be paid for by the government rather than by the employer. Instruction would also be available to the nonemployed. They would receive 33 kronor per hour, except for youths 16 to 18 years old and those over 65, who would receive 13 kronor per hour while learning Swedish. Instruction would be financed by a general payroll tax for those who are employed and by the government for others.[13]

Another big question about language training concerns the younger generation: How should immigrant children be taught? Much of their future in the labor market and in the larger society hinges on their ability to master Swedish. It is in this area that the most dramatic policy changes have occurred.

Assimilation or Diversity?

Initially the attitude was that immigrants' children should learn Swedish as quickly as possible. They could learn their parents' native languages later in life, if at all. For both pragmatic and ideological reasons, attitudes and policies have changed. Children who came to Sweden after learning their native language frequently did better at Swedish than Swedish-born children of immigrants, who were often found to do poorly in two languages. Now the feeling is that immigrant children should first learn their mother tongue and then learn Swedish, to give them a firmer grasp of both languages. This is a major shift from a pure assimilationist model of immigration to one that stresses preservation of multicultural and ethnic diversity. It is felt that this will also enhance the development of the child's sense of identity, contact with parents, and respect for parental language and culture.[14]

This is in keeping with new guidelines for immigration policy unanimously adopted by Parliament in 1975, based on three objectives: cultural *freedom of choice* for immigrants; *cooperation* and solidarity between the native Swedish majority and ethnic minorities; and *equality* between immigrants and Swedes.[15]

This policy is now reflected in the school system. Since 1977 all children—from 6 year olds in preschool to students in upper secondary school—have had the right to instruction in the language spoken at home. It only applies to a few hours a week, however, which some feel is inadequate. The National Immigration and Nationalization Board contends that it also begins too late in the children's lives and that it should start in day-care centers.[16] A large number of experiments are now in progress with teaching completely or partly in the home languages, an approach that appears to be most feasible for major ethnic groups in places where there are large numbers of immigrants. Critics of monolingual instruction in foreign languages think this will isolate immigrant children, but supporters feel otherwise. "The idea is not that they should live apart," says Anna-Greta Leijon, Social Democratic member of Parliament and until 1976 deputy minister in charge of immigrant affairs in the Social Democratic cabinet.[17] They will attend a Swedish school, she explains, and after the first few years will be given a "gentle transition to regular Swedish groups."[18] Karin Andersson, Center party member and minister of immigration in the Center-Liberal coalition stresses the security that the children get from their language and culture as a result of these classes. Without it, she contends, "their chances of adjusting to Sweden are reduced."[19] And that makes home language instruction the most important immigrant issue of her party. The existence of home language instruction in more than fifty different languages stands in sharp contrast to a time not long ago when immigrant children were encouraged to speak only Swedish at school and at home.[20]

It is too soon to know the ultimate impact of this and other policies designed to preserve diversity and to ease the immigrants' transition to life in a new and often very different society. Examples of other policies include state grants to immigrant organizations and newspapers, funding of public libraries for the purchase of foreign books, courses for interpreters, and even a basic education program for adult illiterates that started in 1977.[21] Although the average education level of immigrants is about the same as for Swedes, certain smaller groups of immigrants have serious educational deficiencies, and some are unable to read or write. The handicap that such illiteracy presents in Swedish society, and especially in its labor market, is self-evident.[22]

An immigrant—whether unemployed or not—can learn about the basic features of labor-market programs from an AMS brochure that tells about labor-market training, vocational guidance, rehabilitation, relocation grants, the public-employment service, and unemployment benefits.[23] This publication, like many similar ones that provide information about housing, social insurance, schools, traffic, outdoor life, and so forth, is available in Swedish—but also in Finnish, English, German, French, Spanish, Portuguese, Italian, Greek, Turkish, Serbo-Croatian, Polish, Hungarian, and Czech—the major immigrant languages.[24] In larger towns and cities, interpreters also are often available, usually through the local immigration office. In Norrköping, for example, there are 140 interpreters on the list maintained by the immigration office. They speak thirty-six languages, which means that 94 percent of the immigrant population will be able to understand them.[25] Other government offices, including the Employment Service, utilize their services when required.

Labor-Market Policies

Many immigrants have benefited from labor-market programs, although they are far from problem-free. Labor-market training is used extensively by foreign nationals, who make up 5 percent of the labor force but 10 percent of the unemployed and about 20 percent of labor-market trainees.[26] An immigrant's labor-market training often starts with Swedish lessons. The popular preparatory course on working life and education also has been adapted to the special needs of immigrants. Formerly given at Labor Market Training Centers, since 1980 it has been given at Labor Market Institutes. The course aims to increase the immigrants' limited knowledge of work and training opportunities in Sweden prior to choosing their occupational training. Furthermore, regular courses are also available at the training centers.

The dropout rate from training programs, however, is higher among immigrants than for others. It is not uncommon for them to have difficulty benefiting from courses because of their inadequate knowledge of Swedish, which the short course at the training center may not be enough to overcome. They are also less likely than others to get jobs after completing training.[27]

Immigrants are also eligible for relief work but are underrepresented in these jobs. With more relief jobs in white-collar fields, those with language problems are at a disadvantage.

Sometimes the training and education immigrants received before coming to Sweden is not sufficiently utilized. In an attempt to rectify this situation, AMS has gathered information about educational systems in the countries from which the immigrants come in order to provide better guidance. Experiments with a bilingual vocational-guidance staff from Finland are also being undertaken, with preliminary evaluations showing positive results.[28]

Labor-Market Discrimination

Even an immigrant who knows the language may not be hired. For most white-collar occupations, employers will not employ applicants who do not have a *very* good knowledge of Swedish, even if there are no other applicants for the job.[29] This can extend to other kinds of employment as well. The immigrant editor-in-chief of a publication concerned with migration contends that "a competent immigrant can be denied employment by a municipality as a domestic helper because he does not speak 'pure' Swedish."[30]

Kjell Öberg, chief of the Swedish Commission on Prejudice and Discrimination, which has been given the task of documenting the extent of racial and ethnic discrimination in Sweden, cites an example of a serious form of discrimination that occurs privately against well-qualified people—for example, the civil engineer who may end up a foreman in a factory.[31] There is no specific law banning ethnic or racial discrimination in the labor market similar to the one banning sex discrimination and promoting affirmative action in the workplace that became effective in July 1980. Antidiscrimination law now relies on a provision in the Swedish penal code adopted from the U.N. convention prohibiting ethnic discrimination, which does make it an offense for a businessman or public servant to discriminate on racial and ethnic grounds. Although this would cover, for example, a restaurant owner or a boarding-house keeper who refused to serve or to rent a room to someone, there is a gap in the Swedish law: it would not be an offense for an employer to refuse to hire or promote someone because of his or her racial or ethnic origin.[32] Furthermore, Öberg feels that Sweden lacks effective administrative machinery to handle even those complaints that are covered by law.[33]

The Future

A crucial issue affecting Sweden's immigrants is whether occupational segregation that exists today is transitional or whether it will be handed down to their children—a situation that would also have dire implications for Swedish society.

Studies of economist Eskil Wadensjö suggest that immigrants who have been in Sweden for a longer time are less occupationally segregated than those of the same age who arrived more recently.[34] Many earlier immigrants, however, were highly educated political refugees from northern and central Europe. More recent immigrants who have come to work—many from southern Europe—may face greater discrimination. To a large extent the future of the immigrant population hinges on the fate of their youth, who, along with other young people, face a harder time in the labor market than in the past.

Youth Unemployment

It is no exaggeration to say that youth unemployment is one of the most discussed problems in contemporary Sweden. Its magnitude is so small compared with the problem in the United States that one might wonder whether there is any problem at all. But the problem is real. Swedes deplore the fact that *any* young people cannot find work. Their unemployment is considered a blemish that must be removed if these youngsters are to feel that they are part of society. Rising alienation, crime, alcoholism, and drug abuse are considered possible consequences of the problem.

In the United States, youth unemployment has festered for decades. But in post-World War II Sweden the problem is a later development. As recently as the mid-1960s, jobs were plentiful for most Swedish youngsters, regardless of whether they had completed only the nine-year comprehensive school, which is compulsory for 7- to 16-year-olds; or upper secondary school, which follows; or had graduated from a university.[35]

Official jobless figures reflect this situation. When overall unemployment hit a low of 1.2 percent in 1965, the rates for 16- to 19-year-olds and for 20- to 24-year-olds were only 2.9 and 1.9 percent, respectively; and the rates in other years in the 1960s seldom went above 5 percent for the younger group or above 3 percent for 20- to 24-year-olds (table 8-2).

Table 8-2

National and Youth Unemployment Rates in Sweden, by Age and Sex, 1963-1981

Year	National All Ages, Both Sexes (%)	Rate of Unemployment (%)[a]					
		16- to 19-Year-Olds			20- to 24-Year-Olds		
		Both Sexes	Male	Female	Both Sexes	Male	Female
1963	1.7	3.8	2.9	4.7	2.2	2.1	2.3
1964	1.6	4.4	3.7	5.1	2.0	2.1	1.8
1965	1.2	2.9	1.9	5.1	1.9	1.2	2.9
1966	1.6	3.7	2.7	4.8	2.2	2.0	2.3
1967	2.1	5.2	4.7	5.8	3.2	3.0	3.5
1968	2.2	5.7	5.0	6.5	3.0	3.0	3.0
1969	1.9	4.6	3.8	5.4	2.8	2.6	3.0
1970	1.5	4.3	3.4	4.8	2.2	2.5	2.4
1971	2.5	7.7	7.1	8.4	3.7	3.7	3.8
1972	2.7	8.2	7.8	8.7	4.5	4.2	4.9
1973	2.5	6.8	5.8	8.0	4.4	4.2	4.7
1974	2.0	6.6	5.2	8.1	3.2	2.7	3.8
1975	1.6	5.5	4.2	7.1	2.8	2.1	3.5
1976	1.6	5.5	4.1	7.0	2.7	2.2	3.4
1977	1.8	6.7	5.4	8.1	3.2	2.9	3.5
1978	2.2	7.9	7.1	8.7	4.3	4.3	4.3
1979	2.1	7.4	7.0	7.9	3.7	3.6	3.8
1980[b]	2.0	7.6	6.5	8.8	3.7	3.5	3.9
1981	2.5	9.4	8.2	10.5	4.7	4.8	4.6

Source: Sweden, Central Bureau of Statistics, Labor Force Surveys.

[a]Rate of unemployment as a percentage of the labor force.

[b]Because of a labor market conflict, includes first, third, and fourth quarters only.

As one Swedish expert put it, youth thought that "unemployment was something that happened to those working in factories that closed down, people in rural areas, construction workers, those with social problems. But young people hardly imagined that they too could become unemployed."[36]

The Origin of Youth Unemployment

Then it happened. In the 1970s, job prospects became less promising. Sweden's first recession of the 1970s, starting in 1971, drove the annual unemployment rate up to 2.5 percent and slightly higher for several consecutive years. Youth was hard hit. In 1971 unemployment among 16- to 19-year-olds climbed to nearly 8 percent, and for 20- to 24-year-olds it average nearly 4 percent—high figures for Sweden. Although the unemployment rates for these young people declined slightly in the mid-1970s, by the end of the decade it was again hovering around the 1971 levels (table 8-2). Thus since the early 1970s Sweden has had a youth-unemployment problem that, though modest compared with the one in the United States, is severe for a country with high expectations.

Unlike that of the United States, the youth population of Sweden was not growing when youth unemployment became part of the Swedish landscape. Between 1970 and 1978 the number of 16- to 24-year-olds actually declined by 10 percent. Not until 1979 did it start to increase for the 16- to 19-year-old group, reflecting an increase in the birth rate in the early 1960s. This growth is expected to last into the 1980s; before the mid-1980s, as these youngsters start to grow older, the number of 20- to 24-year-olds will start to rise.[37] Although their numbers did not grow, the labor-force participation rate of 16- to 24-year-olds did rise in the 1970s. But their population decline more than offset that increase. As a result, they made up a somewhat smaller proportion of the total labor force in 1979 than in 1970—16.4 percent compared with 17.8 percent.

Despite their declining share of the labor force, young people are more at risk of being unemployed compared with adults than in the past. Thus, although youth unemployment rises and falls with the business cycle, the relative gap between youth and adult unemployment rates widened during the 1970s. This is partly because of a decline in the proportion of latent job seekers or discouraged workers among 20- to 24-year-olds—less so for teenagers. Thus more hidden unemployment has been transformed into visible unemployment.[38]

Factors Related to Youth Unemployment

But many other factors are involved. During this period, apprenticeships practically disappeared, and most companies that had once provided on-the-job training for youngsters no longer did so, since educational changes meant that many received training in the secondary schools.

In the 1970s manufacturing employment stagnated as a result of productivity gains that reduced labor requirements, recessions, structural problems that beset important export industries, and the tendency of Swedish transnational corporations to locate more manufacturing jobs abroad. Thus many blue-collar jobs that might have been available to working-class youngsters simply were not there. Gone, too, were other jobs, such as delivering packages, that once gave some employment in small businesses. Most job creation was in the public sector, but some fast-growing areas—for example, hospitals—were often out of bounds for persons under 18 years of age, who cannot work at night, drive vehicles, or do other work unsuitable for them. For some jobs, housewives, who entered the labor force in large numbers, were hired in preference to the young.

In slack labor markets, lack of experience became a more important barrier to employment, and employers often claimed that wages for youths were too high.[39] Unlike the United States, Sweden has no minimum-wage law. The negotiated contracts that set most wages allow youths to earn less than adults. Partly as a result of the wage-solidarity principle, the youth-to-adult wage differential narrowed. Yet this has taken place over three decades; and, as Gösta Rehn points outs, some of the narrowing reflects the fact that the average age of young workers has risen because longer schooling is now the norm.[40] To the extent that this is a factor, subsidies that reduce the cost to the employer of hiring the young have been used in preference to lowering the differential. Swedish unions, it should be noted, present no barriers to employment of the young since anyone who is hired is accepted as a member.

Although some have alleged that nowadays Swedish youths are work shy, studies show that very few shun work and that most jobs listed as un-filled at the Employment Service for a long time are not really available to the young.[41] Employers sometimes contend that employment-security laws caused the problem. Youth unemployment worsened before the advent of these laws, however, although employers may now be more reluctant to hire any workers but those perceived to be prime. Interestingly, the law also per-mits hiring for a probationary period if this is sanctioned by a collective-bargaining contract, which usually is the case.

If "no firing" became more of the rule in the 1970s, many firms also had "no-hiring" policies in effect at times, especially in the middle of the decade. These hurt new entrants into the labor market.[42] Along with many labor-market policies aiming to maintain employment, recovery from a recession has often meant that some additional demand for labor could be met without additional hiring.

As in the United States, youth unemployment is uneven in its impact. As table 8-1 shows, young women have higher unemployment rates than young men, and the rates for teenagers exceed those for 20-to-24-year-olds. Within these groups the least educated and the youngest—the 16- and 17-year-olds—are hardest hit.

In the early 1970s about 70 percent of Swedish comprehensive school graduates went directly to upper secondary school, and that figure rose to about 85 percent by the end of decade.[43] Secondary school is more special-ized and more vocationally oriented than in the United States. There are more than twenty different lines or courses of study that last from two to four years. Lines are practical or theoretical (academic) and are meant to prepare for further education, although some higher education is now also open to those who study practical lines.[44] Teenagers who leave school at the age of 16 or who drop out of secondary school without a skill are very vulnerable in the labor market: in addition to their lack of skills or ex-perience, they are often too young for many jobs.

National policy now stresses recurrent lifetime education—interspersing periods of work and schooling—so that these youngsters can (and some do) return to school later on. Youngsters from lower socioeconomic back-grounds are more likely to take shorter, more practical courses and to drop out along the way, or not to enter secondary school at all.[45] Thus youth unemployment has a class as well as an age dimension. Some unemployed teenagers, especially in the south, where there is typically less unemploy-ment, have other social problems. And those who do not have them, Swedes fear, will develop them, especially alcoholism, about which there is much concern.

Changes in higher education during the 1970s also worsened the relative position of the youngest and least educated by increasing the supply of better-educated young people in the job market. Unemployment among university graduates led to a substantial decline in enrollment in higher edu-cation, which added to the competition in the job market. Some college graduates had to take lower-level jobs than in previous years, including ones that previously had gone to secondary-school graduates. These better-educated young people were often preferred by employers, and this caused a chain reaction that reverberated down the line and ultimately affected even the comprehensive-school graduate.[46] Reforms that encourage students with work experience to enter universities have had a similar result. This is because relatively fewer students are admitted directly from secondary school and extra credit is given to applicants with work experience, making it easier for them to gain entrance. This induces more students to work for a few years before going on to higher education.

Young women, especially teenagers, experience relatively more unem-ployment than their male counterparts; and gender is still a strong determi-nant of their fields of study and job preferences. In 1980 girls made up from 93 to 97 percent of applicants to the nursing, social-service, clothing-manufacture, and consumer lines in secondary schools, but only 2-6 percent of applicants to the building and construction, forestry, workshop, motor-engineering, operating-engineering and maintenance, electrotechnical, woodworking, and technical lines.[47] With so many applicants, the nursing line has the lowest acceptance rate of all.[48] In the labor market, young women usually seek a limited number of very traditional female jobs, some of them not open to the very young—for example, in hospitals—or with few openings for the untrained, as in day nurseries.

Immigrants are least likely to continue beyond comprehensive school because of their lower socioeconomic status, language problems, difficulties in school, family pressures to earn money, and so on. This tendency is even more pronounced among immigrant girls, some of whom come from cul-tures far removed from either the goal or the practice of equality for women.[49] Once in the labor market, immigrant youths suffer relatively more unemployment. In 1979 joblessness among foreign citizens 16- to 24-years old was 7.8 percent compared with 4.8 percent for Swedes. Immigrant children who enter upper secondary school more often take shorter, practical lines, either out of preference or because some theoretical lines have stiffer requirements, including better English (mandatory from the third grade of comprehensive school) or are otherwise more difficult to get into.[50] Immigrant women, for example, would be less likely to get into the nursing line because it requires such high grades. Paradoxically, many immigrants are handicapped not only because of problems in Swedish but also because a good knowledge of English is needed for many jobs and academic pursuits. University admission generally requires excellence in both Swedish and English.[51] Mastering one foreign language is difficult enough. Mastering two is even more of a barrier.

With the average young immigrant entering the job market with less education and with different education than the nonimmigrant, the stage is set for continuing occupational segregation, even without the additional problem of overt discrimination.

Policies to Combat Youth Unemployment

Policies to combat youth unemployment are wide ranging and include those directly targeted at youth as well as those targeted at specific kinds of unemployment for which young people are significant beneficiaries. General economic policies, needless to say, are particularly important, since recessions inevitably hit the young harder than adults. Policies toward immigrants and women are also important.

Though not a youth policy, regional-development efforts play a crucial role, since youth unemployment is most severe in the north. More than 40 percent of those hired as a result of job expansion stimulated by development policies were under 25 years old.[52] The other side of the coin is that youths also migrate for jobs. In the last half of the 1970s, about 60 percent of persons who used geographic-mobility allowances were under 25 years old.[53]

Within the school system there are efforts to inform students about the world of work. For example, visits to a variety of work sites are conducted in the last years of comprehensive school. There are vocational guidance officers in all schools, and Employment Service personnel also talk to secondary-school students and at parents' meetings. As part of its broad educational effort, AMS also prepares printed material and radio and television programs.

There is a good deal of cooperation between the local Labor Market Boards and the boards of education. Special courses may be developed in the adult municipal school system, or in folk high schools (a uniquely Scandanavian form of adult education: a type of boarding school run by local governments, churches, trade unions, temperance societies, and other non-profit organizations with no official syllabus or compulsory subject matter).

They also cooperate to develop courses in the ordinary school system and in labor-market training centers. Since 1977 there have been planning councils for youth in all municipalities. These are headed by local school authorities and include representatives of other municipal agencies, the Employment Service, labor, and management. Under this arrangement, schools are responsible for maintaining contact for two years with all students who leave compulsory school without continuing their education. Until these youths are 18 years old, they must be guided and advised about jobs or other educational opportunities that may arise, such as the special courses or the availability of additional openings in particular lines in the regular school system.[54] The aim is to prevent out-of-work 16- or 17-year-olds from drifting aimlessly on their own.

Attempts to break down occupational sex-tagging of jobs is considered a very important part of the fight against youth unemployment. Young women already in the labor market are encouraged to consider nontraditional jobs; and greater efforts are being made within the school system, among employers, within the family, and in the mass media to change sex stereotypes.[55] Similarly, young immigrants in the labor market are affected by a whole constellation of factors, including discrimination and inadequate schooling. There is, however, a strong hope that home language instruction will help them receive a better education and aid them in the job market.

Cash assistance—unemployment benefits that are granted to some people who have never worked or are otherwise ineligible for regular benefits—was introduced with the young and women in mind. Persons who have finished secondary school or the equivalent are eligible for these benefits (which pay less than regular unemployment insurance) if they have unsuccessfully sought work for three months through the Employment Service. Those who have not completed secondary school and who are at least 16 years old must have worked for at least five months. Although just over half of all recipients of such support at the end of the 1970s were under 25 years old, only 30 percent of the unemployed in that age group received benefits.[56] However, some may have been receiving regular benefits. But unemployment insurance is hardly seen by the Swedes as a solution, especially not for the young. At best, it provides a temporary income until something more substantive can be arranged—preferably a job or training for a job.

The Employment Service tries to help in the job search, and intensified placement efforts have sometimes been made for youths. When employers demand a great deal of experience or high levels of skills, there may be little gain. Telephone follow-ups and even personal visits by placement officers, however, have occasionally proved helpful in placing young people in jobs.

Until the 1970s there were few young people in labor-market training or relief work. With a few exceptions, training was reserved for persons 20 and over, beyond normal secondary-school age; and its major thrust was to help adults in the work force adapt to changing demands for labor. With rising youth unemployment, the proportion of trainees under 25 years old rose from 30 percent in 1969 to 38 percent in 1979.[57] There was some relaxation of the age limit, with about 10 percent of the training slots taken by teenagers, especially in short courses.[58] The popular course in working life and education was redesigned once more, and youngsters uncertain about their occupational choice were encouraged to try several types of jobs before deciding on further training or more formal education. Special programs were developed for those with special problems who were alienated by ordinary schooling. Groups of about eight young people were given alternating periods of general education and work: two weeks of education followed by six to eight weeks of relief work, repeated but with a different job each time.

The biggest expansion was in relief jobs for the young at regular wages. Between 1970 and 1978 the proportion of persons in relief work who were under 25 years old rose from 4 percent to 68 percent. As mentioned in chapter 7, these jobs were particularly important for young women. In 1979, 83 percent of women but only 57 percent of men in relief work were in that age group.[59] In the public sector, office work, maintenance and repair work, environmental conservation, and care of children and the elderly were popular, to cite some examples. Private-sector employers who hired young people referred by the Employment Service were also able to provide relief work, with a 75-percent subsidy, if these jobs were in addition to their regular recruitment and included some useful training. The hope that they would also offer regular jobs after the six-month maximum for relief work often did not materialize. Sometimes a succession of relief workers was taken on for six months, and there was a feeling that training was sometimes lacking or cursory.

In the case of 16- and 17-year-olds, the government feared that labor-market training, and especially relief work, would compete with regular schooling and might even induce students to quit school for short-term jobs. Secondary-school students in Sweden receive a stipend—in 1979, 208 kronor a month. Relief jobs paid 3,000-4,000 kronor a month to these teen-agers.[60] Would high pay lure students into these temporary jobs but fail to improve their basic situation?

New Policy Directions

That, along with questions about the reliability of some of the training, were major reasons for the policy changes toward 16- and 17-year-olds approved by Parliament in June 1980. Relief work was considered inappropriate for youths under 18 years old, as was labor market training; and such youths are no longer eligible for these programs. They are encouraged to return to school as regular students in secondary school. As an alternative, they are offered additional vocational education and training within industry or some flexible arrangement of education and practical work experience, with the responsibility shifted from AMS to the educational authorities. The stipend paid is the same as for other secondary-school students.[61]

The Social Democrats opposed ending relief work and felt it was a retreat from the goal Parliament had declared in 1976 of a youth guarantee to ensure either training or employment for all out-of-school youth.[62] The new approach is less costly, which may have been a consideration of the government. Since the legal age at which compulsory schooling ends is 16, 16- and 17-year-olds who do not wish to attend school are in an ambiguous position, as are those who wish to work and return to school under the philosophy of recurrent education. These issues remain unresolved. The success of the new program, however, will surely hinge on the adequacy of the training and the ability to attract back into the program students who had become alienated from the educational establishment. Not enough time has elapsed to confirm the results, but early reports are positive.

Sweden's youthful population will increase in the 1980s, unlike the 1970s, so attempts to find solutions to the problem of youth unemployment are especially compelling. The ability to absorb the young into the labor market, however, will also depend on the state of the economy.

Older Workers: To Work or Not to Work?

It may seem paradoxical to consider older workers in a chapter on the disadvantaged, since they are much less likely to be unemployed than are young workers. For both men and women, unemployment declines steadily with age until it reaches a trough of about 1 percent among 45- to 54-year-olds and then rises to about 2 percent among 55- to 65-year-olds. (see table 7-1). Beyond that age there appears to be no unemployment. Labor-force participation is very low after age 65, however—only 14 percent for men and 4 percent for women (1979), about half the rates for 1970. Those who lose their jobs slip into retirement, since the pensionable age was lowered to 65 during the 1970s.

Although older workers are less likely to lose their jobs—the 2-percent jobless rate of 55- to 64-year-olds is low, especially compared with that for people just entering the labor force—they are out of work longer than those who are younger. This pattern is the same as in the United States.

The situation of older and handicapped workers started to deteriorate in the late 1960s and early 1970s—partly because of the demand for higher productivity, LO contends.[63] Also, whenever there was a plant closing or cutback in production, most of those who lost their jobs found others. But, even in nonrecession years a residual group was left without work—mostly older workers and the handicapped. The recession of the early 1970s made their plight worse. Many of the laws protecting these workers came after that period, partly in response to these developments in the labor market.

Policies toward older workers fall into two main categories: those that seek to maintain employment and those that seek to maintain income when there is no work.

Policies to Maintain Employment

Much of the sweeping labor legislation of the 1970s aimed at increasing the security of all workers. The vulnerable status of older workers and the handicapped was recognized, however, and they were given special protection. As mentioned in chapter 6, the Security of Employment Act not only requires prior notice of dismissal.[64] The length of time that must be given to a worker varies with age, reaching a maximum of six months for employees over 45 years old. Seniority determines the order of dismissal, a provision that tends to protect older workers. The computation of the length of service for those over 45 is also governed by more generous rules. Finally, the act states that there must be reasonable grounds for dismissal. Illness and reduced work capacity are not generally considered sufficient grounds, except if an employee is no longer capable of doing work of any significance. Such workers are given disability pensions. The employer has the duty to find less demanding work for the others. Thus there is great job security for older (and disabled) workers whose capacity to do certain work has diminished or who cannot perform their old jobs but could do something else.

The Promotion of Employment Act, also discussed in chapter 6, helps both older and handicapped workers by requiring that the County Labor Market Board must be notified before any layoff or plant closing.[65] The employer must, if requested, provide the board with information about the number of employees above a certain age or with diminished work capacity. Special plans can then be made for their reemployment, although they are usually retained unless the plant actually shuts down. The act also gives the County Labor Market Board the day-to-day responsibility for consulting with employers—even when no dismissals are involved—in order to improve the situation of elderly or handicapped workers already within firms and to promote their recruitment.

Thus the primary thrust of policies toward older workers is to prevent their unemployment by maintaining their existing jobs. Though not specifically designed for them, such measures as in-plant training and the stockpiling subsidy also benefit older workers.

Labor market training is not used extensively for older workers. During the 1979-1980 fiscal year, for example, about 15 percent of the unemployed were over 55 years old, but only 2 percent of those in labor-market training (excluding in-plant training) were in that age group.[66] In most cases the problem that confronts the older worker is not lack of skill but lack of an employer who will hire someone that old. Relocation is not much used either, since these persons have strong ties to a locality and relatively few working years left. Relocation also requires that one be able to get a job. In the north the older person who loses a job has a slimmer chance of finding another one than elsewhere.[67]

Some older workers are in relief work. Those 45 and older held about 45 percent of all relief jobs in 1975, but the large expansion of relief work in the late 1970s was aimed at persons under 25. Thus, although the *number* of persons 45 and over holding these jobs changed little, they represented only 13 percent of relief workers by the beginning of 1979.[68] A disproportionate number of handicapped workers are older, and special measures to create subsidized jobs for them are discussed later in this chapter.

Policies to Maintain Income

Despite the protection given to older employed workers, unemployment does occur, particularly when plants close. Then income support plays an important role. As mentioned in chapter 6, regular unemployment benefits are usually payable for up to sixty weeks but for persons from 56 to 64 years old, they are payable for ninety weeks, if necessary. Cash labor-market assistance, available to someone who has exhausted regular benefits, also varies with age, rising from thirty weeks for persons under 55 years old to sixty weeks for those between 55 and 59; for those 60 and over and for some structurally unemployed persons, benefits can be paid until their sixty-fifth birthday, when the normal retirement pension begins.

Unemployed workers over 60 often can qualify for a disability pension. The medical test is much more lenient for older workers than for younger persons. Equally important, if a person is regarded as permanently unemployed, there is no medical test at all if he or she has exhausted regular benefits or has received cash labor-market support for ninety weeks.[69] Liberalization in the granting of disability pensions is the result of concern on LO's part at the end of the 1960s, when older workers began to encounter increasing difficulties in the labor market. Statutory amendments were passed in the early 1970s to change the rules that govern eligibility for disability pensions. Eskil Wadensjö estimates that a worker earning the average wage receives about 88 percent of prior after-tax income from a government disability pension; one earning half the average receives about 117 percent;

and one earning twice the average receives about 66 percent. For most workers there is also a union-negotiated disability pension. Thus the living standards of older workers who leave the labor market in this way are maintained.[70]

Although there is much talk in the United States about increasing the age of eligibility for full Social Security retirement benefits from 65 to 68, Sweden has been going in the opposite direction. In 1976 the pensionable age for full benefits was lowered from 67 to 65, and reduced benefits can be received from the age of 60. Unlike a U.S. worker, a jobless Swede is not forced to take early retirement, with its permanently reduced benefits, because there are no alternative sources of incomes. The disability pension can maintain income until the age of 65, when the old-age pension would start. The most interesting option for an employed worker who wishes to reduce working gradually prior to full retirement is the partial pension that was introduced in 1976. Partial pensions are geared to part-time work. The rule is that working hours must be reduced by at least five hours a week and after the reduction must still be at least seventeen hours weekly. The worker must also have been employed for at least ten years after the age of 45.[71] (Because of these rules, the partial pension has been used disproportionately by men.) The partial pension pays 50 percent of the loss of earnings that results from the reduction in hours.[72] The actual after-tax disposable income from the combined partial pension and part-time earnings is substantial, however, because of Sweden's high marginal tax rates. Unlike early retirement benefits, a partial pension does not lead to a smaller old-age pension at age 65, when the partial pension stops. Then a worker might retire and collect a full old-age pension. A person between the ages of 65 and 70 who continues to work can receive a full old-age pension without any retirement test. It is also possible to postpone collecting all or part of the old-age pension up to the age of 70. If that is done, the pension will be larger when payments finally start. The longer the wait, the higher the pension.

The partial pension has proved to be extremely popular, providing a bridge between the world of work and full-time retirement. Many people who retired faced a shock—an abrupt change in their way of life after a lifetime of work. They missed their friends and social contacts at work. Doctors and psychologists supported unions in their desire to facilitate a more gradual transition into retirement. It is interesting that the main argument against disability pensioning for the older unemployed worker in Sweden is based not on economics but on the feeling that this leads to social isolation and a self-identification as disabled.[73] The partial pension avoids these problems and also is available to workers not threatened by unemployment. Further, it enables some workers who might not be able to function on a full-time basis to avoid disability pensioning. Thus the partial pension increases the individual's freedom of choice about the age and extent of retirement. It does not, however, resolve the problem of those older workers whose jobs are eliminated by a plant closing: one cannot work part time at a nonexistent job. Nor does it resolve the problems of older jobless workers who still have not reached the age of 60.

The Continuing Search for Jobs

In the 1970s job security was enhanced for most older workers and their range of options about retirement expanded. Swedes, however, exhibit great concern for those who nevertheless become unemployed and thus have fewer options. Labor-market and social policy in Sweden have always given first priority to jobs—those who want to work should be able to work.[74] Failing to live up to its own goal to provide work for all, Sweden has used pension policy more extensively as an alternative approach to the problem of unemployment in the later years of life. Swedes do not consider it an ideal solution. Therefore, the quest to provide jobs for older workers continues. Some of the methods used are discussed in the next section.

The Handicapped in a Full-Employment Labor Market

In Sweden the concept of full employment also applies to the handicapped. Disability pensions, generous by U.S. standards, are not regarded as a substitute for work for those disabled persons who want jobs. Work is considered necessary for the integretion of the individual into society. Thus a handicapped person who wants to work but is unable to secure employment is viewed as someone who may be cut off from an important part of life: from friendships formed at work and from a feeling of usefulness.

Prevention

Before discussing the techniques used to place Sweden's handicapped in jobs, we should note that Sweden's long-standing neutrality has virtually eliminated war as a source of disability. And the general thrust of Swedish society is to emphasize prevention. National health insurance, which covers the whole population, stresses prenatal and childhood medical care and the prevention or early detection and treatment of conditions that might be more likely to lead to adult disabilities in the United States.

Several other examples of this emphasis on avoiding disabilities will be cited. The law requires the use of automobile seat belts, and compliance is widespread. Strong legal sanctions against driving after drinking prevent many auto accidents.[75] Although per capita alcohol consumption is somewhat lower than in the United States, alcoholism is a national concern that is discussed in Sweden more often and more openly than in the United States. Alcohol was rationed until 1955, but steep taxes on it since then have failed to curb consumption.[76] A twenty-five-year plan to decrease cigarette smoking per capita by 80 percent, launched by the government in 1973, does appear to be working.[77] Occupational-safety and -health laws are strict, as is compliance, in which workers are actively involved. The Work Environment Act of 1978 requires every workplace with five or more employees to have a safety steward, who is given free time to carry out legal duties. These stewards have the right to participate in negotiations and to receive other information necessary for their work. They can also stop work in acutely dangerous situations, if management takes the opposite view.[78] High on labor's agenda are the democratization and humanization of working life, which are considered necessary adjuncts to reducing the prevalance of certain mental and physical disorders. Wildcat strikes in the late 1960s and early 1970s awakened LO's leaders to the intensity of rank-and-file feeling on these issues and were a catalyst for the far-reaching labor legislation of the 1970s.

Policies toward the Occupationally Handicapped

Much is done to try to provide the disabled with work. The aim is to place as many as possible in regular jobs, although various techniques are used for those who cannot be placed in the open labor market.

Labor-market policy focuses on the occupationally handicapped. In Sweden this means anyone who encounters or is expected to encounter a problem in getting or keeping a regular job because of a physical, mental, intellectual, or sociomedical disability. The latter category includes alcoholics, drug abusers, and ex-offenders. The concept is a broad one, and the occupationally handicapped are an extremely heterogeneous group that can also include older persons with job-related problems.[79] The nature of the handicap and the person's work are important in determining whether a specific condition is an occupational handicap. Alcoholism may be a problem in almost any kind of stable employment. An orthopedic disability, however, might be a handicap for a construction worker but not for a white-collar worker. Depending on conditions in the labor market, an employer may or may not consider a particular disability a barrier to employment. About 12 percent of applicants at the Employment Service are occupationally handicapped. They either come directly or are referred by hospitals, doctors, institutions for the care of alcoholics, prisons, social agencies, associations for the handicapped, and similar organizations. Sometimes extensive preparation is necessary before they can actually work.

Rehabilitation and Training

Labor Market Institutes, funded by AMS through the County Labor Market Boards that govern them, are located in every county and provide extensive medical and psychological evaluations of work capacity, as well as any work training needed for rehabilitation. (For example, certain types of training for the handicapped and the working-life and education course, previously done at the Labor Market Training Centers, are now carried out at these institutes.)[80]

A few provide specialized rehabilitation. Some, for instance, work with the visually impaired. One, in Sundsvall in the north, serves workers with back problems and emphasizes teaching trainees to condition their minds and bodies to prevent and reduce back strains.[81] Unlike most hospital rehabilitation centers, the Sundsvall institute pays much attention to the workplace. If the disabled person has a job but is unable to work, the staff will investigate the workplace to see if poor working habits or workplace design are at fault. If so, the person will be taught correct working positions; and, if necessary, the workplace may be designed to prevent the problem from recurring after he or she leaves the center. The County Labor Market Board will pay all or part of the cost of the redesign.

Most centers, however, are not specialized. An example is JAVI in Östersund, which serves all of one northern county.[82] It accepts the physically and mentally handicapped, including alcoholics, drug addicts, and those with behavior problems, but not the mentally retarded. There is a good deal of physical training, as well as intensive interviews and guidance to determine the kind of work rehabilitants want to practice. Trainees are encouraged to try out different kinds of work on the premises or at work sites to see what they find most appealing.

While at these centers—the stays range from several weeks to as long as a year—rehabilitants are relieved of the kind of financial pressure that so often accompanies illness and disability in the United States and that can exacerbate the physical or mental condition. Rehabilitation is provided without cost to the trainee, who also receives either a labor-market training grant or a payment from the general health-insurance scheme.

The main purpose of these centers is to improve physical, mental, and social functioning rather than to provide occupational training, which the handicapped can receive elsewhere along with the nondisabled. Much of the occupational training takes place at labor-market training centers, where about one out of three students has some kind of handicap.[83] There the handicapped take regular courses adapted to their special needs, as well as some specially designed courses such as "Adaptation and Training," which lasts a year and prepares those with visual, motor, or hearing defects for daily life, other training, and useful employment. Special driver-license courses serve those with impaired mobility, and there are even special courses for homemakers who are wheelchair-bound or have other infirmities, as well as special training for students with poor eyesight prior to their entering a university.

Subsidized Employment and Other Measures

Unfortunately, neither rehabilitation nor occupational training necessarily leads to a regular job. In recent years handicapped persons have encountered more difficulty in securing regular employment, a finding stressed in a 1978 report of the Swedish government's Commission on Long Term Employment Policy.[84]

Sweden has long had programs to aid the occupationally handicapped who are unable to obtain regular employment. Sheltered employment, semisheltered employment, and archive work, as well as relief jobs, are the leading forms of subsidized work.[85]

Sheltered employment, work that is shielded from the competition of regular applicants, does not carry the same demands for profitability as regular work and is mainly done in special sheltered workshops—usually subcontracting for industrial firms—and in a few cases at home. The wages are the same as would be received by someone doing the same kind of work on a regular job, so heavy subsidies are involved—about 1.7 times the wage costs for the disabled persons.[86] In 1980 sheltered workshops were reorganized and put under the jurisdiction of Swedish Communal Industries (Samhällsföretag), which negotiates with the unions. Persons in this kind of employment usually have less work capacity than those in semisheltered jobs. In 1978, 27 percent of those working in sheltered workshops (including a few homebound workers) had motor handicaps, but 51 percent had some mental, intellectual, or sociomedical handicap. Only a small proportion—5 percent—suffered from cardiovascular disorders or from hearing (1 percent) or visual (1 percent) handicaps.[87]

Semisheltered employment is regular work that is subsidized. The grants are always given on the condition that wages and employment benefits are the same as for others doing the same work, as set by collective-bargaining agreements, and that the relevant union gives its approval. Public and private employers then receive a wage-cost subsidy of 75 percent for the first year, 50 percent for the second year, and 25 percent for the third and fourth years. After that, subsidies are considered on an individual basis. Regular employees who become disabled are sometimes transferred to semisheltered employment, in which case the Labor Market Board grants a 25 percent subsidy, usually contingent on the employer hiring another handicapped person referred by the Employment Service. The subsidy for a handicapped young person can go as high as 90 percent of wage costs; but AMS reported in 1979 that it had not been used much, "which suggests that not even very generous subsidies are sufficient to break down resistance to employing handicapped persons."[88] Despite the upturn in the economy that year, AMS reported that the number of persons in semisheltered jobs had not increased to the extent envisaged because employers had demanded such high qualifications.[89]

Archive work is a form of partly or wholly subsidized employment that is for disabled white-collar and professional workers and a small proportion of refugees who are not disabled, and for whom it was originally developed. Usually it is done for national or municipal authorities or for nonprofit organizations, which receive a subsidy from AMS. Jobs range from simple clerical tasks to research. The pay is the same as for other workers and is set by collective agreements in the same way as for semisheltered workers. A few archive workshops specialize in printing and copying and take orders from government and business firms. In 1980 these were transferred to the same Communal Industries that is now responsible for sheltered workshops. At that time regular archive work and semisheltered employment were merged into one program called *work with wage subsidy*, with a 100-percent subsidy for government employers, 90 percent for nonprofit organizations, and the same as before for semisheltered work.

Some special relief work programs also provide employment for older and handicapped workers, as does industrial relief, described in chapter 6. These were also put under the jurisdiction of Communal Industries in 1980.

Although the ideal of Swedish labor-market policy is to have handicapped workers in all subsidized programs eventually move on to regular, nonsubsidized jobs, in reality that seldom happens. The programs are actually a form of permanent employment.

Some indication of the relative size of these measures in June 1980 is as follows:

Archive work	13,959
Semisheltered work	15,464
Sheltered workshops	18,280
Sheltered office workshops	1,500
Total	49,203[90]

Thus slightly more than 1 percent of the Swedish labor force of about 4.3 million were in one of these special job programs for the handicapped. (These figures exclude about 5,500 occupationally handicapped persons in various forms of relief work.) In the United States, with a civilian labor force of 105 million in 1980, that would be comparable to more than 1 million persons.

Other Labor Market Board Grants
to Improve Employability

The Labor Market Board also uses other measures to improve employability. The disabled can get grants and loans to purchase or adapt an automobile needed to get to work, or can receive technical aids, such as a machine that translates books from ordinary print into braille. Grants and loans also enable some to go into business. At JAVI (which does some occupational training as well as rehabilitation), older and disabled forestry workers unable to continue at their old jobs are taught woodworking, given grants to purchase tools, helped by JAVI to design furniture—and then helped to market it after they return to their home-workshops in the woods. Employers can also get help. They may be given up to 50,000 kronor (1979) to redesign a workplace—that is, to install a special elevator or redesign tools or machinery—to enable an individual handicapped employee to work.[91] Employers can also get a subsidy for the time of a *work assistant*, if a co-worker is needed to help a disabled person do his or her job.

Supportive Efforts in Other Areas of Society

Efforts in the workplace are backed up by a panoply of measures in areas such as housing, transportation, and social services.[92] All mesh with Sweden's philosophy that the handicapped should be enabled to be part of the community and to live as normally as possible. For example, codes require most new buildings and major renovations (but not private homes) to be accessible to the handicapped, who also get grants for remodeling existing dwelling units to meet individual needs. There are ample reserved parking spaces and subsidized rides in taxis or special vehicles—free in some municipalities—for those with reduced mobility—the solution until all public transportation is made accessible. That issue is being pushed by the handicapped. Some public transportation is already accessible. Stockholm's subway, for example—in sharp contrast to New York's—has elevators and escalators as most stations and is thus more usable by those in wheelchairs or those who cannot manage stairs because of impaired mobility or cardiovascular problems. Older stations without these features are being renovated. For the visually impaired, the letters on station signs are equivalent to the big E on the Snellin Eye Chart—simple, but lacking even in the new and modern transit system of Washington, D.C.

Recognition that such programs are essential for the disabled has grown in the United States, where the handicapped themselves are demanding changes, as they have been doing for a longer time in Sweden. An example is Section 504 of the Rehabilitation Act of 1973, requiring accessibility where federal funding is involved; but recognition has been slow and fraught with controversy.[93] The Swedes are more committed and have already gone further toward providing a barrier-free environment.

Thus affordable transportation costs or inability to get to work are far less likely to be barriers to employment than in the United States. Furthermore, non-means-tested handicap allowances of varying amounts are also paid to the disabled 16 and over who need assistance in everyday life or in order to work or study, or who have other extra disability-related expenses. If a person is eligible, these are paid whether or not he or she works or collects a disability pension—and they are always paid to the blind, the deaf, and those with other serious hearing defects.

Disability pensions are generous relative to those in the United States. As noted in the discussion of older workers, they replace about 88 percent of after-tax earnings of the average worker and are almost always supplemented by union-negotiated pensions. Handicapped persons who meet the medical criteria but have never worked can also get the government disability pensions, which are smaller than those for disabled workers but not means tested. By contrast, in the United States, welfare—in the form of Supplementary Security Income—is the main program for the disabled without work experience who, with some exceptions, are ineligible for Social Security disability benefits.

Pensioning is relatively more common in areas of high unemployment. Feelings are strong, however, that pensions should not be used to "solve" unemployment problems; and some believe that the younger disabled should be given work, regardless of cost or degree of disability, to prevent their social isolation.[94] Even when both provide the same income, most of the disabled express a preference for sheltered or semisheltered work over pensions.

Adjustment Groups

The Security of Employment and Promotion of Employment Acts, already discussed, give special protection to the elderly and disabled. Sometimes, however, special measures are needed to enable a worker to continue employment; and the problems of unemployed disabled workers remain unresolved by job security of the employed.

Thus the Promotion of Security Act also provides a legal framework for *adjustment groups*, workplace teams that are given the task of devising practical ways to help the handicapped get and keep jobs and to promote positive attitudes toward them. They are usually made up of from three to seven people—representatives of labor, management, the Employment Service, and if necessary a medical doctor or psychologist. Some existed even before the act. Now they are found in all workplaces with fifty or more employees. But how do they work? To what extent do they positively alter the status of the handicapped and elderly?[95]

Let us look at one of the oldest adjustment groups. It is in Sundsvall, at the Sunds plant, headquarters of a large Swedish transnational corporation specializing in the manufacture of equipment for the pulp and paper industry. Larger than most, and considered one of the more active and successful groups, it meets regularly. Some do not. Its members include representatives of the company, the Employment Service, and the three unions at the plant, as well as a foreman, a plant-safety officer, and the company doctor.[96]

The following are some examples of problems the Sunds Adjustment Group has dealt with, and their solutions:

A young worker with asthma and allergies was given a separate work area in which special equipment was installed that purified the offending allergen. The County Labor Market Board paid for most of the cost, and Sunds paid for the rest.

A deaf-mute worker was unable to communicate with co-workers. The foreman, who cooperated willingly, was sent to school to learn sign language. The County Labor Market Board paid for his salary during his absence from work.

A worker with diabetes was unable to handle shift work and there were no appropriate openings at the mill where he worked, which was owned by the mother company. He was transferred to the Sunds plant.

Back problems have been solved by raising or lowering work tables.

In a pattern noted throughout Sweden, physical problems seem easier to solve than those related to sociomedical handicaps. Some of the toughest ones are never considered by the group because workers, who must voluntarily ask for help, may be reluctant to discuss personal problems such as alcoholism. (In a new program, a County Labor Market Board can pay someone at work to look after such a handicapped person—for example, to call up or stop by the home of an alcoholic who is absent. Co-workers might be willing to act as such "guardian angels" without pay, but AMS though they should be reimbursed 2,000 kronor annually for extra expenditures and efforts.[97])

Adjustment groups can play a useful role in raising the consciousness of regular workers to the needs and special problems of the handicapped. Like the Sunds Group, however, many of them have primarily dealt with the disabled already on the payroll and have engaged in little recruiting of those without jobs.

Future Policy Directions

In contrast to the employed disabled worker, the unemployed disabled worker still has a tough time. Employers do the hiring, and they generally defend their reluctance to employ the handicapped on the basis of profitability or lack of suitable work. As in the United States, when given the opportunity to choose, they usually choose the nondisabled.

In the summer of 1979, with the economy again on the upswing, a big issue was who would be hired. Would traditional hiring patterns persist, or would the disadvantaged be hired? For the most part, the handicapped were not hired. To take one example, Volvo claimed a shortage of labor but preferred to recruit prime-age, ablebodied men in the north and in Finland. LO decried the practice, claiming there was no shortage except in the eye of the beholder and contending that available groups such as the handicapped and women were simply not wanted.[98] The disabled themselves were clamoring for jobs, reminding the government that they too were part of the jobs-for-all promise.

All the while, an important provision of the Promotion of Employment Act had never been used. The act gives the County Labor Market Boards the authority to negotiate with firms to increase their employment of the elderly and the disabled. A company that does not comply may be required to increase the number of handicapped among those it hires. As a last resort, an employer can be banned from hiring anyone who is not referred or approved by the Employment Service. This part of the act had never been implemented. In some circles quotas were being called for, something that SAF strongly opposes.

Policy changed. Starting in the fall of 1979, AMS ran a big campaign to place the disabled in jobs. The County Labor Market Boards were told to start discussions in adjustment groups and—in firms where a reasonable proportion of handicapped and elderly persons were not taken on—to use the Promotion of Employment Act to get better results. As a consequence, between November 1979 and April 1980 the number of handicapped persons who secured employment on the open market (including those with wage subsidies) rose by 50 percent compared with a year earlier.[99] Some of that hiring may have been due to the economic recovery, but it is thought that the threat of legal sanctions produced the encouraging results. Guidelines for hiring the handicapped and elderly also were worked out with some major employers, including the state railways, public insurance offices, and banks.[100] Continued implementation of these action programs represents a major breakthrough in the use of the law to support hiring of the handicapped.

The disabled do particularly poorly during recessions. It is clear, moreover, that even during periods of economic recovery, they stand at the end of the line and can be bypassed as long as there is a ready source of ablebodied workers from other areas or nations. Thus, by drying up the supply of able-bodied workers available to migrate, more development aid to the north would benefit the disabled in that region and also throughout Sweden. In coming years, the problems of the handicapped will have to be resolved both through traditional means and through firm application of legislation requiring employers to increase their employment of the disabled. The alternative, which some feel has already started, is to accept the pension as a "solution." Since that runs counter to the wishes of most of the disabled and to the philosophies of equality and normalization, it will not be accepted easily. Present indications suggest that efforts to secure more opportunities will be stepped up rather than ideology altered. But the task will be more difficult in a recessionary era.

Concluding Comments about the Disadvantaged

As chapters 7 and 8 show, a major effort is made to translate the still unfulfilled commitment of jobs for all into reality for the disadvantaged. This had been made harder by a weakening economy. In contrast to the increased security gained by most Swedish workers in the 1970s, the situation of the weakest members of the labor force was worsened by a slowdown in economic growth, recessions, and the slight secular decline in industrial employment. In the case of women these factors were offset by the expansion of public-sector jobs and greater provision of child-care facilities.

Despite adverse economic factors, the commitment to full employment expanded during the 1970s. It is interesting to see that measuring unemployment in a way conceptually similar to that used in the United States has not prevented public policy from looking beyond official jobless figures. Labor-force participation is considerably higher in Sweden than in the United States, but concern for those outside the labor force is strong. In 1979 the Swedish government Commission on Long-Term Employment Policy found a potential labor force of persons who would be willing and able to work if certain impediments were removed—for example, lack of social services, child care, jobs, work experience, or part-time employment opportunities.[101] Part-time work among women has often been viewed negatively in Sweden, but the commission recognized that some persons outside the labor force only want or can only do part-time work. And it felt that they should have that opportunity.[102] These are not just mothers of young children but also some of the elderly, especially women, and some of the disabled, the commission found, as did economist Marianne Pettersson in her study of part-time employment.[103] The commission, in an approach similar to Russell Nixon's analysis of genuine full employment in chapter

1, stressed that statements about increasing employment should always show *how* the demand for labor is to be created and *how* the different groups are to be enabled to take the job opportunities offered.[104]

The underlying philosophy that everyone should be able to live according to the norms of the society emerges once again in these chapters. For example, in public policy, the importance of jobs with regular wages and working conditions extends even to those of the handicapped incapable of attaining average productivity. Subsidized wages are preferred to risking an inadequate income. By contrast, many sheltered workshops in the United States can legally pay below the federal minimum wage because of the low productivity of their disabled workers, thus giving work to these disabled persons but also helping to wed them to poverty.[105]

Sweden's unemployment is very low by international standards. Rarely, during severe recessions, it hovers around 3 percent, a rate that might be dubbed *over* full employment by many U.S. economists who consider full employment to be anywhere from 4 to 7 percent unemployment, and possibly higher. But even when Sweden's unemployment has been 2 percent or lower, which is usually the case, special policies have proved essential for this disadvantaged. There are still some major gaps—for instance, the need for stronger antidiscrimination legislation for immigrants. In the 1970s, however, the need to strengthen and expand special policies for the disadvantaged was widely recognized and incorporated into labor-market policies in the attempt to make full employment and jobs for all a meaningful outcome for all who wanted work.

Notes

1. "Immigrants in Sweden," *Fact Sheets on Sweden* (Stockholm: Swedish Institute, 1978), p. 1.

2. Ibid., p. 1.

3. Ibid., p. 2.

4. Peter Evans, "A Place of Refuge," *Sweden Now* 2 (1980):49.

5. David Schwarz, "Sweden, an Immigrant Country—as I See It," *Current Sweden,* no. 208 (Stockholm: Swedish Institute, January 1979), p. 5.

6. Unless otherwise specified, all data on the labor force in this chapter are taken or derived from *Arbetsmarknadsstatistick Årsbok, 1979-1980 (Yearbook of Labor Statistics, 1979-1980)* (Stockholm: Liber Förlag, 1980), or from unpublished data, Sweden, Central Bureau of Statistics, Labor Force Surveys, various years.

7. Schwarz, "Sweden," p. 7.

8. Eskil Wadensjö, "Occupational Segregation of Migrant Workers in Sweden," *Växjö, Migration Studies,* no. 5 (Växjö: Universitetsfilianen i Växjö, 1976), pp. 3-5.

9. Schwarz, "Sweden," p. 7, and Wadensjö, "Occupational Segregation," p. 7.

10. "Immigrants in Sweden," p. 1.

11. Eskil Wadensjö, "The Act Concerning 240 Hours' of Swedish Lessons and Unemployment among Foreigners," *Committee of Experts on Immigration Policy,* Report no. 1: *Proceedings of Nordic Seminar on Long Term Effects of Migration,* 27-29 May 1974 (Stockholm, 1976), pp. 303-305.

12. Swedish Trade Union Confederation-LO, *Report on Labor Market Policy* (Stockholm: Swedish Trade Union Confederation, 1975), pp. 108-109.

13. Eskil Wadensjö, Swedish Institute for Social Research, personal correspondence, Stockholm, 9 February 1982. For proposals of the Swedish Governmental Committee on Education in Swedish for Foreigners, see Sweden, SOU 1981: 26, and SOU 1981:27.

14. Lise Blomqvist, "Second Generation Issues Are the Most Important in Swedish Immigration Today," *Social Change in Sweden,* no. 15 (New York: Swedish Information Service, January 1980), pp. 4-5.

15. "Immigrants in Sweden," p. 2.

16. Blomqvist, "Second Generation Issues," p. 4.

17. Christina Kelberg, "Immigration Policy," *Election Year '79,* no. 5 (New York: Swedish Information Service, July 1979), p. 3.

18. Ibid., p. 3.

19. Ibid., p. 3.

20. "Immigrants in Sweden," p. 2.

21. Ibid., p. 2.

22. Swedish Trade Union Confederation-LO, *Report,* p. 110.

23. *Information for Immigrants: The Public Employment Service in Sweden* (Solna: National Labor Market Board of Sweden, 1978).

24. Ibid., p. 23.

25. Evans, "Place of Refuge," p. 49.

26. Leif Tallskag, Research Department, National Labor Market Board, personal interview, Solna, 31 August 1979.

27. Ibid.

28. Sweden, National Labor Market Board, *Swedish Employment Policy 1979/80,* Annual Report Reprint (Solna: National Labor Market Board, 1980), p. 14.

29. Wadensjö, "Occupational Segregation," p. 3.

30. Schwarz, "Sweden," p. 8.

31. Cited in Evans, "Place of Refuge," p. 50.

32. Ibid., p. 50.

33. Ibid., p. 50.

34. Wadensjö, "Occupational Segregation," p. 8.

35. Eva-Lena Ahlqvist, "Youth Unemployment in Sweden," *Current Sweden,* no. 216 (Stockholm: Swedish Institute, April 1979), p. 3.

36. Ibid.

37. Gösta Rehn (Sweden) and K. Helveg Peterson (Denmark), *Education and Youth Employment in Sweden and Denmark,* Study prepared for the Carnegie Council on Policy Studies in Higher Education, 1980), p. 6. This comprehensive study of Swedish youth deals with all aspects of behavior, attitudes, education, employment, and unemployment.

38. Ibid., p. 70.

39. This paragraph draws heavily on ibid., pp. 75-77.

40. Ibid., p. 75.

41. Ibid., p. 77.

42. Ibid., p. 74.

43. "The Integrated Upper Secondary School in Sweden" (Stockholm: National Board of Education, 1976), p. 1, and "Primary and Secondary Education in Sweden," *Fact Sheets on Sweden* (Stockholm: Swedish Institute, 1981), p. 4.

44. Ibid., pp. 3-4.

45. Rehn, and Peterson, *Education,* pp. 140-141.

46. Sten Markusson, Swedish Confederation of Professional Associations (SACO/SR), personal interview, Stockholm, 3 September 1979, and Ahlqvist, "Youth Unemployment," p. 3.

47. Sweden, National Labor Market Board, *Jämställdhet på arbetsmarknaden: Statistik (Equality in the Labor Market: Statistics)* (Solna: National Labor Market Board, 1981), table 14, pp. 19-20.

48. Rehn, and Peterson, *Education,* table 20, pp. 133-134.

49. Sweden, National Committee on Equality between Men and Women, *Step by Step: National Plan for Equality,* SOU-56 (Stockholm, Liber Förlag, 1979), p. 26.

50. Ibid., p. 26.

51. "Higher Education in Sweden," *Fact Sheets on Sweden* (Stockholm: Swedish Institute, 1981), p. 2.

52. Rehn, and Peterson, *Education,* p. 88.

53. Ibid., p. 89.

54. For more details, see Sweden, National Labor Market Board, *Unemployment among Young People in Sweden—Measures and Experience* (Solna: National Labor Market Board, 1979), p. 3.

55. National Committee on Equality, *Step by Step,* chap. 2.

56. Ahlqvist, "Youth Unemployment," p. 7.

57. Rehn, and Peterson, *Education,* p. 92.

58. Ibid., derived from data on p. 91.

59. Sweden, *Yearbook of Statistics,* table 2.14.6, p. 179.

60. Ingrid Jonshagen, National Labor Market Board, personal interview, Stockholm, 29 August 1979.

61. Rehn, and Peterson, *Education,* p. 90.

62. Ibid.

63. Swedish Trade Union Confederation, *Report,* pp. 15-17; see also Sweden, Swedish Government's Commission on Long-Term Employment Policy, *Employment for Handicapped Persons: A Summary of the Commission's Report, January 1978 and of Five Research Projects* (Stockholm: Ministry of Labor, 1978), p. 3.

64. For the detailed contents of this act, see Sweden, Ministry of Labor, *Swedish Laws on Security of Employment, Status of Shop Stewards, Litigation in Labour Disputes* (Stockholm: Ministry of Labor, 1977), pp. 1-2, 6-20.

65. For the detailed contents of this act, see ibid., pp. 2-3, 21-24.

66. Derived from Sweden, Central Bureau of Statistics, Labor Force Sample Survey, unpublished data, and Sweden, National Labor Market Board, *Swedish Employment Policy,* 1979/80, p. 16.

67. The proportion of persons on disability pensions has also been found to be higher in municipalities with higher jobless rates. See Commission on Long-Term Employment Policy, *Employment for Handicapped Persons,* pp. 25-29.

68. Sweden, National Labor Market Board, *Swedish Employment Policy 1978/79,* Annual Report, Reprint (Solna: National Labor Market Board, 1979), derived from table for diagram 1, p. 23.

69. Lennart Lagerstrom, *Social Security in Sweden* (Stockholm: Federation of Social Insurance Offices, 1976), pp. 33-34.

70. Eskil Wadensjö, "Disability Policy in Sweden: The Swedish Contribution to the Cross National Disability Study" (Stockholm: Swedish Institute for Social Research, March 1981), table 4.7, part 4, p. 22. This comprehensive study is from Victor Halberstadt and Robert Haverman, eds., *The Economics of Disability Policy: A Cross National Perspective* (tentative title), forthcoming.

71. Wadensjö, "Disability Policy," part 3, pp. 33-34.

72. "Old Age Care in Sweden," *Fact Sheets about Sweden* (Stockholm: Swedish Institute, 1981), p. 2.

73. Wadensjö, "Disability Policy," part 5, p. 3. According to Wadensjö, newly published sociological studies have not confirmed the hypothesis of the socially isolated pensioners. (Eskil Wadensjo, Swedish Institute of Social Research, personal correspondence, Stockholm, 21 December 1981.)

74. Wadensjö, "Disability Policy," part 5, section 5.1, pp. 1-6.

75. For details, see "Traffic Safety in Sweden," *Fact Sheets on Sweden* (Stockholm: Swedish Institute, 1980).

76. Swedish Council for Information on Alcohol and Other Drugs (CAN), *The Alcohol Question in Sweden* (Stockholm: CAN, 1978), pp. 4-7, provides data giving international comparisons and trends within Sweden. See also Thomas Nordegren, "Alcohol and Alcoholism in Sweden," *Social Change in Sweden,* no. 23 (New York: Swedish Information Service, December 1981).

77. Don Hinrichsen, "Smoking Ourselves to Death," *Sweden Now* 1 (1981):32-35.

78. See, for instance, "Occupational Safety and Health in Sweden," *Fact Sheets on Sweden* (Stockholm: Swedish Institute, 1979), and Terrence Greenwood, "The Law at Work," *Sweden Now* 6 (1980):16-19. For comparison of policies in the United States and Sweden, see Steven Kelman, *Regulating America, Regulating Sweden: A Comparative Study of Occupational Safety and Health* (Cambridge, Mass.: MIT Press, 1981). For the situation before the 1978 law, see *Report on the Workplace Environment,* prepared jointly by the Swedish Trade Union Confederation (LO) and the Swedish Central Organization of Salaried Employers (TCO) (Stockholm: LO and TCO, 1974).

79. Commission on Long-Term Employment Policy, *Employment for Handicapped Persons,* pp. 1-2. This report provides an excellent overview.

80. National Labor Market Board, *Swedish Employment Policy 1978/79,* p. 11.

81. Description based on the author's visit to Rygginstitutet (the Back Pain Institute), Sundsvall, Sweden, 24 August 1979, and on an interview with Mona Wohlin, director.

82. Description based on the author's visit to JAVI, in Östersund, 21 August 1979, and on interviews with Kerstin Johansson and Christer Ägren.

83. Sweden, National Board of Education, *Labour Market Training: A Presentation* (Stockholm: Liber Lärmodel, 1975), p. 5.

84. Commission on Long-Term Employment Policy, *Employment for Handicapped Persons.*

85. A detailed analysis of subsidized employment is given in Wadensjö, "Disability Policy," part 3, section 3.4, from which this draws heavily. See also "Support for the Disabled in Sweden," *Fact Sheets on Sweden* (Stockholm: Swedish Institute, 1981), and Sweden, National Labor Market Board, *Vocational Rehabilitation in Sweden* (Solna: National Labor Market Board, 1978).

86. Wadensjö, "Disability Policy," part 3, section 3.4, p. 48.

87. Sweden, National Labor Market Board, unpublished data.

88. National Labor Market Board, *Swedish Employment Policy 1978/79,* p. 21.

89. Ibid.

90. National Labor Market Board, *Swedish Employment Policy 1979/80,* adapted from data on p. 20.

91. Curt Landén, director, Public Employment Service, Sundsvall, personal interview, 24 August 1979.

92. A more detailed description is given in "Support for the Disabled in Sweden."

93. For details on laws in the United States, see President's Committee on the Employment of the Handicapped, *The Law and Disabled People: Selected Federal and State Laws Affecting Employment and Certain Rights of People with Disabilities* (Washington, D.C.: U.S. Government Printing Office, 1980).

94. Wadensjö, "Disability Policy," part 5, p. 3.

95. For a description of adjustment groups, see Sweden, National Labor Market Board, *Adjustment Groups* (Solna: National Labor Market Board, May 1978).

96. Discussion of the Sunds adjustment groups is based on the author's interview with the Sunds team in Sundsvall, 24 August 1979.

97. Ingeborg Jönsson, National Labor Market Board, personal interview, Solna, 30 August 1979.

98. Göran Borg, Labor Market Department, Swedish Confederation of Trade Unions (LO), personal interview, Stockholm, 30 August 1979.

99. National Labor Market Board, *Swedish Employment Policy, 1979/80,* p. 19.

100. Ibid., p. 20.

101. Swedish Government's Commission on Long-Term Employment Policy, *Policy for Employment for Everybody: A Summary of the Final Report,* May 1979 (Stockholm: Ministry of Labor, 1979), p. 6.

102. Ibid., p. 8.

103. Marianne Pettersson, *Deltidsarbetet i Sverige (Part-time Work in Sweden)* (Stockholm: Arbetslivscentrum/Akademilitteratur, 1981).

104. Commission on Long-Term Employment Policy, *Employment for Everybody,* p. 8.

105. See Sar A. Levitan and Robert Taggart, *Jobs for the Disabled* (Baltimore, Md.: Johns Hopkins University Press); and Barbara L. Wolfe, *Impacts of Disability and Some Policy Implications* (Madison, Wis.: University of Wisconsin Institute for Research on Poverty, 1979).

**Part III:
Coda**

9

The Future of Full Employment

In a world beset with uncertainty, one cannot predict with certainty the future of full employment. Nevertheless, it is still worthwhile to explore possible future directions.

Sweden

Studying full employment in Sweden makes it clear that the engine that propels the system is political commitment. There is nothing inherent in the Swedish economy that produces full employment or even low unemployment, especially since the beginning of the 1970s. If not for extraordinary effort and willingness to make full employment a national priority, Swedish unemployment would easily be more than double its actual rate.

What about the future? That depends on a constellation of political and economic factors.

Sweden's full-employment policy was initially the product of Social Democratic ideology and trade-union support. The Social Democrats were at the helm of government, either alone or in a coalition, for about four and a half decades. Political continuity over a long period of time made it possible to implement policies and to gain broad acceptance. Nonsocialist governments after 1976, as we have seen, continued to pursue full-employment policies. The shift in political power from the Social Democrats was actually very slight, however. A serious erosion from the Social Democrats or from labor could weaken the commitment to full employment. That does not seem likely, at least not in the near future, especially since the victory of the Social Democrats in the September 1982 election.

Immigrants also pose a large problem for the future. Sweden's full-employment policy was originally developed when its labor force was homogeneous. That is no longer the case. Because of their relative youth compared with Swedes, the proportion of immigrants and those of foreign descent will increase in the future even without more immigration.[1] So far there has been a commitment by the government to equality for immigrants, as already discussed. Still, there are possible danger spots. Relatively high unemployment rates (around 3 percent in mid-1982) could foreshadow trouble especially among immigrant youths. Some newcomers have been called

"black heads," and there have been scattered skirmishes between immigrants and Swedish youths.[2] Immigrants are sometimes blamed for
unemployment. Racism in Sweden and confrontations between Swedes and
immigrants have often been blown out of proportion by newspapers; in
fact, contact between Swedes and new ethnic groups is not always filled
with conflict. More often, according to an official of the National Immigration and Naturalization Board, it is simply nonexistent.[3] Many Swedes
probably have not yet come to grips with the concept of a multiethnic country. Firm measures against discrimination are still lacking. Moreover, as in
other countries, children of immigrants will probably be more likely than
their parents to resent occupational segregation if it persists. Thus, if immigrants and their children are not integrated into Swedish society and into
the labor movement as active members—as LO is trying to do—some fear
that they will become a permanent underclass.[4] That could lead to a
breakdown of traditional working-class solidarity, create exceptions to the
full-employment goal, and give rise to acceptance of "tolerable" levels of
unemployment. If Swedes can learn anything from the U.S. experience, it is
that racism and acceptance of high unemployment among "them" are incompatible with the ideology of real full employment.

Sweden's full-employment concept has encompassed women. As in the
case of immigrants, however, rising unemployment could prompt acceptance of more unemployment, especially hidden unemployment, among
women. A slowdown in public-sector growth could also affect women
adversely through fewer job opportunities and fewer services and child-care
options. Any rise in unemployment would disproportionately harm *any* of
the disadvantaged groups and make it more difficult to eliminate youth
unemployment, which has been such a concern to Swedish society.

Political factors are crucial in determining the commitment to the goal
of full employment. Economic factors, however, determine the ease with
which the goal can be attained. Like most Western nations, Sweden entered
the 1980s with a long list of economic problems. At the September 1981
Social Democratic party Congress, a year before the party's electoral victory, the country was described as facing a crisis.[5] In the background was a
depressing international scene, characterized by a deepening recession with
rising unemployment, currency instability, rising oil prices (at the time), and
the pursuit of restrictive policies by other nations. On the domestic front, in
addition to an acute increase in unemployment, other problems were
cited—for example, structural problems in basic industries, inflation,
foreign debt, a large domestic budget deficit, a trade deficit, and a low level
of industrial investment.

Sweden's economic problems will have to be overcome with decreasing
emphasis on nuclear power. Despite the lack of oil, a strong environmental
and antinuclear movement led to a national referendum in 1979 on the

future of nuclear energy, which was originally developed under Social Democratic governments. As a result of the referendum—which was only advisory but is being abided by—nuclear energy is slated to be phased out within twenty-five years.[6] Though a heavy oil importer, Sweden is already much more energy efficient than the United States, consuming only a little more than half as much energy per capita (1978).[7] Now, however, there is a heavy emphasis on conservation and on finding nonpolluting substitutes for oil, as Sweden strives for economic growth, jobs, *and* a good environment.[8]

Labor-market policy will remain an integral part of planning for full employment, as it has for several decades. Industrial policy, however, has now also become a necessary adjunct. In the 1970s active government intervention was needed to prevent the collapse of some industries, such as steel. Unlike that of the United States, the Swedish government has not been content to watch the shutdown of steel plants passively. Instead, firms were brought together and merged into one large enterprise capable of surviving and remaining profitable.[9] This required a massive infusion of capital from the government, which then became a majority stockholder. It was also predicated on shrinking the industry in a planned way while simultaneously working out alternatives for the affected workers, all of whom were given at least two years to seek other jobs, training, or relocation assistance. In line with Sweden's law on worker participation, unions played an important role in the whole process, gaining three out of twelve seats on the board of the new company.

The general decline in industrial investment in Sweden is partly related to decisions made by multinational corporations. Swedish industrial companies have been expanding investment and employment more rapidly abroad than within Sweden. LO, fearing that Sweden runs the risk of industrial impoverishment, has called for more democratization of the economy, with more state and worker control over multinationals, to face up to this challenge.[10]

The Social Democrats never made nationalization an important part of their ideology. Instead, as Rudolph Meidner notes, the "rallying cry was full employment, economic growth, fair division of national income and social security."[11] Intervention in the sphere of production was considered unnecessary. Indeed, most industry is still privately owned, but there has been an increasing call for more social control of investment and production. Wage-earner funds are the focal point of this issue.

The formal debate about wage-earner funds has been especially intense since 1975, when a report by Meidner, commissioned by LO in 1971, was released.[12] It suggested that part of a company's profit should be transferred to collectively owned employee funds. One of the main reasons for the proposal was to counteract the tendency for the wage-solidarity policy to lead to even more economic concentration. The explanation for this phenomenon is simple. Wage bargaining is centralized and emphasizes equal pay for equal work and reducing wage differentials between workers doing the same work in different firms. Thus workers in the most profitable firms do not push for wages as high as their firms could pay, since less profitable firms would not be able to meet these wages. Therefore, some firms capable of paying more reap additional profit, which accelerates economic concentration and power. Wage-earner funds were proposed as a means of continuing the wage-solidarity policy without these undesired consequences. They were also proposed as a way of giving the community and unions more of a say in allocating profits and in ownership of productive assets. With the decline in industrial investment, wage-earner funds have also been considered an important potential means of raising investment capital and ensuring more democratic control of its use. There is a feeling that there will be a great need for capital in the future and, if sacrifices have to be made by workers to ensure capital formation, they and the larger community should be entitled to an influence over these funds.

The different forms that wage-earner funds might take have been debated in Sweden.[13] LO endorsed the idea of wage-earner funds in the mid-1970s, and the Social Democrats committed themselves to a form of wage-earner funds in 1981.[14] The funds are strongly opposed by employers and by conservatives, who contend that they would eventually mean a takeover of all private industry. Supporters feel they will lead to increased industrial democracy and a somewhat different form of mixed economy. Whether or not some version of wage-earner funds is eventually adopted in Sweden, the issue is sure to be prominent and hotly contested in the 1980s.

In the past Sweden has met a considerable number of challenges by retailoring policies, without dropping its commitment to full employment, which is so strongly embedded in Swedish society. The big question for the future is how the challenges will be met—and whether they can be met if the economic crisis facing all Western countries deepens and keeps a small country like Sweden from being the master of its own fate.

The United States

Both past experience and present realities give little cause for optimism about the future of full employment in the United States.

In Sweden, public policy has made a substantial difference in reducing unemployment. With a strong political commitment, the Swedish economy has been pushed toward full employment for long periods of time, even if that goal has not been reached. In the United States, however, public policy has often been geared toward maintaining and even creating unemployment. If anything, the movement away from full employment has been *greater* since passage of the Humphrey-Hawkins Act.

Full employment cannot be viewed in isolation from other issues or from the general economic and political climate, which has deteriorated under the Reagan administration. At this writing, there is a major recession with very high unemployment. There are also high interest rates, deep cuts in social programs (including jobs and training), a tremendous budget deficit caused by a combination of huge increases in the military budget and projected revenue shortfalls (from unprecedented tax breaks favoring the rich and corporations) and from the effects of unemployment itself, as explained in chapter 4. The commitment to equal opportunity and to the disabled has seriously eroded. Environmental and occupational safety and health programs are under assault. The list could go on and on.

Much of the future of full employment hinges on the political response to this situation. It may be weak, defensive, splintered, and ineffective. The crisis, however, might stimulate new political activity and directions and the development of linkages between groups that could eventually lead to significant political changes, especially within the Democratic party.

Not only is political power required to pass a strong law, but it is also needed to enforce the law. To get this kind of power, there must be a greatly expanded grass-roots full-employment movement coupled to a much broader electoral base, both united in a common political platform.

In contrast to Sweden, where voter turnout is usually around 90 percent or more, a large and growing proportion of voting-age Americans (nearly 48 percent in 1980) stay home on election day; even more do so on primary day.[15] In Sweden those from the least favored groups generally vote for the Social Democrats. Paradoxically, in the United States, many of those who would benefit most from full employment and related programs are outside the political system and exert little power. They are the very ones who are overrepresented among nonvoters: blacks, Hispanics, blue-collar workers, the young, the jobless, and the less affluent.[16] Their nonparticipation may stem partly from a feeling that it doesn't make any difference what they do.

A bold Democratic agenda that stresses full employment, income security (including strengthened Social Security), a national health program, more affordable housing, genuine tax reform favoring lower- and middle-income individuals, and related programs might attract some nonvoters.

Not everyone who would benefit from these programs necessarily or automatically supports them, however. Hence there is a constant need to increase the level of consciousness about full employment and related issues. It is unlikely that full employment can be achieved unless it is part of a larger package of reform measures. Although each reform had its own history, the Social Security Act, the National Labor Relations Act, the Fair Labor Standards Act, and other significant reforms of the New Deal era were politically feasible because they were part of a package put together in a favorable political and social climate.

A widespread movement for full employment and jobs now—much more extensive than the one that took place during the drive for the Humphrey-Hawkins Act, but drawing on that experience—could help create a favorable climate. Local groups linked through national networks could press for full employment and jobs now. This kind of movement could engage in electoral politics such as lobbying, local and national demonstrations, and education about full employment. It would, however, also have to build *electoral strength* at conventions, in primaries, and in congressional and local as well as presidential elections—for without continuing political strength, political promises will often mean little. In that way it could become a force for change, along with other movements. Is such a movement possible?

Full employment is a difficult issue on which to organize. In addition to the many problems discussed in chapter 3, there is another one. The issue often seems too abstract, especially if the focus is only on the national economy. The need for jobs and the benefit of providing jobs can often be grasped more readily if also posed in terms of the communities in which people live. How, specifically, will full employment affect Cleveland? Flint, Michigan? Vermont? rural Mississippi? rural Wisconsin? Harlem? Great Falls, Montana? a Navaho reservation in Arizona? Los Angeles? How many jobs would we need? What kind of work needs to be done? In sum, there is a need to set local as well as national goals.

In the wake of the Reagan policies, Representative John Conyers (D-Michigan), a member of the Black Congressional Caucus from Detroit, is proposing locally based national planning for full employment.[17] Conyers regards this measure as a way to strengthen and enforce the Humphrey-Hawkins Full Employment and Balanced Growth Act. Using this approach, there would be national *employment* as well as *unemployment* targets. These national targets, moreover, would be translated into employment and unemployment goals for every town, city, county, and region—including rural, suburban, and urban areas. In larger cities, employment targets would be built up from the neighborhood level.

There is no way of getting or implementing such legislation in the present political climate. Thus Conyers sees his proposal (in the embryonic stage at this writing), as a consciousness-raising and educational tool, and as a possible way to activate a broad movement for jobs. The hope is that in the future it may be part of a new Democratic agenda, along with other progressive measures.

The essence of Conyers's approach to locally based planning for full employment is to democratize the planning process. Through broad citizen participation, there would be an assessment of each area's needs, which would vary from place to place. High priority would be given to employment in certain fields, such as rural and urban transportation, renewable energy sources, housing rehabilitation and construction, agriculture, natural resources, a high-speed national train system, and beefing up a deteriorating public infrastructure. Basic public services—which might include badly needed day care, services for the aged, health care, and education—also get high priority, as do artistic and cultural activities and a number of other areas—in particular, efforts at reindustrialization, which are often dependent on a better infrastructure.

An area's needs would be matched against a locally conducted survey of unused labor, with numerical job goals debated and established all over the country, in U.S. towns, cities, counties, and states. These targets for jobs—perhaps 260,000 new jobs for Conyers's own Detroit, for example— would provide the basis for short- and long-term planning by private and nonprofit employers, as well as by all levels of public employers—not just the federal government.

Does this mean that the federal government would be opting out of its responsibilities for full employment? Not at all. As Bertram Gross and Stanley Moses explain it, although the inspiration for this kind of planning would "come from the bottom, the federal government would also have a vital role."[18] It would, for example, finance projects, promote special assistance to distressed areas where unemployment is deeply entrenched, provide technical assistance, coordinate decentralized plans, and carry out plans of a regional and national scope. In addition, it would help establish and promote local groups and would require citizen participation and full-employment planning as partial conditions for federal aid to states and localities. An important feature of this proposal is that it would also be binding on the board of governors of the Federal Reserve System.

The proposal is broad ranging and provides for special, focused efforts for groups with more than their share of employment problems, such as victims of discrimination, the physically and mentally handicapped, ex-prisoners, alcoholics, and drug addicts. Areas with special problems would also receive special help. This means that the problem of plant closings and capital flight, which was not explicitly considered in the Humphrey-Hawkins Act, would receive specific focused attention. There would also be planned conversion from military to civilian production to prevent any adverse impact on workers or areas currently dependent on these jobs.

The last point is an important part of Conyers's proposal since it is part of the answer to two questions that are sure to be asked about this bold approach to full employment: Isn't it inflationary? And how will it all be financed?

The inflation issue haunted supporters of full-employment legislation in the 1970s. Conyers tackles it head on, with a call for cuts in the inherently inflationary budget. He would take away those parts that represent waste and overkill. Along with that, he advocates selective price controls to curb corporate price-setting power, as well as standby controls for other prices. A complementary incomes policy would cover executive salaries and dividends, as well as wages. Credit allocation, prevention and alleviation of bottlenecks, democratization of the federal reserve system, and staged reduction of real interest rates are also proposed. Could support for such a program—one that includes a slash in Pentagon funding and wage-price controls—come from labor, or would those issues prevent the formation of a broad coalition? In the case of military expenditures, the answer is not clear cut. The AFL-CIO seems to be reconsidering its previous position on military expenditures. How far it would go in this direction is an unresolved issue of the 1980s. Support for the idea is already evident from unions such as the International Association of Machinists (IAM), and the American Federation of State, County and Municipal Employees (AFSCME). The rapid growth of the nuclear-disarmament movement provides a basis for guarded optimism that this trend will continue. As for controls, the AFL-CIO's opposition to them during the struggle over Humphrey-Hawkins stemmed from a negative experience with inequitable controls. Since then the federation has publicly supported full economic controls covering *all* sources of income—not just wages and prices, but also profits and dividends.[19]

To finance full employment, Conyers proposes a number of measures, including (but not limited to) redirecting some military expenditures to useful civilian purposes, a major tax reform that would make the rich and corporations pay their share, and more social control over workers' pension funds, with federal guarantees of their investments.

Nothing like the Meidner plan for wage-earner funds is on the agenda in the United States. Organized labor, however, has been demanding a more effective voice in the investment and control of collectively negotiated pension funds, many of which are unilaterally controlled by employers. The AFL-CIO executive council already supports the use of these funds to increase employment through reindustrializing the nation's economic base. Most funds are invested in the largest corporations, and labor has been increasingly concerned that many of these same corporations have transferred a large portion of their production abroad and are increasingly hostile to unions at home.[20]

Labor's interest in gaining some control over use of pension funds might open the entire issue of social control over private investment decision. Although there were some exceptions—for example, Michael Harrington, then the chairperson of the Democratic Socialist Organizing Committee—during the debate over full employment prior to passage of the Humphrey-Hawkins Full Employment and Balanced Growth Act, this issue was rarely raised by proponents of full employment.[21] Not even the earliest version of Humphrey-Hawkins tackled this issue. Yet without more public restraints on investment decisions, any attempt to reach full employment could be frustrated. As long as capital retains unlimited power to shift operations overseas or to leave an area without warning, regardless of the employment impact, it can continue to transform entire communities and even regions into depressed areas. The tax system, which encourages these practices, would obviously have to be altered. Labor recognizes this but at present lacks sufficient political power to effect the change.

Political power is an absolute necessity if there is to be full employment, and a strong movement could go a long way toward reopening the issue in the 1980s. The active involvement of people clamoring for full employment in their own towns, neighborhoods, and regions could provide an essential ingredient for a successful movement. Without a national focus, such as the proposed national legislation, however, a locally based movement could lead to extreme narrowness—to concern over full employment in my area but not in yours, to the belief that full employment has arrived when it comes to Cleveland, whether or not it has come to Detroit. That would be analogous to concern about unemployment when it affects whites but not blacks, the young but not the old, men but not women, the ablebodied but not the disabled. That is why a movement for genuine full employment would have to operate on all levels—local, state, and national—and become involved in electoral and nonelectoral politics at all levels, working in tandem with other progressive movements.

There are ways that a movement can operate at the local level to begin to raise consciousness, and community groups may even locate some funds for job creation in advance of federal action. A proposal in the New York City Council, for example, would promote more jobs through use of public-employee pension funds.[22] This proposal also calls for more stringent control of real-estate tax abatements. Proponents contend that these have often been used to finance skyscrapers—ones that would have been built anyway—in the most desirable Manhattan locations. The proposed law would use these extra taxes to finance jobs or the infrastructure for jobs or to promote small and medium-sized business, which have been known to be incubators of jobs. Full employment cannot be achieved without national policy, but local initiatives could become part of a national movement. The danger is that some purely local approaches could end up robbing Peter to pay Paul, if the focus is on luring jobs from another place rather than on increasing the number of jobs. Or, for example, a purely local approach might be to fight for a larger military budget so that a locally affected economy might get more military contracts.

Presumably, a movement for full employment would be made up of many of the same groups that participated in the drive for the Humphrey-Hawkins Act, possibly with more involvement from antiwar and neighborhood groups and with more emphasis on individuals who are not affil-

iated with any organization. Will the negative experience of having worked
for a law that was watered down and then ignored make it more difficult to
generate activity? That is a real question. It may shift more of the emphasis
onto demands for concrete national programs that are needed and that, if
implemented, would provide jobs as a result. Housing, rebuilding of
railroads, and day-care centers are examples. The approaches, however, are
not mutually exclusive; they are reinforcing. Full employment, after all,
aims both to meet the needs of society and to provide jobs. Conyers's approach calls for both.

Organized labor could play a vital role in such a movement. Faced with
an increasingly hostile environment, labor has been changing, especially
since the death of George Meany and the onset of the deepening crisis.
Solidarity Day in September 1981 reflected a growing awareness of the need
for broad coalitions to achieve goals, and the AFL-CIO has already
recognized the need for greater political activity. However, even with additional funds, unions cannot match the huge sums available to corporations
for campaign expenditures. But they do have a vast untapped potential for
mobilizing large numbers of people into political action in local communities. If that grass-roots potential is actually mobilized, it could spell a
major difference in effectiveness. So would a major expansion of the labor
movement itself, if more blue- *and* white-collar workers were organized. At
present, the opposite is likely, with the flight of jobs to nonunionized areas
of the country and overseas, tougher employer tactics, the contraction of
traditionally unionized industries like auto and steel, the trend toward white-
collar employment (which is scarcely unionized), recessions, and government actions such as the Reagan assault on the Professional Air Traffic
Controllers Organization (PATCO). In the 1930s, through struggle, unions
expanded and were revitalized during a period of economic hardship but
political ferment. If this happens in the 1980s, it could help create a climate
conducive to a new agenda for the Democrats, since labor's political power
would be greatly enhanced.

The AFL-CIO has begun, in a modest way, to question the size of the
military budget. Pressure from some unions, especially in the public sector,
for extensive cuts in the military budget and for more socially useful jobs
could also help to effect change. That, along with pressure from some
leaders, like William Winpsinger, president of the IAM, who are already
outspoken on the issue, might succeed in reversing the AFL-CIO's historic
support for large military budgets. This would put pressure on the
Democratic party to support full employment without excessive military expenditures, something that was barely part of the debate over Humphrey-
Hawkins. Winpsinger, disappointed by the failure of the Democratic party.
to fight for full employment and related issues, acknowledges that the
trade-union leadership, himself included, is still committed to trying to be

effective within that party. However, he warns that if the party does not move to the left, his union will reconsider its commitment to the Democrats.[23] That would also put pressure on the Democrats. The growth of a strong third-party movement advocating progressive issues would also put pressure on the Democrats, but that does not seem to be on the national horizon.

What Can Be Learned from the Swedish Experience?

Full employment is not just around the corner. It would still be useful, however, to consider some major lessons about full employment from the Swedish experience and to pose some questions about the ability to achieve full employment in the United States.

Judging by the Swedish experience, full employment would require massive federal participation in the economy. Except for military expenditures, the political appeal in the United States has been to reduce the role of government. In Sweden, along with the development of other parts of the welfare state, full-employment policy has led to a public sector much larger than that in the United States. Any movement for full employment would have to confront that issue. Can the American bias against public spending in favor of private be overcome? A more equitable tax system might make Americans more willing to support public expenditures. Sweden is a high-tax economy. Its citizens' greater willingness to support high taxes stems from a feeling that tax dollars are well spent. Proportionately less is spent on military expenditures than in the United States—only about 3.5 percent of GNP—and less on pathologies such as crime that are associated with unemployment and poverty and that drain so much from our public purse in the United States. Public facilities and services are of very high quality in Sweden, which reinforces public support.

There are other possible reasons for this difference, however. One of them is the U.S. emphasis on individualism. Can the American ethos of individualism be altered? Attitudes toward social welfare are instructive in this matter. When young adults between 18 and 24 were asked about the greatest accomplishment of their nation by a Japanese survey team, 60 percent of Swedish youth, but only 24 percent of American youth, mentioned social welfare as one of these accomplishments. A majority of Swedes believe that society has a major responsibility for the individual's social welfare.[24]

Part of the political appeal of Sweden's social-welfare state has been that it bestows benefits on large groups of people without the stigma of means testing. As noted in chapter 6, this philosophy has been maintained in job and training programs. They are not just for the poor, but are for all those who need jobs or training or retraining. A worker whose plant is closing does not have to become destitute to qualify for retraining, if it is needed. In the United States, programs created only for the poor are most politically vulnerable. Thus Social Security has more political strength than welfare programs. When CETA was reauthorized to serve only the most severely disadvantaged, it became more politically vulnerable and a likely candidate for extinction. Means-tested programs invite backlash: Why should "they" get jobs and training but not "us"? When race is associated with low income, as it is in the United States, this makes the programs even more vulnerable. A universal approach requires more resources to accommodate all groups. Otherwise, the disadvantaged will lose out to others. But a universal approach is not incompatible with special programs that focus on special needs and problems of different groups. *Indeed, the Swedish experience shows that special efforts are required if all groups are to attain full employment.* Discrimination does not vanish because unemployment is low, although it is easier to overcome at such times; separate patterns of employment and education for the sexes do not vanish simply because unemployment is low. In the United States, where patterns of racial discrimination have such a long history, it would be naive to believe that racism would disappear automatically in a full-employment economy. Positive efforts would have to continue for minorities and other disadvantaged groups. The Swedish experience also shows that even small rises in unemployment worsen the labor-market position of disadvantaged groups.

Judging from the Swedish experience, government expenditures and special efforts in the labor market would be required even at very low levels of unemployment. Are Americans willing to admit the need for these programs when unemployment is at 2 percent—if that should ever happen? If not, then they probably cannot have real full employment in the sense of a job for everyone who wants to work. In that respect, power alone would not be sufficient. As Meidner has observed, "organizational strength without ideology is form without content."[25] Without a focus on full employment as a moral issue, without a feeling of solidarity, a political movement for full employment is likely to dissipate. It would work until employment is fuller, but not full. It would work until unemployment declines, still leaving some without work. And these ranks would be peopled by those who have always occupied the least favored spots in the U.S. economy and society.

The conditions stipulated by Meidner do not exist in the United States. Moreover, the United States is far from achieving even the interim goal of 4 percent unemployment set by the Humphrey-Hawkins Act, let alone 2 percent unemployment. And the United States is not Sweden. But even as advocates of full employment work toward the immediate task of ending the near-depression of the early 1980s, they should also study the Swedish system. It is not too soon to *propose* certain policies that might be introduced when there is a more favorable political climate. The struggle to obtain these policies would also help to build ideological and institutional underpinnings of a full-employment society.

Should not Americans have the opportunity to consider an extensive system of publicly subsidized child care, parenthood leave, and a family policy that considers the needs of working parents and their children? a commitment to youth? advance planning of public jobs? security of employment legislation, including advance warning before layoffs or dismissals? more attention to the needs of disabled workers? regional-development policies? relocation grants? extended unemployment benefits? partial pensions for older workers? jobs and training programs without means testing and with decent wages and stipends? The list could go on and on. Most important, should we not consider the *goal* of decent jobs at decent wages for those who want to work and decent income support for those who cannot work? If all the facts were known, these programs would be positively regarded by many persons in the United States because they meet real needs. Starting a national debate on these issues would bring us closer to full employment.

Notes

1. Lise Blomqvist, "Second Generation Issues Are Most Important in Swedish Immigration Policy Today," *Social Change in Sweden*, no. 15 (New York: Swedish Information Service, January 1980), p. 3.

2. Peter Evans, "A Place of Refuge," *Sweden Now* 2 (1980):49-50, and John Vinocur, "Swedes Discover Their Dark Side: Racism," *The New York Times*, 4 February 1980, sect. 4, p. E.5.

3. Blomqvist, "Second Generation Issues," p. 6.

4. Swedish Trade Union Confederation, *Report on Labor Market Policy* (Stockholm: Swedish Trade Union Confederation, 1975), pp. 102-115, and *Swedish Trade Union Confederation* (Stockholm: Swedish Trade Union Confederation, 1978), p. 32.

5. Ingvar Carlsson, "The Future for Sweden," Press Service, Swedish Social Democratic party Congress, 28 September 1981.

6. See Per Ragnarson, "Before and After: The Swedish Referendum on Nuclear Power," *Political Life in Sweden*, no. 5 (New York: Swedish Information Service, September 1980).

7. U.S. Bureau of the Census, *Statistical Abstract of the United States: 1980* (Washington, D.C.: U.S. Government Printing Office, table 1594, p. 917.

8. See, for instance, William Dampier, "Energy in Focus: The Cold, Hard Facts," *Sweden Now* 4 (1981):28-30.

9. Jeffrey Burton, "The Swedish Steel Merger: Government and Worker Participation," *Working Life in Sweden*, no. 21 (New York: Swedish Information Service, November 1980), and Anders Davisson, "Swedish Industrial Policy at the Beginning of the Eighties," *Current Sweden*, no. 262 (Stockholm: Swedish Institute, December 1980).

10. Swedish Trade Union Confederation, *The Trade Union Movement and the Multinationals* (Stockholm: Swedish Trade Union Confederation, 1976).

11. Rudolph Meidner, "Our Concept of the Third Way: Some Remarks on the Socio-Political Tenets of the Swedish Labour Movement," *Economic and Industrial Democracy: An International Journal* 1 (August 1980):345. This article gives an excellent analysis of the ideological underpinnings of Sweden's labor movement, as well as the conflicts between the market economy and the wage-solidarity policy and the subsequent thrust for economic democracy and wage-earner funds.

12. Rudolph Meidner, *Employee Investment Funds: An Approach to Collective Capital Formation* (London: Allen & Unwin, 1978). This is the translation of the original 1976 report.

13. See, for example, Rolf Eidem and Bernt Öhman, *Economic Democracy through Wage-Earner Funds* (Stockholm: Swedish Center for Working Life, 1979), esp. pp. 37-58.

14. Chris Mosey, "Swedish Socialists Endorse Plan to Collectivize Industry," *Christian Science Monitor*, 5 October 1981, and Alan Otten, "Swedish Socialists' Comeback Drive Is Imperiled by Their Plan to Let Labor Control Many Firms," *The Wall Street Journal*, 17 June 1982. The plan approved by the Social Democrats differs from the original Meidner proposal. For example, it would set up twenty-four regional wage-earner funds that would buy stock in Swedish companies.

15. *Statistical Abstract of the United States: 1980*, table 851, p. 515.

16. "Over the Years 'None of the Above' Got More Votes," *The New York Times*, 21 September 1980, p. 60.

17. See Bertram Gross and Stanley Moses, "Building a Movement: Full Employment Planning from the Bottom Up," *The Nation*, 10 April 1982, pp. 424-425, and idem, "Some Anti-Crime Proposals For Progressives," *The Nation*, 6 February 1982, p. 140, from which this section draws heavily.

18. Gross and Moses, "Building a Movement," p. 424. See also Bertram Gross and Stanley Moses, *How to Plan for Full Employment* (Washington, D.C.: Institute for Policy Studies, forthcoming).

19. AFL-CIO, *The National Economy: Background and Policy Recommendations for 1982* (Washington, D.C.: AFL-CIO, n.d.).

20. The Industrial Union Department of the AFL-CIO now puts out a monthly publication, *Labor and Investment: The Publication on Labor,*

Pension and Benefit Funds and Investment (Washington, D.C.: Industrial Union Department of the AFL-CIO).

21. See Michael Harrington, *Full Employment: The Issue and the Movement* (New York: Institute for Democratic Socialism, 1977), pp. 22-32. The Democratic Socialist Organizing Committee is no longer in existence. It has merged with the New American Movement into a new organization, also headed by Harrington, the Democratic Socialists of America.

22. "Community-Based Planning for Jobs and Balanced Growth Act," Intro. no. 1022, was introduced into the city council of New York City in 1981.

23. William Winpisinger, "Looking at a Democratic Socialist Strategy in the U.S. Trade Union Movement," Speech at a Conference on World Systems of Labor and Production: Challenges to Social Democracy in the 1980s," Hobart and William Smith Colleges, Geneva, New York, 13 May 1982.

24. Hans Berlind and Merl Hokenstad, Jr., "Sweden's Demogrant: A Model for the U.S.?" *Journal of the Institute for Socioeconomic Studies* 6 (Autumn 1981):77-78.

25. Rudolf Meidner, "Our Concept of the Third Way: Some Remarks on the Socio-Political Tenets of the Swedish Labor Movement," *Economic and Industrial Democracy: An International Journal* 1 (August 1980):350.

Index

About the Author

Helen Ginsburg graduated from Queens College and received the Ph.D. in economics from the New School for Social Research. She is associate professor of economics at Brooklyn College of the City University of New York, where she specializes in labor, poverty, social-welfare, and urban economics. Professor Ginsburg has also taught at Long Island University and has been research associate professor at the New York University Center for Studies in Income Maintenance Policy, where she conducted research on unemployment and subemployment; and research associate at the New School for Social Research, where she was engaged in one of the first major studies of poverty in the United States in the post-World War II era.

Professor Ginsburg's publications include *Poverty, Economics and Society* (1972 and 1981), a textbook, and *Unemployment, Subemployment and Public Policy* (1975). She has also published numerous articles and reviews in such publications as the *Monthly Labor Review, Industrial and Labor Relations Review, Policy Studies Journal, Journal of Current Social Issues, The Nation, America,* and *Current History.*

In the 1970s Dr. Ginsburg was involved in efforts to secure full-employment legislation in the United States. In 1979 she was one of thirteen Americans to be awarded a Swedish Bicentennial Fund Grant, which enabled her to study, first hand, Swedish labor-market policies for full employment.

Professor Ginsburg has been a consultant and frequent lecturer to many organizations and plays an active role in public-service activities. She is a member of the Task Force on Employment in New York, of the Greater New York Community Council, and has given testimony before congressional committees in connection with full-employment and other employment legislation.

DATE DUE